TRAIL *of the* WILD WEST

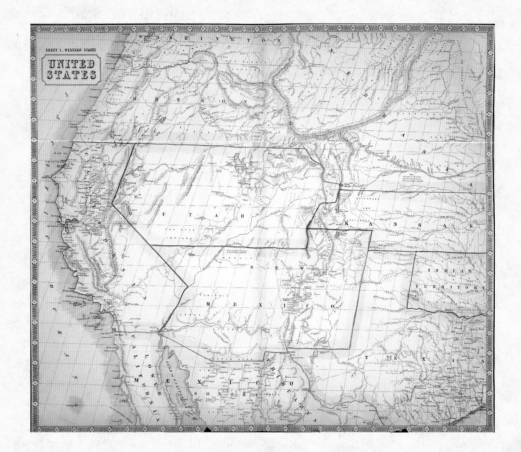

"These mountains are very high
and steep, and he who travels them…
must labor hard if he would
reap the golden harvest."

REPORT FROM COLOMA, APRIL 18, 1849

TRAIL
of the
WILD WEST

Paul Robert Walker

National Geographic Society

To my beloved Marlene,
who held down the fort while I followed the Trail.

Library of Congress CIP data: page 232

Sutter's Mill, 1849

Contents

An Introduction

THE WILD WEST IS THE GREAT AMERICAN MYTH, created as events occurred, first in newspaper accounts and official reports, later in dime novels and melodramas—only to be distorted further in twentieth-century films and television shows. Every American knows the basic components of this myth: A brave, white-hatted lawman faces a cowardly, black-hatted outlaw on a dusty street at high noon; the blue-coated cavalry arrive just in time to save the beleaguered settlers from Indian attack; the tired yet happy cowboys sing around the campfire, and the old grizzled prospector leads his burro in an endless search for one big strike; the tough-talking dance-hall girl hides a heart of gold.

LIKE ALL MYTHS, THE MYTH OF THE WILD WEST overlays a bedrock of truth. There were brave lawmen, and the cavalry did occasionally save the settlers from Indians. Cowboys did sing songs, prospectors did search for that big strike, and some dance-hall girls surely had hearts of gold. But the story of what really happened in the West is far more complex—and far more interesting—than any of these simple stereotypes. It is a story of an extraordinary people driven westward by the twin forces of greed and adventure, a story of their triumphs and tragedies, a story of the battles they fought—with the land, with each other, and with the Indian people who had come before them.

THIS BOOK IS AN ATTEMPT TO TELL THAT STORY IN WORDS AND PHOTOGRAPHS, with a point of view aimed at bringing the people, the events, and the land itself into focus for the modern reader. Unlike many general works about the West, which attempt to cover the entire 19th century, my story begins with the discovery of California gold in 1848 and ends with the stampede to the Klondike in 1898. The half-century demarcated by these events—filled with frenzied mining rushes and railroad building, bloody Indian wars and gun battles, dusty cattle drives and cowtowns—put the "wild" in the Wild West, and it is this wilder side that forms the heart of the tale. The *Trail of the Wild West* is not a single trail across the land but a trail in time, connecting the flash points on the edge of white civilization.

IN ORDER TO BETTER UNDERSTAND THIS STORY, I traveled throughout the West, following the trails of miners and settlers, visiting the sites of battles and boomtowns. I shivered in a rainstorm at Sutter's Mill and dipped my hand into the cold, clear water of Bonanza Creek in the Yukon. I gazed into the undulating hills above the Little Bighorn and slept in a Lakota tepee near Wounded Knee. I walked the streets of Abilene and sat in the living room of Jesse James. In Johnson County,

Wyoming, I climbed up into the old barn of the TA Ranch and peered out through rifle holes cut in the wooden walls by an invading army of cattlemen and Texas gunslingers. I sailed through the mist-shrouded waters of Alaska's Inside Passage and flew in a tiny plane over the Chilkoot Pass, so close to blue-ice glaciers that it seemed I could reach out and touch them. I visited archives and museums as well, poring over diaries and old newspapers, examining photographs and artifacts, searching for the authentic voices of those who walked this trail before me.

As important as the places I saw were the people I met, who offered frontier hospitality, professional expertise, and in some delightful cases, a living link with the past. Most of these men and women are mentioned in the acknowledgments, but I would like to single out one special person. His name is Alex White Plume, and he lives on the Pine Ridge Reservation not far from Wounded Knee. Alex has two great dreams for his people: to see herds of buffalo grazing again over Lakota land and to preserve the Lakota language for future generations. Alex and his partner Phillip Jumping Eagle keep a small buffalo herd of their own, and they allowed me to join them in a wild chase for a lost buffalo over the rocky, rolling, exquisitely-beautiful land, while Alex shared his insights on the long history of hatred and misunderstanding between his people and white America. "What can I do?" I asked. "Just tell the truth," he replied.

Just tell the truth. Easy to say, difficult to do—not only in telling the story of the native people, but in telling the story of the West. In 1897, journalist Tappan Adney rode the first wave of the Klondike stampede to Dawson, where he met an experienced miner—a sourdough in local parlance—who had spent many years amid the harsh conditions of the Yukon. "The longer a man stays in this country," he said, "the less he knows. If he stays here long enough he gets so he don't know nawthin." In writing this book, there were times when I felt much the same about the history of the West. The more we penetrate the layers of myth and memory, the more we discover about any given event, the less certain the truth of that event becomes. Dr. Rodman W. Paul, who collected original sources relating to the California gold discovery, addressed this issue in a statement that could be applied to the history of the West as a whole: "The story of what happened at Sutter's Mill is…in a sense the victim of a relentless search for the truth—a search that has inevitably inspired controversy even as it has uncovered additional information. But that is the essence of history."

IN THE END, IT IS THAT ESSENCE, THAT UNCERTAINTY AND CONTROVERSY that gives the story of the West such power. Each of us can read the story as we wish to read it; each of us can see something of ourselves in the words and actions of men and women long passed. For the Wild West is more than a myth; it is a crucible in which a more modern America was formed. And even as we look forward to a new millennium, we have much to gain by looking behind us, by understanding our antecedents and walking once again on the trail of the Wild West.

Paul Robert Walker

GOLD IN THE HILLS

"Monday 24th this day some kind of mettle was found in the tail race that looks like goald."

HENRY W. BIGLER, JANUARY 24, 1848

GOLD IN THE HILLS

─────── 1848-1854 ───────

THE AMERICAN RIVER RISES AMONG THE RAGGED GRANITE PEAKS OF THE SIERRA NEVADA. IT IS A THREE-FORKED RIVER, LIKE THE MUDDY MISSOURI THAT CARRIED LEWIS AND CLARK INTO THE HEART OF THE CONTINENT; BUT THE AMERICAN RIVER FLOWS CLEAR, DOWN FROM THE MELTING MOUNTAIN SNOWS, CARVING DEEP AND SPECTACULAR VALLEYS THROUGH ROLLING FOOTHILLS WHERE OAK, ASH, PINE, AND FIR BATTLE FOR SUPREMACY—GREEN IN THE SPRINGTIME, GOLDEN IN THE FALL. • THE SOUTH FORK BEGINS BELOW ECHO PEAK, NOT FAR FROM THE SOUTHERN SHORE OF LAKE TAHOE.

IT TUMBLES WESTWARD, CUTTING ITS WAY THROUGH SEDIMENTARY ROCK FORMED ON THE FLOOR OF AN ANCIENT SEA, AND MASSIVE GRANITE, PUSHED UPWARD AS MAGMA FROM DEEP WITHIN THE EARTH. IN THE AGE OF MOUNTAIN BUILDING, THE AWESOME HEAT OF THIS RISING, MOLTEN GRANITE DROVE HOT WATER THROUGH ROCKS BENEATH THE EARTH'S CRUST, LIQUEFYING QUARTZ AND GOLD AND PROPELLING THEM TOWARD THE SURFACE. THERE, AS THE WATER COOLED, THE MINERALS SETTLED TOGETHER IN MILKY WHITE VEINS THAT RUN ALONG THE WESTERN SLOPES OF THE SIERRAS—INCLUDING A BROAD

Previous page: Mount Humphrey towers over Golden Trout Lake in California's Sierra Nevada Range. Opposite: Wagon trails cut into the steep slopes of the Sierras remain visible some 150 years after hopeful miners followed them west. The beauty of the landscape belies the harsh life that awaited prospectors like the one above.

band that begins just north of the South Fork, a unique 120-mile network of riches that came to be known as the Mother Lode.

John Augustus Sutter knew nothing of mother lodes and little of quartz veins. Nor did he know that the South Fork of the American River—like countless other rivers over millions of years—had eroded the hard quartz, picking up pieces of gold like a precious hitchhiker, carrying it downstream only to drop the heavy load in gentle eddies and gravel bars where anyone could find it. What Sutter knew was that he had too many debts in Switzerland, his creditors were hounding him, and people in his own village were singing the praises of a magical land called America. So he left his wife and five children and sailed west, arriving in New York in 1834 and quickly reaching the Missouri frontier—where he invented an aristocratic military title of "Captain" and developed a vision of empire. Back in Switzerland, a warrant was issued for Sutter's arrest.

I Have Found It!

Within a decade, Sutter had established himself as lord and master of New Helvetia, the New Switzerland in the near-mythic land of California. "I had power of life and death over both Indians and white people," he later bragged, and for a time at least, the statement was true.

From his sprawling adobe fort on the high ground near the confluence of the American and Sacramento Rivers, Sutter ruled a personal fiefdom of over 225 square miles, made up of two separate land grants from the Mexican government—which had empowered him to judge and execute criminals, issue passports, perform weddings and funerals, and dole out parcels of land. He employed hundreds of Indians in a variety of enterprises and played generous host to the trickle of Americans who had begun to cross the mountains, including a moody yet capable craftsman named James Marshall, who first arrived at Sutter's Fort in 1845. Craftsmen were few on the California frontier, and two years later, when Marshall asked for work after the Mexican War, John Sutter put him in charge of a project he'd been considering for some time: a sawmill in the foothills of the Sierra Nevada.

In May 1847, led by an Indian boy, Marshall and his party worked their way up the South Fork of the American River until they came to a small, beautiful wooded valley that the native Maidu-speaking people called "Cullomah." Even today—after its earth has been turned upside down by those who came in Marshall's wake—the valley is a place of almost primeval splendor, where deer run through the morning mists that hang upon the hills and sunlight sparkles on the rushing waters below. It is Eden-like, a place of pure and natural possibility. So it seemed to James Marshall that spring, and though he didn't know it, the possiblities he saw would change not only his own life, but the lives of his countrymen for generations to come. For it was in this valley, where the river emerges from a steep canyon and bends toward the northwest, racing over a bed of softly-rounded rocks, that James Marshall decided to build John Sutter's sawmill. It was in this valley that the Wild West was born.

Construction began in September, with a workforce of Indians and whites, including a handful of Mormons recently discharged from the Mormon Battalion formed during the Mexican War. By mid-January 1848, the mill was near completion, but the tailrace—where water ran out of the mill and back into the river—needed deepening to allow the great mill wheel to turn properly. So Indian workmen cleared the channel of rocks and debris during the day, while each night the water was allowed to rush through the ever-deepening channel.

On the afternoon of January 23, Marshall went to inspect the tailrace. Drawn to some crumbling granite at the bottom, he asked for a tin plate—a strange request his workmen thought, and it seemed even stranger as they watched the mill boss swirl some of the sand and gravel and water around in the plate. Although he found nothing of interest, he remarked to one of his Mormon workers that he believed the rock contained minerals and suspected there was gold in the surrounding countryside. He could see "the blossom," he explained, the white flintlike quartz that was present throughout the hills. In fact, Marshall had suspected that the valley contained precious minerals from his first visit, but he believed that the primary mineral was silver.

Now, he was dreaming of gold.

Ordering his men to "turn on a good head of water" during the night in order to wash away the debris, Marshall returned the following morning—clear, cold, and full of promise—to see what he could see. Almost a decade later, he told the story:

> …about half past seven…I went down as usual, and after shutting off the water from the race I stepped into it, near the lower end, and there, upon the rock, about six inches beneath the surface of the water, I discovered the gold. I was entirely alone at the time. I picked up one or two pieces and examined them attentively; and having some general knowledge of minerals, I could not call to mind more than two which in any way resembled this—sulphuret of iron, very bright and brittle; and gold, bright, yet malleable; I then tried it between two rocks and found that it could be beaten into a different shape, but not broken.

Marshall gathered several pieces of the bright, malleable metal in the crown of his old slouch hat and showed them to William H. Scott, who was working at the carpenter's bench.

"I have found it!" Marshall announced.

"What is it?" someone asked; perhaps it was Scott, perhaps it was Alexander Stephens, who was cutting timber nearby.

"Gold," Marshall answered.

"Oh! no," returned Scott, "that can't be."

James Marshall replied with conviction, "I know it to be nothing else."

Four days later, in the midst of a driving rainstorm, James Marshall and John Sutter huddled over a dripping package of glittering flakes and grains in Sutter's office at the fort, running a series of tests until they were convinced that they had, in Sutter's words, "the finest kind of gold." They agreed to keep their find a secret, but it didn't last for long. By March, Sutter's workers were deserting, and a group of Mormons had discovered even richer diggings further down the American River at a place that became known as Mormon Island. Still, the rush was a trickle

GOLD IN THE HILLS
1848-1854

State and territory borders as of 1850
Present-day state names in gray

By the 1850s, innumerable mining towns had sprung up around rivers like the American, Feather, Yuba, and Stanislaus. The gold rush made California the 31st state in 1850, and its early political history was dominated by figures from the gold regions.

Leland Stanford, for example, made a fortune selling supplies to prospectors, and he used his money to propel him to the California statehouse in 1861. From Sacramento he used his political clout to build a second fortune in railroads. Stanford and his three partners—all

of whom grew wealthy during the gold rush—were the driving force behind the Cental Pacific Railroad, which built the western half of the transcontinental railroad.

Tools of the Trade

MANY OF THE earliest California miners simply picked gold out of crevices with knives, but they soon adopted other tools and techniques, some learned from experienced men who had worked in the gold mines of Georgia, some developed in California itself. All of these "placer mining" methods used gravity to separate the heavier gold from the lighter impurities that surrounded it. The pan (below) was a tin or iron plate about ten to fourteen inches across with a flat bottom and sloping sides. A miner would fill the pan with dirt, dip it into the water, then lift it out while slowly swirling it around, allowing the heavier gold to settle to

the bottom while sand and soil were washed over the sides.

The cradle was a wooden box about twenty inches wide and three or four feet long, mounted on rockers. At one end was a sieve, at the other end a series of cleats, called riffles. Miners would dump dirt into the sieve and wash it through with water while gently rocking the device back and forth, sending the dirt over the riffles while the gold remained in the cradle.

As many as six miners working together might use a long tom, a 10- to 30-foot-long inclined trough that ended at a sheet of perforated metal called a riddle. The miners would wash large loads of dirt, sand, and gravel down the trough, and gold would pass through the riddle unto a riffled box similar to a cradle. When a long tom was extended by a series of riffled boxes at the end, it was called a sluice, requiring from five to twenty men to operate and processing more dirt than any of the other devices. ■

until May 8, 1848, when 29-year-old Mormon elder named Sam Brannan—who owned a store at Sutter's Fort, a newspaper in San Francisco, and was soon to be excommunicated for keeping the tithes he collected—stepped off the San Francisco wharf and held a small bottle aloft for everyone to see, shouting, "Gold! Gold! Gold from the American River!"

By the end of the month, San Francisco was all but empty. Brannan's competitor, the *Californian*, ceased publication on May 29, announcing, "The majority of our subscribers and many of our advertising patrons have closed their doors and places of business and left town....The whole country, from San Francisco to Los Angeles and from the sea shore to the base of the Sierra Nevada, resounds with the sordid cry of 'gold! gold! GOLD!!!' while the field is left half planted, the house half built, and everything neglected but the manufacture of shovels and pickaxes...." Brannan's own paper, the *California Star*, lasted two more weeks, but he was hardly concerned; his store at Sutter's Fort took in $36,000 worth of gold between the 1st of May and the 10th of July.

In the weeks that followed, soldiers deserted their posts, sailors jumped ships, and servants ran away from their masters. Wages shot through the roof, for why would a man work for wages when he could earn far more by picking up gold from the ground? A U.S. Army sergeant named James Carson, stationed in Monterey when he caught his first glimpse of raw gold, later expressed the prevailing feeling of the time:

A frenzy seized my soul....Piles of gold rose up before me at every step; castles of marble, dazzling the eye with their rich appliances; thousands of slaves bowing to my beck and call; myriads of fair virgins contending with each other for my love...in short, I had a very violent attack of the gold fever.

Within an hour, Carson had obtained a furlough, mounted an old mule, and headed for the mines.

At first the natural inclination was to gravitate toward Coloma and Mormon Island, but the prospectors of 1848 discovered that there were riches waiting in almost every river, stream, and gulch on the western slopes of the Sierras and in the Trinity mountains to the north. The richest of the early finds was at Dry Diggings, located in a narrow gulch about ten miles over the steep foothills north of Coloma. There, a careful observer estimated that by the end of July some one thousand miners, including hundreds of Indian laborers, had pulled $3,000,000 worth of gold from the seasonal ravines. This at a time when gold traded for no more than $16 an ounce, and the miners worked with the simplest of tools: knives, picks, shovels, pans, baskets, and a small wooden washing machine called a rocker or cradle.

GOLD MANIA RAGES

Those who were fortunate enough to be in California during the summer of 1848 remembered it as an idyllic time. James Carson praised the "morals of the miners of '48," who never dug on Sundays, but instead prospected, played poker, sang songs, and drank whiskey, all in the spirit of "harmony, fun, and goodwill." Though prices were outrageous and the whites often cheated their Indian laborers, outright crime was rare. What was the point in stealing another man's gold when all you had to do was poke your jackknife into a crevice or turn a few shovelfuls of dirt to mine your own?

The peace and harmony began to fade by the fall, however, as "outsiders" arrived in the mines, first from the Hawaiian Islands, then from Oregon, Mexico, Chile, and Peru. In early October, at the sawmill in Coloma—now used as a makeshift miners' dormitory—a drunken ex-American soldier stabbed and killed another American who had recently arrived from Hawaii. Murders had occurred in California before, but this one, coming as it did in the very spot where gold had been discovered, reverberated like the original sin in the Garden of Eden. The *Californian*, which had resumed publication, urged the people to unite rather than let "red murder stalk through the land," and unite they did, though it is difficult to say if justice was served.

In January 1849, at Dry Diggings—which had sprouted into

Over 150,000 miners staked claims near rivers like the American (above). Rivers and streams were the easiest places for prospectors to look for gold, not only because they carried and deposited the gold where it could be easily found, but also because the water aided the miner in processing his precious gold-bearing "dirt." To mark a parcel of land as his own, a miner would drive stakes into the ground to delineate the boundaries of his property. Eventually the miners created a bureaucracy to protect their claims, dividing the countryside into mining districts, with each miner allowed one claim per district. District officials settled claim disputes, and sometimes criminal matters as well.

a booming town in a few short months—a gambler named Lopez was attacked by five men after a lucky night at the gaming tables. The robbers were captured, and the miners organized themselves into an ad hoc vigilance committee, trying, convicting, and sentencing each of the five to 39 lashes. After the public flogging, an anonymous miner shouted that three of them—all foreigners—were wanted for robbery and attempted murder on the Stanislaus River to the south. Another trial was immediately held, with the now-drunken miners sentencing the three men to death and hanging them from a large oak tree behind the Jackass Inn. From that moment on, Dry Diggings became known as Hangtown.

There were perhaps 14,000 non-Indians in California in the summer of 1848 and approximately 20,000 by the end of the year, a substantial increase by the standards of the underpopulated frontier, but only a small glimpse of the deluge to come. By the end of 1849, there would be almost 100,000; three years later, close to a quarter million; and by 1860—on the eve of the Civil War—the free state of California would have a population of 380,000. It was one of history's greatest mass migrations, kicked off, appropriately enough, by the President of the United States.

That summer and fall, rumors of the California gold discovery slowly filtered to the east, eliciting more incredulity than excitement. Then on December 5, 1848, outgoing President James Polk, who had seen the official report of the military governor of California, confirmed the richness of the gold fields in his final message to Congress. Two days later, as if to gild Polk's words, a military courier arrived carrying a Chinese tea caddie bearing over 230 ounces of incredibly pure California gold. There was no turning back. "The gold mania rages with intense vigor," proclaimed the *New York Herald,* "and is carrying off its victims hourly and daily."

From Maine to New Orleans, from New York to Missouri—and in time from Europe to China—tens of thousands of men, with a smaller number of women and children, made preparations to head for California. As in all the rushes that followed, the merchants reaped the first bonanza, offering for sale every imaginable article that might be of use in the California gold fields—and many more that were completely useless, including a bogus "Goldometer" that would supposedly locate the precious mineral, and a "California Gold Grease" that allegedly allowed the miner to pick up gold by simply rolling naked down a hill.

SEEING THE ELEPHANT

Bizarre modes of transportation were offered as well: An "Aerial Locomotive" was scheduled to leave New York City on April 15 and carry its passengers "through by day-light, without stopping" for $50, wines included. Some 200 people actually signed up for the voyage, but in truth, there was no easy way to California in 1849. Most who left from the East Coast chose to go by ship—either the long, traditional route around Cape Horn and up the coast of South America, or the shorter, but more dangerous passage that included an overland trek through the fever-infested jungles of the Isthmus of Panama.

The restless farmers and townspeople of the inland valley region chose the wagon routes across what was then called the Great American Desert, some taking southern trails through Mexico or Santa Fe and Los Angeles, most following the Oregon-California trail across the heart of the continent. It is the journey along this route which came to symbolize the California gold rush; and it was this journey—with all its hardships and triumphs—that led, in time, to raging warfare on the Plains and the ultimate settlement of the West. But in 1849 America had just won a war with Mexico, and her adventurous sons and daughters set out to see the greatest prize: California, the new El Dorado, the land of golden riches. They called it "seeing the elephant," an expression drawn from a strange little story of the time about a farmer who, upon hearing the circus had come to town, loaded his wagon with fresh vegetables to sell at the market and met the circus parade along the way, led by an exotic elephant. The farmer was overjoyed by his first glimpse of the giant pachyderm, but his terrified horses bolted at the sight, turning over the wagon and spilling vegetables across the road. "I don't give a hang," the farmer said, "for I have seen the elephant."

In the spring of 1849, at least 35,000 emigrants gathered near the Missouri River towns of St. Joseph, Independence, Westport and Council Bluffs. One of them was Sallie Hester, a bright, wide-eyed 14-year-old newly arrived with her family from Bloomington, Indiana. "As far as eye can reach," she wrote of St. Joseph, "so great is the emigration, you see nothing but wagons. This town presents a striking appearance—a vast army on wheels...." The following year, another emigrant described much the same scene in more caustic terms: "Never, probably since Peter the Hermit preached the Crusade had such a motley groupe of men been collected together."

> ## *"The accounts of the abundance of gold in that territory are of such an extraordinary character as would scarcely command belief were they not corroborated by the authentic reports of officers in the public service...."*
>
> President James K. Polk, December 5, 1848

Like the booming mining camps that waited at the end of the trail, the trailhead towns featured the violence, bad whiskey, and crooked gambling that we've come to associate with the Wild West. More than one "Californian" lost his grubstake before crossing the Missouri River. A few were buried with a bullet. But the greatest threat of all was cholera—epidemic in 1849,

still lethal in 1850, when a physician from Ohio named Mendall Jewett left his home with the blithe notion that "an overland journey will be likely to improve my health." Within a month, the doctor found himself stuck on a Missouri River steamboat, up to his elbows in dying patients:

Called at 3 o'clock this morning to see a man by the name of Finch....Found him purging violently and suffering from excruceating cramps in all the mussles with vomiting and lividity of countinance shrunken skin in fact all the symptoms of Aceatic Cholera...by 3 o'clock P.M. was dead.

The cholera continued along the broad valley of the Platte all the way to Fort Laramie, perched on the high, windswept plains of what is now eastern Wyoming. No one knows how many died of the dread disease in the early years of California migration; estimates range from 200 to 5,000 in 1849 alone. "The cholera is raging," Sallie Hester wrote in early June as her family camped along the Platte. "A great many deaths; graves everywhere." By the time the overland migrations were over, some 39,000 graves—marked and unmarked—would line the trail from the Missouri frontier to the Pacific coast.

Fueled by rumors, partial truth, and prejudice, many emigrants feared Indians as much as they feared disease; but in the early years at least, the native people were more likely to watch in silence or steal livestock than to seriously attack a wagon train. One historian calculated that out of a quarter million pioneers who crossed the Plains between 1840 and 1860, Indians killed 362 whites while the emigrants killed 426 Indians, insignificant compared to the deaths from disease—even more devastating to Indians than whites—or the violent warfare that would ultimately follow the mass migrations.

Even in the early stages of the journey, the trail was strewn with the leavings of those who tried to lighten their load, discarding and arguing over possessions they thought would be essential in the new El Dorado: pianos and stoves, blacksmith tools and mining equipment. The trail itself took its toll; those

The California Indians
TROUBLE IN PARADISE

WHEN SPANISH missionaries first arrived in 1769, there were perhaps 300,000 Indians living in the area that would become the state of California. They were a diverse people, living in more that 500 village-states, speaking over 100 different languages and dialects. Most had plenty of food, whether they fished along the Pacific coast, farmed in the Colorado River valley, or gathered acorns in the foothills of the Sierras. Though some were among the greatest basket weavers in the world, their material culture was simple. And they were so blessed by natural riches that they had little need of war.

Because of their simple and peaceful ways—and their dark complexions—many viewed the California Indians as primitive creatures, a "degraded and brutish class," in the words of one correspondent. Yet these Indians had a complex spiritual and social culture that many never recognized. They provided a capable labor force, first for the missions, then for the vast ranchos of Mexican Californios and newer arrivals like John Sutter, a fair man for his time, who paid them in his own currency which they could exchange for food and supplies at his store.

By the time of the gold rush, much of the native culture had been destroyed by white encroachment, and diseases introduced by early settlers had already cut the total Indian population in half. The people of the Sierra foothills, however, including the Maidu-speaking Nisenan who lived in the Coloma Valley, had been relatively untouched by these early troubles; they generally accepted the miners and helped them find the gold. During the summer of 1848, military governor Richard B. Mason estimated that half the 4,000 miners then working in the goldfields were Indians. "They make the most who employ the wild Indians to hunt it for them," wrote an observer. "There is one man who has sixty Indians in his employ; his profits are a dollar a minute." For early Californians, whether ranchers or goldseekers, the Indians offered a cheap labor supply.

The relationship changed for the worse with the arrival of men from Oregon who had developed a deep enmity toward Indians in the north. In the spring of 1849, after five Oregon miners were murdered on the American River, the Oregonians waged all-out war against the Nisenan near Coloma, killing over seventy-five in a series of raids and executions. When James Marshall intervened on behalf of the Nisenan, the Oregon men threatened to kill him as well.

Brutal attacks continued throughout the gold regions, with some local governments paying a bounty on Indian scalps. "A war of extermination," an early Californian called it, "shooting them down like wolves, men, women and children." Yet deaths by violence were insignificant compared to those resulting from the destruction of the natural environment and the rampant spread of white diseases, including typhoid, cholera, measles, and syphilis.

By 1860, there were less than 30,000 Indians in the state of California, a tenth of the population of a century before. They were a shadow people, stripped of legal rights, driven from the mines, forced into indentured servitude or onto ill-conceived reservations, with no real place in their native land and no real future in the new California society. ■

Once the domain of California Indians, Snowslide and Lower Caribou Lakes (opposite) are now part of Maidu State Park in the Sierra foothills. The Indians were casualties of the gold rush; petroglyphs carved in stones (above) testify to their once-thriving culture.

The Donner Party

AMONG THE EMIGRANTS bound for California in 1846 was a group of men, women, and children led by a wealthy 62-year-old Illinois farmer named George Donner. After easily crossing the Plains and Rockies as part of a larger group, the Donner Party decided to set off on their own to take a cutoff that appeared in *The Emigrants' Guide to Oregon and California* by Lansford W. Hastings.

Although he had promised to lead them, Hastings was out on the trail with another wagon train by the time the Donners arrived at Fort Bridger, Wyoming. The party wasted 18 precious days pushing through a boulder-strewn canyon in the Wasatch Mountains, only to face the harsh, hot deserts of Utah and Nevada—where they lost livestock to the elements and Indian raids.

On October 19, a man they had sent ahead returned from Sutter's Fort with supplies and two Indian guides, and four days later the group began the long climb over the Sierra Nevada. It was here their luck failed completely. Winter came early, and a storm that raged virtually unabated for three months buried them, in makeshift cabins and tents, under thirteen feet of snow. By the time relief arrived in February 1847, many had starved to death, while some of the rest had resorted to cannibalism, alluded to by survivor Patrick Breen in his diary:

"Mrs. Murphy said here yesterday that thought she would Commence on Milt. & eat him....The Donnos [Donners] told the California folks that they [would] Commence to eat the dead people 4 days ago, if they did not succeed that day or next in finding their cattle...." A few weeks after the rescue, General Stephen W. Kearney arrived at the site—now known as Donner Pass—to find dismembered bodies and bones stripped of their flesh.

Of the 89 people who followed George Donner or joined the party along the way, only 48 survived, including 12-year-old Virginia Reed, who wrote to a cousin, offering sage advice to anyone making the journey west: "...never take no cutofs and hury along as fast as you can." ▪

who left later in the spring often met others returning to the East, giving up their dreams of California gold before they had reached the mountains. "They have seen the tail of the Elephant," wrote one 49er of his discouraged brethren, "and can't bear to look any farther. Poor, forsaken looking beings they are...But our motto is 'Go Ahead!'" And go ahead they did—most of them—until the great California Caravan stretched for some 600 miles, from the sod-covered roofs of Fort Kearny in central Nebraska to the broad, sloping, mountain-shadowed plateau of South Pass in western Wyoming.

Mercifully, the cholera disappeared beyond Fort Laramie, as did thoughts of turning back; but the worst part of the emigrants' journey came later, in the seemingly endless trek along the Humboldt River and deserts of Nevada, where alkali dust burned their eyes and bad water made them sick, leaving a trail of dead animals and more discarded possessions as they rolled on day after weary day. Here the passage took on new urgency, not only because of the harsh conditions, but because of the treacherous Sierra crossing yet to come. The tragic tale of the Donner Party, caught in a Sierra snowstorm in October 1846, was fresh in the emigrants' minds, and no one wanted to repeat the mistake—including the U.S. Army, who sent out search parties to find and help over 8,000 stragglers still on the trail in the fall of 1849. The snows came late that year, and with the Army's aid, even the stragglers managed to reach California.

Sallie Hester crossed the Sierras in mid-September 1849, earlier than the stragglers, later than the swift. "It was night when we reached the top," she wrote, "and never shall I forget our descent to the place where we are now encamped—our tedious march with pine knots blazing in the darkness and the tall majestic pines towering above our heads. The scene was grand and gloomy beyond description...another picture engraven upon the tablets of memory." For Sallie, California proved an exciting, if strange sort of place, where she found herself the center of attention as a young woman in a world of young men. "I am invited out so much," she wrote that March, "that I am beginning to feel quite like a young lady. Girls are scarce; I presume that is the reason. Young men are plenty."

For the plentiful young men, however, who set off with wild-eyed dreams of gold, the new El Dorado often proved a bitter disappointment. By the time the first overlanders arrived, the easy pickings were gone. Mining was hard work, they discovered, and prices outrageous. Alexander Ramsay, who left Indiana to forget a broken heart, arrived in the mines on September 17, 1849, to find bleak prospects:

…in the morning by a great deal of hard labor we got into the gold mines the place which we had come three thousand miles in serch of and the prospect looked much more like starving in than making a fortune there are now probably three hundred persons now in these mines one third of whom are sick one third doing nothing or preparing to leave, one third digging gold and obtaining from nothing up to fifty dollars per day each…it looks as if they had left no stone unturned.

A few days later, Ramsay dug five dollars worth of gold and wryly noted that, prices being what they were, "if I had been a very hearty eater I could have eaten the value of my five dollars during the day."

MONEY IS OUR ONLY STIMULUS

When Mendall Jewett arrived in July 1850, it was even more difficult to make a living as a miner, but Jewett didn't take the time to find out, giving up after a single day at Mormon Island. "First tryed Mining," he wrote. "Diggins poor for any body, but especially new beginers…the hardest Kindest kind of labour. It is not the work for me." Returning to what he knew best, the poor-spelling doctor ministered to miners and sold hay on the side. Doctoring was a booming business in California; gold rush diaries are full of physical complaints, from dysentery and scurvy to typhoid and mysterious mountain fevers. It's no wonder; the men were already sick and worn from the rigors of the trail, and then set straight to the harsh reality of mining, closer to digging ditches than anything else they might have experienced in the East.

Though a crude device by modern standards, the long tom used by the miners above represented a significant leap in mining technology. With a continuous supply of water from a nearby stream, a team of miners could sift through a far greater volume of soil than they could process individually with rockers or hand-held pans. Such innovations helped make 1852 the most lucrative year in the gold rush. The hills yielded over eighty million dollars in gold that year, but the average take per man was less than a thousand dollars.

They slept on the hard ground at first, or curled up in canvas tents, only gradually building more permanent structures to protect them from the driving California rains. They ate rancid bacon, jerked beef, and stale flapjacks for breakfast and had them again for dinner, laboring six days a week, often in cold water up to their waists, pausing briefly to smoke a pipe at noon. The only relief came on Sundays, when the unkempt men cleaned up a little and headed for the nearest town, perhaps a single muddy, garbage-strewn street lined with slapdash storefronts, where they traded their golden "poke" for supplies and spent what was left on liquor, gambling, and—if the town and poke were large enough—maybe a woman's comfort, before heading back to the diggings, broke and hungover, to do it all again.

It was enough to discourage the weak of body and spirit, but for the young and healthy, it was the experience of a lifetime. A 20-year-old 49er named John Ingalls wrote to his brother back in Connecticut, "How I wish you could have been here with me this winter. I think you would have enjoyed it first rate." Others expressed similar sentiments, but for most, the enjoyment was directly related to the amount of gold they averaged each day. "How it made my back-ache when I only got an ounce a day," wrote another early prospector, "but when one gets three or four ounces a day he don't feel any back-ache."

What drove them on was the prospect of rich diggings to come, the golden dream of "making a pile" and heading back to "the states" for a new life of wealth and luxury. The Great California Lottery, the miners called it, and so it seemed to those who toiled in vain, only to hear reports of astounding riches around the bend. A sober, hard-working farmer from New York State named William Swain gave up after a year in California with a grand total of $500 in gold—though he had worked several promising claims and spent months damming the Feather River to work the stream bottom. Yet a group of men on the same river earned $8,000 each, sold their claims for $12,000, and went home as heroes; while a woman in Downieville—on a tributary of the Feather called the Yuba—was said to have gathered $500 in one day while sweeping her earthen kitchen floor and worked the same ground until she "acquired a fortune."

Most California fortunes were made by those who supplied the miners—men like Sam Brannan who expanded his network of stores, bought vast tracts of land, and became California's first millionaire. The "Big Four" who later built the Central Pacific Railroad—Collis Huntington, Mark Hopkins, Charles Crocker, and Leland Stanford—all established their original fortunes as gold rush shopkeepers. Levi Strauss made pants from canvas, Philip Armour ran a butcher shop, Domingo Ghirardelli made chocolate, and John Studebaker used the money he earned selling wheelbarrows in California to expand his wagon works back in Indiana.

The great gold-rush historian Rodman W. Paul called California "the theater in which Americans learned how to supply and serve a newly populated wild region and how to provide that minimum of property law and criminal justice needed to prevent total disintegration." Driven by the powerful engine of profit, gold-rush merchants easily solved the problem of supply, but it was up to the miners themselves to establish that minimum of law and justice. As in the early incident at Hangtown—now known by the more genteel name of Placerville—the immediate and permanent justice of "Judge Lynch" was often questionable, tainted by prejudice, drunkenness, and the whims of the mob. Yet it was better than no justice at all on a wild frontier without jails or established judicial processes. "Lynch law is not the best law that might be," admitted the *Alta California* in 1851, "but it is better than none, and so far as benefit is derived from law, we have no other here." This despite the fact that a state government had been established the previous year.

In the remote mining camps, where men often left their gold and supplies lying unprotected, thieves were dealt with as summarily as murderers. "Arrest, trial and punishment rarely occupy more than a few hours," wrote one prospector. "No warrants, indictments or appeals delay proceedings....The miners are anxious to get back to their work and the prisoner is not long kept in suspense." On the Yuba River, a thief died after receiving 150 lashes, while on the North Fork of the American River, another prospector reported, "a man stole $300 and had both his ears cut off and the letter 'T' branded in his cheek.

Theft consequently is of rare occurrence."

Far more numerous than thieves were those who separated the California miners from their hard-earned dust by more subtle means. Gambling, brothels, and saloons flourished in every major mining camp, but the biggest, wildest "camp" of them all was San Francisco, the first Wild West boomtown. A sleepy hamlet of 850 before the rush, it had a permanent population of over 20,000 by the fall of 1849, with thousands more passing through. "Hotels and houses spring up like mushrooms; every day brings a change in the appearance of the place," a New York correspondent wrote, "and a man who absents himself for a week is utterly lost on his return."

"Gambling, drinking and all kinds of excesses are the main occupations of the diggers."

REPORT FROM WOOD'S CREEK, APRIL 22, 1849

The changes continued as the business district burned and rose again six times by the summer of 1851, canvas tents and the hulks of abandoned ships giving way to handsome brick buildings with fireproof iron doors and shutters. A man with gold could buy almost anything in San Francisco, including mock turtle soup, good cigars, and the services of a French mademoiselle, "fair but frail" in the euphemism of the time, who would sit beside him at the gaming tables for an ounce of gold an evening, or spend the whole night privately for the generous sum of $200 to $400. It was said that one young lady amassed $50,000 for her efforts.

Respectable women were rare in the early days of the rush, but those who came found opportunity as well. Some mined beside their husbands, a few dressing in men's clothes, while others used more traditional feminine pursuits to amass small fortunes of their own. One anonymous woman claimed to have made $18,000 baking pies for the miners, one third of it "clear profit." Luzena Wilson progressed from baking biscuits around a campfire to running a prosperous hotel in Nevada City, where she graciously took her husband into partnership. "Mrs. R" of Rich Bar earned a hundred dollars a week doing laundry, more than many men earned mining gold.

The opportunity to make money was the lure of the California experience for both men and women. "Money is our only stimulus," admitted a man from Missouri, "and the getting of it our only pleasure." Although the Missourian and other moralists lamented the golden obsession, for many, the freedom to search for gold—whether it was found in a gravel bank, a store, or a bawdy house—was part of a larger and delicious liberty that broke the chafing bonds of eastern social convention. "It is all the same whether you go to church or play monte," wrote a joyful Mary Jane Megquier, who left three children in Maine when she accompanied her husband to California in 1849. Six years later, after two visits home, she still felt much the same, crowing that "the very air I breathe seems so very free that I have not the least desire to return."

For all its genuine glories, the free California air proved stifling for foreigners, particularly if they spoke Spanish or Chinese. Among the first acts passed by the newly-formed California legislature in 1850 was the Foreign Miner's Tax, which set off a near riot in Sonora and drove thousands of Mexicans and Chileans from the southern mines. Even after the tax was repealed, violent confrontations continued, mostly in the south, where the foreign miners developed the dry, yet productive diggings, but occasionally reaching as far north as the pine-covered slopes of Downieville—where a Mexican woman named Josefa stabbed and killed an American man who had drunkenly broken down her door on the 4th of July, and then called her a whore when she asked him to pay for the door the next morning.

By THE TIME Lola Montez sailed into San Francisco Bay in May 1853, she had already captivated the hearts of Europe—including those of composer Franz Liszt, novelist Alexandre Dumas, and King Ludwig I of Bavaria, who made her the Countess of Landsfeld. As a fervent proponent of democracy, her influence on the elderly king was so powerful that it fermented the Revolution of 1848 during which Ludwig was forced to abdicate while Lola fled from Bavaria, ultimately finding her way to America.

Although Lola's dark-eyed beauty entranced admirers and critics alike, her talents as an entertainer were arguable. She was a lithe and evocative dancer, famous for "La Tarantella," or the Spider Dance, in which she gyrated as if being attacked by spiders. Her attempts at serious acting met with less success, though, and even those who enjoyed her dancing seldom returned to the theater. Her engagement in San Francisco lasted less than three weeks, and she had no sooner taken her final bows than a local troupe mounted a highly successful burlesque of her performance called "Who's Got the Countess?"

Stung by public insult, Lola rushed

Lola Montez
THE SPIDER DANCE

into marriage with a young newspaper editor and moved to Sacramento, where the same pattern was repeated: great enthusiasm for her act at first, followed by empty houses. The marriage broke up quickly, and Lola settled into a comfortable cottage in the booming mining town of Grass Valley.

It may have been a long way from the courts of Europe, but, for a time, Grass Valley suited Lola Montez. She loved to ride through the countryside visiting mines and sawmills, "puffing her cigar with as much gusto as a Broadway dandy," according to one newspaper. Always kind and generous to children, she encouraged the performing talents of a young neighbor named Lotta Crabtree, who went on to become one of the most famous entertainers of the 19th century.

Lola's greatest contributions to Grass Valley, however, were her famous "salons," where she entertained men of substance with intelligent, charming conversation, good brandy and cigars, even a player piano. At the time, the hard-rock mining industry was struggling to establish itself, and the director of the famous Empire Mine, John Southwick, financed Lola's salons as a way of attracting prospective investors to the rough mining area.

Lola's Grass Valley sojourn began to unravel in late November 1854, when she took offense at nasty comments in the local newspaper and went after the editor with a riding crop. The following summer, Montez left for a tour of Australia, and when she returned, Californians commented that her acting had improved and her fiery personality had begun to mellow. Yet she was insulted again in the press and left California for good, dying in New York—at the age of 42—in 1861.

A Hungarian violinist who had accompanied Lola in San Francisco once described her complex, mercurial personality:

"Frivolous, naughty as a little child; can charm with a wink; woe to him who falls into her disfavor. She has a very excitable nature and for the slightest reason her whole body will tremble and her eyes flash lightning." ■

Irish-born Marie Gilbert reinvented herself as Lola Montez (above) and cut a wide swath through European nobility before moving to California in 1853. "Bad, Bad Bodie," California , a ghost town today, (right) boomed on the eastern slope of the Sierras in the 1870s.

The sentence of Judge Lynch was carried out that afternoon, described in a Marysville newspaper:

> She did not exhibit the least fear, walking up a small ladder to the scaffold, and placing the rope around her neck with her own hands, first gracefully removing two plaits of raven black hair from her shoulders to make room for the fatal cord. Some five or six hundred witnessed the execution. On being asked if she had anything to say, she replied, "Nothing; but I would do the same again if I was so provoked."

Over twenty thousand Chinese arrived in 1852, with tens of thousands more to follow. They were taxed as well, treated even worse than the Mexicans and relegated to picked-over diggings that the whites had abandoned as unprofitable, where the patient, industrious "Celestials" managed to eke out a living nonetheless. French miners also faced prejudice—though the women were treasured for their charms—but other fair-skinned Europeans blended more easily into the new California society, and despite its xenophobia, the number of foreign-born actually rose from 24% in 1850 to 39% at the end of the decade. More than any frontier movement before it, the California gold rush was an international affair.

ALL MY GREAT PLANS

The worst treatment of all was reserved for the California Indians, described in an official report to new U.S. president Zachary Taylor as "degraded objects of filth and idleness." The report neglected to mention that it was Indian labor that carried the gold rush in 1848; nor did it point out that the land and its riches belonged to them in the first place. For their efforts, the Indians were driven from the diggings, killed in malice and for sport, while children and "vagrants" were forced into a form of legal slavery by the Indenture Act of 1850. Other repressive statutes, including the Fugitive Slave Law of 1852, severely limited the rights of the smaller, but

The gold rush transformed San Francisco (above) from a sleepy, seaside village to the busiest port in the West. The ships pictured lay abandoned as their crews deserted to search for gold. One ship's captain who passed through San Francisco in August 1848 made it south to Monterey—then the California capital— before desperately reporting to his superiors: "All hands have left me but two; they will stay till the cargo is landed and ballast in, then they will go....All the ships at San Francisco have stripped and laid up....It is impossible for me to give you any idea of the gold that is got here." Many abandoned ships were dragged ashore and used as stores, storage, and living space, providing ready-made "buildings" for a booming city.

significant number of African Americans in the "free state" of California.

And what of John Sutter and James Marshall, the men who started it all? Like the Indians who lived on the land before them, they were swept aside in the fury of the rush. As Sutter's debt-ridden empire collapsed, squatters took his land, stole his horses, and butchered his cattle. He tried mining at Sutter Creek, near the picturesque foothill town that still bears his name, but the charming visionary found more solace in brandy than in the Mother Lode. By 1849, his adult son, newly arrived from Switzerland, had sold the fort for $7,000 to pay his father's debts, and the elder Sutter retired to a farm on the Feather River—where his long-abandoned wife arrived with the other children and set about the difficult task of curbing her husband's lavish spending habits.

"By this sudden discovery of gold, all my great plans were destroyed," Sutter later complained. "Had I succeeded with my mills and manufactures for a few years before the gold was discovered, I should have been the richest citizen on the Pacific shores; but it had to be different. Instead of being rich, I am ruined...."

James Marshall, too, found solace in the bottle, though his defenders say he drank no more than other miners on a spree. Unlike Sutter, however, who ended up moving away from California in his bitterness, Marshall lived out his life in and around the Coloma Valley, watching as the rushing hordes destroyed the pristine eden where he had come to build a sawmill, digging up the earth and riverbed for gold—which ran out faster in Coloma than many other diggings—while building a town of stores, stables, and fine hotels, a town so booming and prosperous for a time that a man who built a toll bridge over the American River collected $20,000 in three months.

Marshall was a resourceful, if cantankerous individual who prospected here and there, grew grapes for wine, did odd jobs, and even went on a lecture tour in his later years. But he never really shared in the prosperity he created and to the end of his life bitterly complained that he had been unrewarded as the discoverer of California gold. In an 1857 letter, James

The Voyage

ALTHOUGH THE arduous overland journey came to define the California gold rush, almost as many gold seekers traveled by sea. Leaving from East Coast ports, they could choose one of two major routes, each with its own dangers and discomforts. The traditional route went around South America through the cold, treacherous waters off Cape Horn, a 13,600-mile journey from New York to San Francisco. The voyage usually took five or six months, but well-heeled argonauts could book passage on fast, graceful clipper ships like the *Josephine*, cutting the travel time to as little as three months.

The second route, across the Isthmus of Panama, was much shorter—only 5,450 miles from New York to San Francisco— but more dangerous and uncertain. The journey began by ship to the Caribbean port of Chagres, set in a malarial swamp where an early traveler wrote, "Bilious, remittent, and congestive fever, in their most malignant forms, seem to hover...ever ready to pounce down on the stranger." Floating by native canoe up the Chagres River, through marshy jungles teeming with "alligators,...small panthers, monkeys, and deadly snakes," the argonaut switched to mule-back for a day-long journey to the Pacific Ocean port of Panama City, where he boarded another ship for San Francisco. At its best, the entire voyage took about five weeks, even less when a railroad was completed across the Isthmus in 1855, but many travelers died of jungle fevers or got stuck for months in Panama City waiting for a ship to the new El Dorado. ■

Marshall succinctly and sarcastically summed up his view of gold rush profits:

Yankeedom, ... $600,000,000
Myself Individually, ... $000,000,000

Marshall's estimate of California gold production up to that time is somewhat higher than most, but no one really knows how much gold was mined in the early years. In all, about 2 billion dollars in gold was taken from California, with almost $650 million by 1860. The peak seems to have come in 1852, when some 100,000 miners produced over $81 million, an astounding annual figure never surpassed in subsequent rushes, yet averaging out to only $810 per miner. Clearly James Marshall was not alone in his frustration.

The year 1852 also marked the peak of the great California migration, with over 50,000 on the overland trails and tens of thousands more by sea. The nature of the migration had changed, from the overwhelmingly male adventurers of 1849 and 1850 to a larger proportion of families who came to settle. At the same time, wives came west to join their husbands, and California children were born. The chaotic census of 1850 reported that women made up only 7½% of the population; by the end of 1853, a contemporary historian estimated that there were 65,000 women and 30,000 children out of less than 300,000. The figures are questionable, but the trend was true. In 1853, one old 49er observed, "Live women are now so plenty that a miner wouldn't take the trouble to drop his pick to look at one."

INDUSTRIALLY DESPERATE

The influx of wives and children had a powerful civilizing effect on the wild California frontier, as on all frontiers before and after. In the raucous boomtown of Columbia, "Gem of the Southern Mines," Clementine Brainard noted proudly in December 1853 that she had attended a large party that included "twenty-five ladies, all married, everything passed off pleasantly, a very good

supper…sayed to be the first party in Columbia where they had no liquors.…" The following year, the city of San Francisco passed its first law against prostitution, a small indicator perhaps—enforced only against Mexicans, Chileans, and Chinese—but an indicator nonetheless. Times were changing.

The business of mining was changing as well. Early Californians engaged in "placer" mining—from the Spanish word for a sandbank—gathering and processing free gold deposited by the forces of erosion. As the easily accessible deposits played out, however, in the first few years of the rush, the placer-mining techniques became more organized and cost-efficient. The rudimentary rocker gave way to the long tom and sluice box, both operating on the same principle of isolating the heavier gold through the flow of water, but each allowing a larger number of miners to process more "dirt." Hydraulic mining took the principle even further, first moving the rivers to mine their bottoms, then moving the mountains themselves with a powerful stream of water that washed everything—earth, rocks, and gold—in its wake.

Most difficult and complex of all was hard-rock mining in which man did the work of Nature, freeing the gold from its prison of quartz with increasingly sophisticated methods and machinery. Although attempted on a small scale as early as 1849, hard-rock mining didn't begin to pay until the mid-1850s, but it continued well into the 20th century. The greatest hard-rock region developed to the north of the original Mother Lode, in the pine-forested mountain slopes of Nevada County, which proved over time to be the richest region in the Golden State. On the high ground above Grass Valley, the Empire Mine alone yielded almost 6 million ounces of gold, extending 367 miles of shafts and drifts over 2 miles into the earth.

Large-scale hydraulic and hard-rock mining were big businesses; no longer could a single miner, or even a small group of miners, hope for fortune from the hills and streambeds of California. Now mining required extensive capital, expensive equipment, and hired labor. In the early days, a miner's "wages" were the worth of the gold he brought forth from the earth each day. By the later 1850s, as often as not, "wages" were what he was paid to work for someone else. The amount of those wages had also changed, from an average of $20.00 in 1848 to perhaps $3.00 in 1856—still more than a man could earn in the eastern coal mines, but with the high cost of California living, hardly enough to spark visions of "castles and fair virgins" as James Carson had once seen, nor enough to send hordes of unprepared adventurers in a mad dash across the continent.

Some men adjusted to the changing times, becoming good laborers, good husbands and fathers, good citizens—even empire builders—of the new state of California. Others returned to their farms and towns in the East, where they tried to settle into the old way of life. But for many, whether in the Golden State or back home, the quest for easy gold had become a strange new sort of drug. John S. Hittell, one of the best contemporary observers, called them the "industrially desperate...ready to go anywhere if there was a reasonable hope of rich diggings, rather than submit to live without the high pay and excitement which they had enjoyed for years in the Sacramento placers."

It was these "industrially desperate," these "Old Californians" as they came to be called, who served as pathfinders in the settlement of the Far West, just as fur traders and farmers had opened frontiers before them. And it was California that served as the crucible for every rush to follow; there would never be another California, but the California experience would be repeated again and again throughout the West.

Less than a decade after the discovery at Sutter's Mill, California was no longer the wild wide-open West; it was the 31st state of a conflicted union. The deciding "free state," troubled by racial issues of its own and separated from the "eastern thirty" by over 1,500 miles of treeless plains, rugged mountains, and scorching deserts, California was a glittering outpost of America's Manifest Destiny. In simple, unromantic terms, the history of the Wild West that followed is the story of settling that vast "empty" land while pushing aside the native people who lived there. And what drove many who came was the same force that drew them west in 1849: the cry of Gold! Gold! Gold!

An outcrop at California's Malakoff Diggins State Historic Park still bears the scars of 19th century hydraulic mining, in which a powerful stream of water blasted away gold-bearing earth. Hydraulic methods brought mining to a new level of production as individual miners working for themselves were replaced by large companies employing small armies of miners. Though lucrative, hydraulic mining was devastating to the land; tailings clogged streams and rivers, causing floods and destroying farmlands. After a long legal battle, the practice was banned in 1884. By then hardrock mining had become the dominant technology, a technique that lasted well into the 20th century.

TROUBLE ON THE TRAIL

"A bigger army than Napolean conquered half of Europe with is already equipping itself for its western march to despoil the plains of their gold."

CHICAGO PRESS AND TRIBUNE, FEBRUARY 4, 1859

TROUBLE ON THE TRAIL

1854-1861

On a hot August afternoon in 1854, an old, lame cow wandered off the emigrant trail near a big bend in the North Platte River, about eight miles east of Fort Laramie. Or maybe the cow collapsed on the trail and was left for dead; perhaps it was taken by force. Accounts differ—some call the cow an ox—but all agree that the animal was killed by a Lakota warrior named High Forehead, who shared the unexpected meat with his hungry friends. • High Forehead was one of over four thousand Lakota and Cheyenne camped near Fort Laramie that August, waiting for the annual dispersal of food and supplies promised in the Treaty of Fort Laramie, negotiated in 1851 between the Plains Indians and the United States government. The treaty provided that the native people would grant white travelers safe passage along the trail, which they came to call the Holy Road because they considered the travelers to be sacred; in exchange, the government promised that the land would belong to the Indians forever and that $50,000 worth of

---

Previous page: Sutter Buttes line the horizon near the Sacramento River valley in California. Opposite: Washington's Yakima County was the stage for bloody battles between Indians and whites, while in Colorado the Arapaho (above) tried unsuccessfully to broker a peace.

supplies would be distributed to the tribes each year for 50 years—a provision that Congress unilaterally reduced to $70,000 for 15 years.

Whether for 15 years or 50, the people who lived along the trail had already come to depend upon the annual influx of food and goods. With the Mormon migration and the massive rush to California, the old Oregon Trail had become a broad highway on both sides of the Platte. The emigrants' livestock ate grass that once fed the buffalo, cutting a swatch miles wide, while the emigrants decimated the game supply and brought white diseases that ravaged Indian villages. In 1853, the respected, tough-minded mountain man Thomas Fitzpatrick—who had helped negotiate the Treaty of Fort Laramie—reported that the Sioux, the Cheyenne, and Arapaho were "actually in a starving state....Their women are pinched with want and their children constantly crying out with hunger."

The annual dispersal of supplies helped ease these hardships, but that August, the government agent in charge of the dispersal was late in reaching the fort. The supplies and provisions remained in a warehouse, while Indian ponies ate what little grass was left and warriors ventured further and further from camp to find meat for their families. So it was that the old, lame cow ended up in the cooking pot.

The cooking pot happened to be in the camp of Conquering Bear, chief of a Lakota subtribe called the Brulé, while High Forehead, the man who killed the cow, was a visitor in the camp with allegiance to another subtribe called the Miniconjou. This complicated the events that followed: Though the Lakota, or Teton Sioux, are often considered a single tribe of the great Sioux nation, in the days when they ruled the northern plains they were much like a nation in their own right, made up of seven subtribes, each powerful and substantial, with its own leaders and allegiances. Although Conquering Bear had signed the Treaty of Fort Laramie as chief of all Lakota—an idea completely foreign to the Lakota, yet insisted upon by the whites—he had no actual authority over the man who killed the cow.

Nonetheless, "the Bear," as the whites called him, knew that the treaty required compensation for wrongs committed by his people. So he rushed to the adobe fort on the treeless, windy plain where the Laramie River flows into the Platte and offered a good pony in exchange for the old, lame cow—more than generous but not enough for the cow's owner, a Mormon emigrant on his way to Utah. The Bear may also have offered to give up the offender, or perhaps he only offered to try and give him up. As in all early negotiations between whites and Indians, cultural differences and bad translation created difficulties for both sides. The young, inexperienced commander of the fort, 2nd Lt. Hugh B. Fleming, left the matter unsettled as Conquering Bear returned to his people.

With Thirty Men

The next day, August 19, another Indian leader named Man Afraid of His Horses, a respected chief of the Oglala subtribe, went to the fort intending to negotiate a settlement. In the midst of a whirling, high-plains windstorm, he watched in confusion and mounting concern as a young officer hurriedly made preparations to march on the Indian camp. "The next thing I saw was a wagon go over to the Adobe Fort," Man Afraid later reported, "and next saw the soldiers draw a cannon out of the fort....Then I saw them clean out the cannon preparing to load it. The officer then went to the store and talked very loud."

The young, loud-talking officer was John L. Grattan. A 24-year-old West Point graduate, he itched to prove himself in the field, convincing Lieutenant Fleming—only a year his senior—to let him bring back the Indian who had killed the cow. That afternoon, Grattan crossed the Laramie River with two cannon, 29 men, and the post interpreter, Auguste Lucien, who, afraid of the Lakota, had begun drinking heavily at the fort and continued drinking along the trail. Man Afraid of His Horses accompanied the expedition and reported that soldiers riding in a wagon were drinking, too. Some accounts claim Grattan was drunk, but Man Afraid said he "did not see the officer drink on the road."

Between Fort Laramie and the Indian camps, the trail climbs high along the sandstone bluffs of the North Platte valley, affording Lieutenant Grattan ample opportunity to survey the vast Lakota encampments—at least 600 lodges stretching for three miles. According to one report, when a white civilian who accompanied the expedition pointed out the extent of the Indian camps, Grattan replied, "I don't care how many there are; with thirty men I can whip all the Indians this side of the Missouri." Descending into the valley, the soldiers arrived at the trading post of James Bordeau, who was married to a Brulé woman and had many Indian visitors camping near his post. The wind had died down, but the drunken interpreter stirred a storm of his own, riding back and forth in front of the Indians, shouting that the Sioux were all women—he would have them killed and eat their hearts before sundown.

Conquering Bear soon arrived, but though two messengers followed him, announcing that High Forehead refused to surrender, the Bear himself was evasive: He had to change his coat before giving an answer; it was his people's custom to ask four times before taking definite action; perhaps Grattan should go to High Forehead's lodge and see what he had to say. Bordeau, who translated this exchange, cautioned the officer against entering the Indian village, but Grattan replied that he had 12 shots in his revolvers and he must have High Forehead. As the soldiers marched on the Brulé camp, just 300 yards away, Conquering Bear rode double on the horse of the interpreter, Auguste Lucien.

In the camp, Grattan's men deployed on either side of the cannons while the officer held another long conference with the Lakota leaders. Lucien's translation was ineffective at best, inflammatory at worst. High Forehead stayed in his lodge, announcing that he would rather die than surrender, offering to fight Grattan man-to-man to settle the issue. In the meantime, young warriors arrived from the Oglala camp, shouting and riding their horses back and forth, just as the interpreter had done at the trading post, while other warriors concealed themselves in a dry creek bed near Grattan's soldiers. The Brulé women gathered their children and fled toward the river. It was almost sunset.

Suddenly, the "loud-talking" Grattan said something the

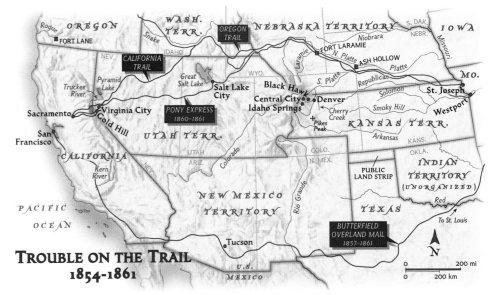

TROUBLE ON THE TRAIL
1854-1861

State and territory borders as of 1860
Present-day state borders and names in gray

By 1860 gold fever had spread from California into Colorado, where prospectors found gold at Cherry Creek, and in Nevada, where silver strikes gave rise to towns like Virginia City. Quick communiction from coast-to-coast was vital. Westbound mail originally traveled by ship to Panama, where it was carried overland to another ship waiting in the Pacific. In 1858 John Butterfield founded the Southern Overland Mail, which carried mail and freight by stage from St. Louis to San Francisco along a route that dipped south into Texas and crossed New Mexico and Arizona Territory, before running north through California. Despite the difficult terrain and the constant threat of Indian attacks, the Southern Overland reliably delivered the mail in a little more than three weeks. The communication lines provided by the Southern Overland, and the short-lived Pony Express, were instrumental in keeping California loyal to the Union when the Civil War broke out.

The Oregon Trail

THE MOST FAMOUS ROUTE from east to west was actually blazed from west to east, by an American named Robert Stuart who in 1812 led a group of fur traders eastward from what is now Astoria, Oregon. At the time, the Pacific Northwest was jointly occupied by the United States and Great Britain, and the Oregon trail helped maintain an American presence in the area.

During the 1830s the trail brought missionaries to Oregon. Jason Lee arrived in 1834, drawn by what he believed was a request from the Nez Percé Indians for the "white man's Book of Heaven." He was followed two years later by Marcus Whitman, Henry Spalding, and William Gray; Whitman and Spalding brought their wives, Narcissa and Eliza, the first white women to cross the Rocky Mountains.

In 1841, a group of 70 settlers followed the trail, the first wave of an American migration that continued for decades. Starting in Missouri, emigrants cut through what is now Kansas and Nebraska, where they followed the Platte and North Platte rivers to Fort Laramie. After stopping to rest and replenish exhausted livestock, they continued through present-day Wyoming, crossing the Rockies at the broad, gentle slope of South Pass. From there, the trail passed Fort Bridger and turned northwest toward the Snake River. The last leg of the journey took the emigrants across the rugged Blue Mountains before rafting down the treacherous waters of the Columbia River to the Willamette Valley—some 4 to 6 months and 2,000 miles from the Missouri frontier.

In 1843, Marcus Whitman guided a group of about 900 settlers called the Great Migration; yet it was dwarfed by succeeding movements, with 3,000 emigrants in 1845 and over 4,000 in 1847—the year after the United States and Great Britain set the international boundary at the 49th parallel. Hordes of gold seekers followed part of the trail to California, while Oregon-bound travelers continued to use it into the 1880s. Today, wagon ruts cut into a sandstone hill (*far right*) are still clearly visible in Guernsey, Wyoming. ■

Indians didn't understand; a moment later a soldier fired and an Indian fell. Someone, probably Man Afraid of His Horses, tried to restrain the warriors, shouting that the whites might be satisfied now that they had drawn Lakota blood, but Grattan ordered a full volley, and Conquering Bear, "paper chief" of all Lakotas, fell dying in front of his lodge, red blood streaming from three separate wounds. The cannons fired, too, Grattan behind one of them; but the charges sailed harmlessly through the tops of the Lakota lodges, landing unseen on the plains beyond.

Now there was no restraint. The warriors swarmed over the blue-coated soldiers, killing them where they stood or hunting them down in retreat, killing 30 men in a matter of minutes; a lone soldier made it back to the fort only to die without telling the story of the battle. According to Indian tradition, Auguste Lucien, the hated interpreter, was last to die, begging and pleading for mercy as he tried to escape on his horse along the emigrant trail. John L. Grattan—brash, brave, and foolish—was found near the cannons, pierced by two dozen arrows including one through his head, his body so mutilated he could only be identified by his pocket watch.

POT-HOUSE SOLDIERS

News of the "Grattan Massacre," as the whites called it, resounded from Fort Laramie to the halls of Congress, where Thomas Hart Benton, the "Lion of Missouri," thundered that the army had destroyed 50 years of peace with the Sioux by "sending our school-house officers and pot-house soldiers to treat the Indians as beasts and dogs." The new commander of the fort stated the same case less dramatically, though no less controversially, reporting, "There is no doubt that Lieutenant Grattan left this post with a desire to have a fight with the Indians...." Yet, despite mounting evidence to support this point of view, the army refused to accept the fact that one of its own had used such poor judgment; instead, they decided to follow the recommendation of another investigating officer, who suggested, "The time has now fully arrived for teaching these barbarians a lesson."

For the task, they turned to one of the most experienced and effective field commanders of the 19th century, Brig. Gen. William S. Harney, a 6'4" white-bearded warrior whom the Lakota came to call "the Butcher." On September 3, 1855, 700 U.S. troops under General Harney attacked a Brulé village near Ash Hollow, Nebraska, just north of the emigrant trail, killing approximately 100 Indians and capturing 70 more. The slaughter was so devastating that it effectively quelled Lakota resistance for a decade, but the damage had been done on both sides. The war between the Lakota and the United States Army had begun.

In an essay entitled, "Into the Sunset," Robert J. Conley wrote, "For the Indians the West was wild only because the white man made it so." While the Indians had fought each other long before the whites arrived, the statement embodies a deep abiding truth: The West was wild because it was a war zone, and it was the whites who forced the battle. The Grattan Fight was not only the beginning of the long conflict between the Lakota and the United States, it was also the opening salvo in a larger war, a war fought on many fronts, from the windswept plains to the sun-baked desert mountains, from the grassy Red River valley to the volcanic Columbia Plateau, a war that would never really stop until all the native people were either dead or relocated to reservations.

The success of General Harney's expedition led to a similar expedition to punish the Cheyenne, who had stepped up their owns raids along the trail. On July 29, 1857, near the Solomon River in western Kansas, Colonel Edwin V. "Bull" Sumner led 300 cavalry troopers against an equal number of mounted Cheyenne warriors, the first full-scale battle fought on the Plains and one of the few times that white and Indian forces met on equal terms in an open field. The Cheyenne believed they had magic that would tilt the scales of battle—under the directions of a medicine man, the warriors had dipped their hands in a lake said to render them invulnerable to the soldiers' bullets. Yet Sumner surprised both Indians and soldiers when he ordered his men to sling their carbines and draw sabers instead. The magic

water offered no protection against cold, sharp steel, and the battle became a rout, troopers slashing away at the warriors and pursuing them in a wild retreat for seven miles.

Further south, along the Texas frontier, the Comanche and Kiowa had been raiding for years, stealing horses and cattle, killing settlers and their families or kidnapping their wives. In 1858, one Texan wrote to his governor: "Now the woods is full of Indian sine in one mile of my house I dare not to leave my house to go one mile on aney business for fear my familey is murde[r] before I can get back I pay my taxes as other citison for protection and has failed to get it." That spring, one hundred Texas Rangers crossed the Red River and drove straight into Indian territory, attacking a Comanche village in the Canadian River valley of what is now western Oklahoma. Although much of the Texas Ranger myth is exactly that, in this case they more than lived up to the legend, battling three hundred warriors for seven hours until the Comanches abandoned the fight, leaving seventy-six dead behind them while the Rangers burned the village. A few months later, a regular army unit crossed the Red River further east and destroyed another Comanche village belonging to a tough old raider named Buffalo Hump.

Although impressive shows of force, the early plains campaigns were temporary measures that resolved nothing and created nothing but enmity. The most extensive and decisive fighting of the pre-Civil War era took place in the Pacific Northwest, where enmity between settlers and native people was so firmly engrained, and the settlers so belligerent, that the army sometimes found itself in the strange position of having to protect the Indians from the wrath of the whites.

Such was the case in October 1855, when Capt. Andrew Smith brought a party of Indian men into Fort Lane, situated in the beautiful, mountainous Rogue River valley of southern Oregon, where gold had been discovered a few years earlier. Although he intended to bring in the rest of the Indian band, Smith's plan backfired when a volunteer company organized by local settlers and miners attacked the village before dawn, killing 23 women, children, and old men. The next day, vengeful warriors ravaged the valley, killing women and children as well.

The Rogue River War came to a climax the following spring, when Captain Smith found himself in the ironic position of facing annihilation at the hands of the Indian people he had once tried to protect. Surrounded for two days on a hilltop called Big Meadows, running low on ammunition, a third of his men dead or wounded and suffering from thirst, Smith's situation was desperate until last minute reinforcements turned the tide of battle, and the Rogue River resistance was broken.

Further north and east, on the rough and desolate Columbia Plateau, fighting also broke out in the fall of 1855, sparked by the murder of several miners who were crossing Indian lands on the way to new gold fields near the Canadian border. The roots of the conflict lay deeper, in a treaty forced upon the Columbia tribes that May by the brash, young and duplicitous Governor of Washington Territory, Isaac Stevens. Although Stevens promised that those who accepted the treaty could stay on their lands until the treaty was ratified by Congress and signed by the President—a process that ended up taking four years—he actually opened the land to white settlers twelve days later, with predictable and tragic results.

Shall I Take a Knife?

The first phase of the fighting was led by Yakima Indians and lasted until the summer of 1856, engaging both volunteer citizen armies and regular forces. The Yakima War proved indecisive and fighting began anew in the spring of 1858, when a column of 164 soldiers under Lt. Col. Edward J. Steptoe marched boldly through the wild Palouse country, only to be surrounded on a hilltop and attacked by hundreds of Indian warriors, much as Captain Smith had been. No reinforcements arrived, however, and Steptoe's command escaped annihilation by sneaking away in the night—a daring, yet embarrassing retreat that forced the army to deploy a much larger, better-armed division under Col. George Wright.

That September, emboldened Indian warriors made the mistake of meeting Wright's army head-on in the open field of the broad Spokane Plain, where the soldiers' artillery and new, long-range rifles prevailed. One artillery officer believed they were aided by a comet that appeared in the sky at that time, "night after night…streaming above us in all its glory. Strange as it may seem, it has exerted a powerful influence with the Indians on our behalf. Appearing just as we entered the country, it seemed to them like some huge besom to sweep them from the earth."

"Return to the old tribal ways! Stay free of the soldiers and the reservation people….Unless you give up the new way, the Indian will die…."

Not willing to rely on comets, Wright continued his campaign, killing hundreds of Indian ponies, destroying food supplies, and hanging alleged ringleaders until the Plateau Indians were forced onto the reservations that Governor Stevens had planned for them.

While Indian military resistance was over, spiritual resistance continued on the Columbia Plateau for decades, best represented in the teachings of Smohalla, one of several dreamer-prophets who arose in the face of white encroachment and eroding Indian values. While others settled uneasily into reservation life, Smohalla preached a religion of sacred dance, vision, tradition, and rejection of white ways, including farming and mining, for these were like destroying the body of his mother earth:

You ask me to plow the ground! Shall I take a knife and tear my mother's bosom? Then when I die she will not take me to her bosom to rest.

You ask me to dig for stone! Shall I dig under her skin for bones? Then when I die I cannot enter her body to be born again.

You ask me to cut grass and make hay and sell it, and be rich like white men! But how dare I cut off my mother's hair?

Though Smohalla and his followers refused to "dig for stone," there were plenty of men in the West—white men mostly—who dreamed of new diggings and new, golden "stones" like they had found in California. The troubles in southern Oregon and the Columbia Plateau had been sparked by small influxes of prospectors, who followed the cry of gold with even less regard for treaties and boundaries than the land-hungry settlers. There were tens of thousands of these men in California, tens of thousands more much like them in the East. Even as the army fought its first major battles with the Indians, these men, these "industrially restless," chafed at the bit, ready to spread throughout the West on the golden trail.

BLASTED BLUE STUFF

In 1855, the year that Harney attacked the Lakota and the Northwest erupted in warfare, false reports of gold on the Kern River, at the southern tip of the Sierras, had drawn 5,000 men from other gold regions before the news got back that there was little or no gold to be found. The strange, irrational force of this brief rush was only a hint of stranger things to come. During the spring of 1858, reports of gold on the Fraser River in what is now British Columbia sparked a rush of over 25,000 adventurers, most of them Californians who set off on a 1,000 mile journey only to discover that, while there was indeed gold, there wasn't enough to warrant the expense of time and money to get there.

The following year, the restless California miners finally found a worthwhile opportunity just over the crest of the Sierras in the high, dry, sagebrush-dotted Washoe Range of what is now

AFTER THE GRATTAN FIGHT, the Lakota moved Conquering Bear to the sandy hills around the upper Niobrara River. Among them was a light-skinned Lakota boy, called Curly for his "hair yellow and soft as a young prairie chicken's." Around twelve, he was old enough to recognize the horror of battle and the approaching death of the Bear, yet too young to participate as a warrior.

Disturbed by all he had seen, Curly fled from the camp on his pony, tethering it in a small grove of cottonwoods while he climbed a nearby hill, searching for a vision—a message from Wakan Tanka, the Great Mystery. For three days and nights, Curly did not eat or sleep, yet still no vision came. It was not surprising; a Lakota vision quest normally involved an older boy who had been prepared by a medicine man. Finally, Curly descended the hill, leaned back against a cottonwood, and fell asleep.

He then had a strange and powerful dream. A man was riding silently toward him, his horse appearing not to touch the ground. The man wore a small brown stone behind his ear and a single feather in his long brown hair. He wore no warpaint and carried no scalps. Although he did not speak, Curly could

Dream of the Warrior
A LAKOTA VISION

understand everything the man thought. Arrows and bullets could not touch this man. A storm cloud rumbled behind him, a zigzag of lightning appeared on his cheek, spots like hail on his body. Then the storm stopped, and a small red hawk circled above his head. A crowd of Lakota people grabbed his arms and tried to hold him back. Yet still the man rode on.

Curly was shaken awake by his father. "What are you doing out here alone?" he demanded. "There are enemies all

around us." Curly wanted to ask the meaning of the dream, for his father was a powerful medicine man, but this was not the time.

Three years later, as Curly and his father camped in the sacred Black Hills near the place where the boy had been born, he told his father about the dream. The older man's heart filled with joy, for he knew that his son had been given a great vision and strong medicine, strong enough, perhaps, to unite the Lakota.

"The man on the horse is you," he explained. "He is the warrior you must become. You must always be first when you ride into battle. You must paint a lightning bolt on your cheek and hail spots on your body. You must tie a stone behind your ear and wear a red-backed hawk above your head. And you must never take a scalp or anything for yourself. If you do these things, bullets and arrows cannot touch you."

The next summer, Curly joined a war party against the Arapaho. He prepared himself as the man of his vision and charged first into battle, untouched by the bullets and arrows that whizzed around him. Killing two enemy warriors, he jumped from his horse and scalped the men, but just as he finished, an Arapaho arrow pierced his leg. He had forgotten the deeper message of his vision—to take nothing for himself. He would never take a scalp again.

When the war party returned to the village, Curly's father sang proudly:

"My son has been against the people of unknown tongue. He has done a brave thing; For this I give him a new name, the name of his father, and of many fathers before him—I give him a great name; I call him Crazy Horse." ■

On a vision quest among the sandy hills (right) near what is now the Nebraska-Wyoming border, a young Lakota called Curly saw his future as a mystical warrior. As the adult known as Crazy Horse, he led the Lakota (above) against U.S. troops until his surrender in 1877.

The Pony Express

*I*N 1860, A NEW company formed by the Kansas freighting firm of Russell, Majors, and Waddell began advertising for "young, skinny, wiry fellows, not over 18. Must be expert riders, willing to risk death daily. Orphans preferred." Despite the hazards, over 200 men of varying ages answered the call and about 80 became riders for the Pony Express.

The Pony Express was a marvel of precision. Starting at St. Joseph, Missouri,

in the east, or Sacramento or San Francisco in the west, a rider would mount a horse outfitted with a special streamlined saddle, ride for his leg of the journey—typically about 75 miles using 3 horses along the way—then hand his mail off to the next rider at a relay station where he would pick up the incoming mail and repeat the trip in the opposite direction. In this fashion the mail traveled between California and Missouri in 8 to 15 days, about half the time it took to deliver the mail by stage. The riders endured blinding rain and swollen rivers, blazing sun and hostile Indians, deep snow and treacherous trails.

Though a logistical success, the Pony Express was a financial failure. Faced with losses somewhere between $300,000 and $500,000 and competition from the newly-completed transcontinental telegraph line, Russell, Majors, and Waddell shut down the operation in October 1861, just 18 months after it began. But in that short time the Pony Express connected the county as it had never been connected before. ▪

Nevada. Excitement began to build in June 1859, when several men working what they judged to be a promising gold claim found themselves battling a strange mix of blue sand and crumbling blue-gray quartz that they called "blasted blue stuff." Finally, a local settler decided to send a sackful of the mysterious mineral over the mountains to Nevada County, California, where two separate assayers concluded it was rich silver ore with a substantial percentage of gold. Before the following dawn, the rush to the Washoe was on.

One of the first men to arrive was an oft-frustrated California miner named George Hearst, who brought back 38 tons of ore through the early mountain snows and earned $91,000 for himself and his partners, establishing the seeds of the Hearst family fortune. There were other successes as well, but most who rushed to the Washoe in 1859 were disappointed to discover that the minimal placer deposits were already claimed and the process of mining the vein itself was beyond their means and abilities. So they turned to wild speculation on mining claims—most of them worthless—buying and selling them by the foot. "Nobody had any money," wrote one chronicler, "yet every body was a millionaire in silver claims....All was silver underground, and deeds and mortgages on top; silver, silver everywhere, but scarce a dollar in coin." What few coins there were, he pointed out, found their way into the gambling houses in the new boomtowns of Virginia City and Gold Hill.

That winter was especially harsh in Virginia City, which hung precariously at an elevation of over 6,200 feet on the steep, sagebrush-covered slopes of Mount Davidson. The high drifting snows cut off all communication, and as they speculated in future millions, the prospectors faced the bleak reality of imminent starvation. Hopes rose in March when the first mule train crossed the Sierras, but in typical Wild West fashion, the "supplies" proved to be liquor and bar fixtures. Fortunately, food soon followed and the Washoe rush was back in business.

The winter of 1859-1860, so difficult for the newcomers in Virginia City, was tragic for the native Paiute people who lived in the shadow of the mines. Though their children died of hunger, the Paiutes refused all offers of food from local settlers for fear that it might be poisoned. Relations between Indians and whites in western Nevada had been poor since the early days of the California gold rush, but now the whites were pouring back over the mountains, building cities and mine shafts, cutting down precious piñon pines that provided an essential native food source.

In May 1860, as Paiute leaders met at Pyramid Lake to discuss their grievances, the poisoned atmosphere erupted in warfare after an ugly incident at a Pony Express station. Accounts vary, but according to one contemporary newspaper, "an old Indian man went to [the station] with a squaw, when four white men tied the buck Indian, and then each committed an atrocious outrage upon the Indian woman. They then let the buck go. He afterwards came back with other Indians, and put a white woman, who was in the house, out of doors, and also three white men who had nothing to do with the outrage. They then bound the four white men who abused the squaw, and burned them in the house." When word reached Virginia City and other Washoe mining towns, the miners formed a ragtag brigade of 105 men to go and fight the Indians. On May 12, the volunteers carelessly rode into a well-planned trap in the narrow gorge of the Truckee River, not far from Pyramid Lake. Surrounded and outnumbered, 46 men—almost half the brigade—fell dead in the trap and the chaotic retreat that followed.

News of the battle sent waves of panic throughout the mining regions. Martial law was declared in Virginia City, where the women and children were herded into an unfinished stone house, newly fortified to withstand attack. Men also sought refuge; a frightened miner from Holland asked his partner to lower him into a 50-foot mining shaft, only to be stranded for three days after his equally frightened partner ran away. Finally, reinforcements arrived from California, and on June 3 a better organized force of 800 men, including 200 regular soldiers, engaged the Indians not far from the earlier battle, killing 25 warriors, capturing 50 horses, and driving the survivors into the hills. Nonetheless, raiding continued for over a year, and through most of June the Pony Express was forced to suspend service, the only time it failed to carry the mail during its remarkable 18-month history.

Gateway Pass at Pikes Peak, which gave its name to the Colorado gold rush despite the fact that it was more than 80 miles from the gold fields. The peak was named for Lt. Zebulon Pike, a New Jersey native who explored vast stretches of the American West. In 1805 he led an expedition to find the source of the Mississippi River, mistakenly declaring it to be Leech Lake in northern Minnesota. Traveling through Colorado a year later, he discovered the 14,110-foot mountain that bears his name. Reaching New Mexico, his party was arrested by Spanish officials, who escorted them back to American soil. He continued to serve with distinction in the Army, reaching the rank of brigadier general, and was killed during the successful assault on York, Canada, during the War of 1812.

The cost of the Paiute War in lives and money shook the already precarious fortunes of the Pony Express. For the Washoe mining rush, however, the war was no more than a distracting interlude. By October 1860, Virginia City was a thriving town with 154 business establishments, including 4 cigar stores and 25 saloons. The rich vein of silver and gold became known as the Comstock Lode, named for Henry T. P. Comstock, a Canadian who had blustered his way into a share of the original discovery claim. Comstock and his partners sold out quickly and cheaply, thinking the strange vein would soon give out, but their thinking was wrong. Over a 20-year period, from 1860 to 1880, the Comstock Lode yielded $300 million in silver and gold.

PIKES PEAK OR BUST

Even before the Washoe excitement, a stranger and more powerful rush had begun to develop a thousand miles to the east, along the magnificent, towering Front Range of the Rocky Mountains. Rumors of gold in the Rockies had been circulating for years, but it wasn't until 1858 that several parties of prospectors set out to investigate. In June, more than a hundred of them camped near the present site of Denver, along Cherry Creek, a tributary of the South Platte River named for the wild chokecherries that grew along its banks. Most went home in disappointment, but one group led by a veteran Georgia miner, William Green Russell, managed to pan a few hundred dollars worth of gold from a "dry pocket" up the Platte. The find played out within a month, and they too headed home for the winter.

That might have been the end of the story but for an imaginative, loose-tongued trader named John Cantrell, who happened upon Russell's camp on his way east from Salt Lake City. He panned about three ounces worth of gold, $48 at the prevailing rate, and when he reached Kansas City loudly proclaimed rich new diggings in the Rockies. The eastern United States was still reeling from the financial panic of 1857, and the Missouri valley had been hit hardest of all. Merchants and newspapers—first in Missouri, then in the East—were only too eager to trumpet the news, hoping for a return of the good

fortune that accompanied the rush to California. And struggling Americans, once so skeptical of the discoveries in the West, were now ready to believe the promise of riches no matter how far-fetched the tale.

As in the past, the first men in were those already in the area: prospectors, traders, and adventurers on the trail or ready to move on the Missouri frontier. By late fall, several hundred of these men were camping along Cherry Creek, side by side with 1,200 Arapaho in the winter camp of Chief Little Raven. Traders by nature, and well-aware of the military expeditions against other Plains tribes, the Arapaho were more inclined to trade with the whites than to resist them, but they watched uneasily as the intruders cut down scarce cottonwood trees to build their log cabins, laying out townsites and hunting on Arapaho land.

One group of adventurous prospectors pushed beyond the Cherry Creek camps into the majestic mountains that rose like craggy giants in the west. They built rough cabins in the beautiful Boulder Valley, where the University of Colorado stands today, and no sooner had they finished than a smaller Arapaho band, perhaps 300 strong, arrived. They were led by an extraordinary chief named Left Hand, who one white pioneer described as "the finest looking Indian I have ever seen....over six feet tall, of muscular build," with hair hanging loosely over his shoulders.

"Go away," he told the startled prospectors in clear, unmistakable English. "You come to kill our game, to burn our wood, and to destroy our grass." Left Hand had learned English as a boy from a white trader who married his older sister and lived among his people. By all accounts, he mastered the language at a time when few Indians on the Plains spoke any English.

Once the prospectors had offered gifts of friendship and promised to move on in the spring, Left Hand gave them permission to stay, though he had to use the full weight of his authority to restrain his angry warriors. It was a situation that he would face again. Like other wise Indian leaders he could see that peace was the only reasonable path in the face of the white onslaught; yet the younger men were eager to prove themselves in battle, as surely as their counterparts in the army. According to one report, Left Hand's peacemaking efforts were aided when the most belligerent of the warriors had a dream that Boulder Creek rose from its banks and washed the Indians away, leaving only the whites upon the land.

"…there was never a viler set of men in the world than is congregated about these mines; no man's life is safe."

MAJOR JOHN SEDGWICK, DECEMBER 1860

Left Hand himself needed no dreams to warn him that a flood was coming. He had just returned from an unprecedented journey to the non-Indian world, working for farmers in Nebraska Territory and Iowa in order to gauge whether his people might adapt to agriculture. Though he returned believing that farming was not for the Arapaho, he saw that the whites were too many and too powerful to fight. He had traveled with one of the first parties of goldseekers heading for Cherry Creek, and he knew that many more such men would follow.

In February 1859, the *Chicago Press and Tribune* proclaimed: "A bigger army than Napoleon conquered half of Europe with is already equipping itself for its western march to despoil the plains of their gold." Estimates of that "army" vary from 50,000 to 150,000, a flow of men and material second only to the great California migration. Many traveled much as the 49ers had traveled, but the shorter distance—about 600 miles from the Missouri frontier—encouraged hordes of "59ers" to simply walk across the plains. A few used more imagination, developing a bizarre vehicle called a windwagon or prairie schooner, designed to catch the zephyrs and sail like a ship across the land. At least three set off in 1859; one almost made it to Denver.

Emigrants with more conventional wagons painted "Pikes Peak or Bust" on their canvas covers, a slogan that only emphasized the absurdity of the rush, which, in the early days at least, was based on nothing but the unpromising finds along Cherry Creek. Those diggings were over 80 miles north of Pikes Peak, but for most Easterners, the name was all they knew of the mountainous western region of what was then Kansas Territory. The 59ers headed for Cherry Creek, where predictably they found frustrated miners who were barely earning a quarter of their daily expenses. That spring, the routes across the plains—along the Platte, the Arkansas, the Republican, and the Smoky Hill rivers—became two-way trails with a long line of angry rushers returning east, even as hordes of hopefuls headed west.

The "Go Backs," as they were called, replaced "Pikes Peak or Bust" with new slogans like "Busted" and "Humbugged." Looking for someone to blame, many of them settled on William Newton Byers and D.C. Oakes, who wrote two popular guidebooks of the time, though the latter's appeal as a villain may have as much to do with the fact that his name rhymed nicely with hoax, creating popular chants like, "Hang Byers and D.C. Oakes/For starting this damned Pike's Peak Hoax." One 59er reported meeting Oakes himself along the Platte, camped near a mound that purported to be his own grave. "Here lie the remains of D.C. Oakes," read the epitaph, "Who was the starter of this damned hoax!"

MY WIFE CAN BE A LADY!

The hoax became reality when experienced prospectors followed the trail of gold into the snowy foothills that began just 30 miles from the Cherry Creek camps. One of them was a young, bright-eyed Missourian named George A. Jackson, who had failed in the California gold fields and was stopping at Fort Laramie when he first heard the news from Cherry Creek. On the day after Christmas 1858, Jackson and two partners, Black Hawk and Tom

Golden, decided to go on a hunting trip, following the twisting canyon carved by a sparkling tributary of the Platte they called the Vasquez Fork. It's Clear Creek today, emerging from the steep mountain walls near Golden, Colorado, named after Jackson's partner, Tom Golden.

The men soon split up, and George Jackson found a campsite on the north fork of Clear Creek, near the present site of Idaho Springs, under a big fir tree where a small stream flowed into the larger one. Noticing that the area contained "good gravel," he built a big fire to thaw the frozen ground; but as he tended the flames, his two dogs, Drum and Kit, got into a fierce and bloody fight with a wolverine who came prowling after the hunter's hard-earned meat. The next day, George Jackson found himself torn between concern for his beloved dogs and curiosity over the thawing gravel. His diary offers an understated glimpse of the moment of discovery:

Jan. 7. Clear day. Removed fire embers, and dug into rim on bed rock; panned out eight treaty cups of dirt, and found nothing but fine colors; ninth cup I got one nugget of coarse gold. Feel good tonight. Dogs don't.

Jackson felt even better that spring, when he returned with 22 partners and set to work on the new diggings, converting their wagon boxes into sluices and netting $1,900 in the first week. In the meantime, he kept the discovery secret, entrusting the news only to Tom Golden whose mouth, Jackson wrote, was "tight as a No. 4 beaver trap."

While Jackson and Golden kept their mouths shut, a smaller find by the prospectors in Boulder Valley offered the first glimmer of hope for the desperate miners at Cherry Creek. The most important discovery, however, was made across the ridge from Jackson's diggings, on the north fork of Clear Creek, by an eccentric, profane-mouthed Georgia miner named John H. Gregory. The details of his initial find are unclear—some say it occurred around the same time as Jackson's, while others say he was actually on his way to Jackson's diggings, panning along Clear Creek as he traveled, and took a "wrong turn" at the fork because the gold signs were stronger. In either case, the real excitement began in early May when John Gregory returned with other men and found four dollars worth of gold in their very first pan. "By God, now my wife can be a lady!" Gregory is said to have shouted. "My children will be schooled!"

Gregory's diggings formed the nucleus of tiny, wealthy Gilpin County, "the Little Kingdom of Gilpin," where the booming towns of Black Hawk and Central City quickly sprang to life. In June, when famed newspaper editor Horace Greeley came to see for himself, some 4,000 miners were working the steep gulches at an elevation of over 8,000 feet; by the end of summer there were 15,000, while thousands more worked the Jackson diggings in neighboring Clear Creek County, as well as the finds in Boulder County to the north. These three regions, along with other discoveries that followed, rescued the Pikes Peak Gold Rush from historical absurdity and thrust a new territory onto the American map. In the census of 1860, after tens of thousands had already returned to the East, a mountain wilderness that had been the province of Indians and trappers only a few years before now had a population of over 34,000.

As You Have Come Here

By this time, the relationship between the miners and the Arapaho had become deeply troubled. There were many ugly incidents, but perhaps the ugliest of all came in the spring of 1860, when a sociopathic ex-convict called Big Phil the Cannibal, who was alleged to have eaten his Indian wife, led a group of drunken miners in a raid on Left Hand's village, then camped near the booming town of Denver. The chief and his warriors were away at the time, and Big Phil and his gang raped the Arapaho women, including Left Hand's sister and probably his wife and daughter.

The better class of Denver citizens were outraged, and when Left Hand and his men returned, he again had to restrain himself and his warriors, eventually agreeing to let the whites punish the miners in their own way. He had reason to believe that justice would be carried out, as he had seen such punishment before;

vigilante justice and the swift verdict of "Judge Lynch" were as much a part of Denver life as other mining camps. Yet in the end, the outrage at what had been visited upon the Arapaho women faded in the mountain air, and Big Phil and his accomplices went free.

In spite of such incidents, or perhaps because of them, many Arapaho and Cheyenne leaders recognized the need to renegotiate their claims to the land promised in the Treaty of Fort Laramie. Even as the whites of Denver debated the atrocities of Big Phil, tens of thousands more were streaming westward over the central plains, killing buffalo and destroying grass, some establishing ranches along the way. There were fewer than 3,000 Arapaho and Cheyenne living south of the Platte; in February 1861, Cheyenne and Arapaho leaders signed a new treaty, deeding a huge region of present-day Colorado, Wyoming, Nebraska, and Kansas in return for a small, barren reservation in southeastern Colorado. The Indians were unclear on the new boundaries; the real inducement was the much-needed food and supplies promised to those who signed. Ten days later, Congress formed the territory of Colorado.

Left Hand wasn't invited to sign the treaty, an unfortunate oversight, as he was the only Indian leader fluent in English, Cheyenne, and Arapaho, very likely the only individual who might have made sense of it all. As it was the treaty solved nothing. That spring angry Cheyenne warriors raided the central plains, while the Civil War broke out in the East, bringing tensions in Colorado to fever pitch.

On April 30, 1861, about a week after news of the war reached the frontier, Left Hand led ten warriors into the Apollo Theater in Denver. After the performance, the tall, charismatic chief jumped up on the stage and addressed the crowd in perfect English, pledging brotherhood and imploring them to do the same. "As you have come here hunting for gold," he told them, "then hunt after the gold and let the Indians alone."

The *Rocky Mountain News* called it a "handsome speech," yet even as he spoke the words, Left Hand—who knew the whites better than any Indian on the central plains—must have realized it was an impossible dream.

This snow-covered Nevada cemetery became the final resting place for many who flocked to Virginia City after the discovery of silver. At its peak, Virginia City had a population estimated at over 30,000, though the highest official figure was far less: 10,917 in 1870. Once the high-grade silver veins were played out, the population quickly dwindled; a century after the discovery of the Comstock Lode, the town's population was a little more than 500. After its mineral riches, Virginia City's other claim to fame is that it fostered the writing career of Samuel Clemens, better known as Mark Twain. Failing as a silver miner, the 28-year-old Clemens went to work as a reporter for the Virginia City Territorial Enterprise *in 1862. Later he would write, "I felt that I had found my legitimate occupation at last."*

Volunteers and Vigilantes

"My own impression is that the Apaches cannot be tamed; civilization is out of the question."

SYLVESTER MOWRY, APACHE AGENT, NOVEMBER 1857

VOLUNTEERS AND VIGILANTES

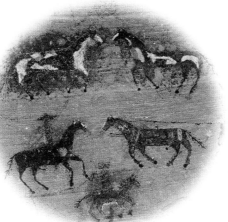

MANGAS COLORADAS WAS A GIANT OF A MAN: SIX-FOOT-FOUR OR MORE, 250 POUNDS OF HARDENED MUSCLE—WITH AN EQUALLY IMPRESSIVE INTELLECT AND TALENT FOR DIPLOMACY. "A NOBLE SPECIMEN OF THE GENUS HOMO," ONE GOVERNMENT AGENT CALLED HIM, "NEARER THE POETIC IDEAL OF A CHIEFTAIN...THAN ANY PERSON I HAVE EVER SEEN....YOU MAY BE SATISFIED THAT HE IS THE MASTER SPIRIT AMONGST THE APACHES." • ONCE IN HIS YOUNGER DAYS, MANGAS CAPTURED A MEXICAN WOMAN AND DECIDED TO MAKE HER HIS WIFE INSTEAD OF A SERVANT, AN IDEA SO ABHORRENT TO HIS TWO APACHE WIVES THAT HE HAD TO KILL THEIR BROTHERS IN HAND-TO-HAND COMBAT, WITH KNIVES IN THE APACHE WAY. AFTER THAT, SHE BECAME HIS FAVORITE WIFE, BEARING THREE ATTRACTIVE DAUGHTERS. LIKE A RENAISSANCE PRINCE, MANGAS EXTENDED HIS INFLUENCE OVER THE SUN-SPLASHED MOUNTAINS AND DESERT VALLEYS BY MARRYING THESE DAUGHTERS TO SELECTED LEADERS, INCLUDING THE FORMIDABLE COCHISE. • PERHAPS UNIQUE AMONG THE FIERCELY INDEPENDENT APACHE, MANGAS HAD A VISION OF UNITING HIS FAR-FLUNG, DISPARATE PEOPLE. IN HIS TIME,

Two views of Arizona's Canyon de Chelly, the Canyon del Muerto (opposite) and the White House ruin (previous page), home first to the Anasazi and later the Navajo. Navajo artists living in the Canyon del Muerto—the "Canyon of Death"—produced beautiful pictographs with paint and charcoal, like the one above.

many Apache bands ranged throughout the Southwest, speaking different dialects, practicing a variety of lifeways. Mangas's own people lived by hunting and gathering, but like most Apaches, they supplemented their livelihood by raiding Mexican villages and pack trains. In return, the Mexicans tried to exterminate the Apache. The northern Mexican states of Sonora and Chihuahua each placed a bounty on Apache scalps; in Chihuahua it was 100 pesos for the scalp of an Apache man, 50 pesos for a woman, and 25 pesos for a child.

When American soldiers first passed though Apache lands during the Mexican War, an old Apache chief suggested that they unite with the Americans against their common enemy. "You have taken Santa Fe," said the chief, "let us go on and take Chihuahua and Sonora; we will go with you. You fight for the soil, we fight for plunder; so we will agree perfectly."

For a time, the Apaches maintained relatively cordial relations with the "white-eyes," as they called the Americans, though it would be an exaggeration to say that relations were trouble free. As travel increased along the southern trail, and as ranchers began to settle and miners searched for gold, scattered Apache raids began to devil the whites north of the border even as they continued to strike Mexicans in the south. By 1854, one U.S. Apache agent was already speaking in terms of extinction, if not extermination: "All that can be expected from an enlightened and Christian government, such as ours, is to graduate and smooth the passway for their final exit from the stage of human existence."

This Yellow Stuff

For Mangas Coloradas the most contentious issue was the presence of white miners in the heart of his territory, at Pinos Altos, in the dry, pine-covered Mimbres Mountains of New Mexico. It was not only the trouble these men caused—hunting game, bringing whiskey mills, even attacking his people—it was a deeper, religious issue that disturbed Mangas, much as it did Smohalla, the Dreamer-Prophet of the Columbia Plateau far to the north. As one Apache leader explained:

This yellow stuff is sacred to Ussen [the Creator]. We are permitted to pick it up from the surface of Mother Earth, but not to grovel in her body for it. To do so is to incur the wrath of Ussen. The Mountain Gods dance and shake their mighty shoulders, destroying everything near. The Mexicans and the greedy White Eyes are superstitious about this stuff. The love of life is strong in all people, but to them it is not so strong as their greed for gold.... It is this stuff that will bring our people to ruin and cause us to lose first our land and then our lives.

In the fall of 1851, Mangas went to the mining camp, offering to lead the miners to richer diggings south of the border. Some say the miners wrongly believed he planned to lead them off and kill them. Whatever their logic, the intruders seized the huge Apache and tied him to a tree, where they beat him with an ox-goad until the proud chief was allowed to crawl away "like a wounded animal." The incident irrevocably turned Mangas against the miners, and by extension against the Americans. As historian Donald E. Worcester wrote in his study of the Apache, "Many a lone miner died slowly, head down over a fire or staked to an anthill, in atonement for the scars on Mangas Coloradas' back."

Like his father-in-law, Mangas, Cochise was bigger than the average Apache, "about six feet tall and straight as an arrow," according to one white who knew him, "built, from the ground up, as perfect as any man could be." Although he may have aided Mangas in early attacks on Pinos Altos, Cochise maintained peaceful relations with Americans in his own territory, the rugged Dragoon and Chiricahua Mountains of what is now southeastern Arizona. His friendship was particularly important to the men at the Butterfield Overland Mail station, a stone building in a mountain pass, later called Apache Pass, with a natural springs that provided essential freshwater.

In October 1860, a half-breed boy, a "coyote" in the Apache term, disappeared from a ranch about 40 miles southeast of Tucson. Though he had no proof, and though Cochise was in fact camping some 80 miles away at the time, the boy's stepfather, John Ward, went to Fort Buchanan, a small outpost not far from the ranch, and announced that he believed Cochise had stolen the boy along with twenty head of cattle. The Apache always suspected it was the cattle that concerned Ward far more than the boy.

CUT THE TENT

The commanding officer dispatched a young, inexperienced second lieutenant named George Bascom with 54 men to settle the matter. On February 4, 1861, Cochise and six followers, including his younger brother, two nephews, and his wife and two children, met with Bascom in his tent near the mail station at Apache Pass. Through a Spanish-speaking interpreter—possibly Ward himself—the Apache chief explained that he believed the boy had been kidnapped by another band and offered his own services to help locate him. Yet even as Lieutenant Bascom served his honored "guest" coffee and dinner, soldiers surrounded the tent, and the officer informed Cochise that he was under arrest. Like a flash of lightning, the tall, muscular Apache whipped out a big knife and slashed the canvas, fleeing through the darkness in a hail of bullets.

Though some dispute the dramatic details of this encounter, the incident was described in local newspapers and the Apache themselves told the story of "Cut the Tent" for many years. Bascom held the other six Apaches hostage, later adding three more Apache men who had nothing to do with the conflict. In the meantime, Cochise took four hostages of his own, including one of the men from the Butterfield station, whom he directed to write a note in English which was then tied to a stake and left where the American soldiers could find it: "Treat my people well, and I will do the same by yours."

It was not to be. Though Cochise made several attempts to negotiate and led a failed attack on the stone station where the soldiers took refuge, Bascom remained resolute. By the time American reinforcements arrived, 12 days after the stand-off began, Cochise and his warriors had fled south of the border, and the soldiers found nothing but the remains of the white

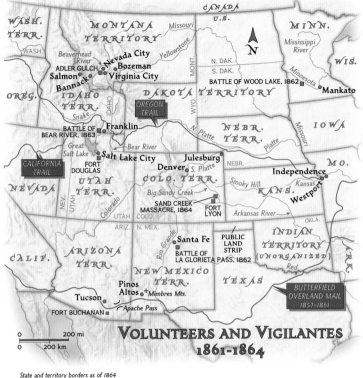

State and territory borders as of 1864
Present-day state borders and names in gray

Largely because of its mineral wealth and the population it attracted, Nevada achieved statehood in 1864, becoming just the fifth state—after California, Oregon, Texas, and Kansas—west of the Missouri River. By that time most of the remaining territories had assumed the shape they would take as states, while miners continued to prospect throughout the mountain regions. At this point the stage was set for large-scale settlement of the West. The Homestead Act, signed by President Lincoln in 1862, provided citizens with free land, and the Pacific Railroad Bill passed the same year, would create quick, cheap transportaion.

hostages, so mutilated and pierced by Apache lances that they were almost impossible to recognize. In retaliation, the soldiers hung the six male Apache hostages from scrub oak trees near the fresh graves of the whites, leaving them dangling for months as a grisly reminder of American justice. While the corpses dried in the desert sun, Cochise plotted his revenge, and from late April to June, Apache war parties ravaged the border region, killing—by the count of one Arizona pioneer—over 150 men, women, and children in 60 days.

That summer, the Apaches watched in satisfaction as the bluecoated soldiers burned their forts to the ground and marched toward the east, while ranchers and miners deserted the land and the Butterfield Mail station closed its doors. Mangas and Cochise had little knowledge of the new war in the East, perhaps no knowledge at all, and they naturally assumed that their own raids had driven the Americans away. In fact, similar activities were occurring throughout the West, as regular soldiers and civilians alike rushed to join the Civil War.

Ironically, this mass evacuation led to a larger and more ruthless fighting force in the West as the poorly educated, often ineffective regular troops were soon replaced by volunteer forces drawn from western settlements. These were a different breed of men—tougher, more motivated, often more educated—serving not for the promise of a regular salary but to defend their adopted homeland. By 1865, there would be 20,000 of such men throughout the West, approximately double the number of western regulars before the war.

In July 1862, the bluecoats reappeared in the land of the Apache, not from the east, but from the west—the advance unit of a California volunteer column under Col. James Carleton on its way to repel a Confederate invasion of New Mexico. Knowing the soldiers would need the water at Apache Pass, Cochise and Mangas decided to make a stand in the rocky gorge. Though their warriors battled the soldiers for two days, fighting with rifles taken in Apache raids, the Indians were no match for American howitzers. "We would have done well enough," one warrior later said, "if you had not fired wagons at us."

Once the spring was secured, the officer in charge sent a

small patrol back to warn the supply train, rolling on the trail behind them. An Apache war party followed and shot the horse out from under one of the soldiers, Pvt. John Teal, isolating him from the other soldiers. From behind the horse's carcass, Teal held off the attackers with his rapid-firing, breech-loading carbine. "In this way the fight continued for over an hour," Teal later remembered, "when I got a good chance at a prominent Indian and slipped a carbine ball into his breast." The Apaches withdrew, taking the wounded warrior with them, while Teal walked back to the supply train with his saddle over his shoulder.

THE GREATEST WRONG

Although John Teal didn't know it, the "prominent Indian" he had shot with his carbine was Mangas Coloradas. The Apache carried their wounded chief all the way to Janos, Mexico, where they grimly informed the doctor that he would either save Mangas's life or they would destroy the village and kill everyone in it. Fortunately for Janos, Mangas survived, but for Mangas himself, good fortune was drawing to an end.

By this time, Mangas was almost 70, perhaps even older, yet as his performance at Apache Pass makes clear, he was still an active warrior and a revered leader. In January 1863, a party of prospectors lured Mangas to Pinos Altos under a flag of truce, perhaps with an offer to exchange supplies for his people in return for permission to work the mines. Other Apaches warned him not to go but Mangas decided to meet the whites, who captured him and turned him over to a detachment of California volunteers, under the command of Gen. Joseph West. According to one soldier, West made it clear that he wanted Mangas to meet an unfortunate end: "Men," he allegedly said, "that old murderer has got away from every soldier command and has left a trail of blood for five thousand miles on the old stage line. I want him dead or alive tomorrow morning, do you understand, I want him dead."

That night, while Mangas slept, soldiers prodded his legs and feet with red-hot bayonets, until the old chief finally rose up to complain. The guards killed him with six rapid shots, later

A Unique Tribe

IN THE 19TH CENTURY, the Shoshone *(woman and child below)* occupied what is now southern Idaho and central Wyoming, as well as parts of Utah and Nevada. It was a young Shoshone woman, Sacajawea, who served as a guide and interpreter for Lewis and Clark in 1805-06. She had given birth less than two months before joining the expedition, but Shoshone women were legendary for their quick recuperation after childbirth. According to one story, a pregnant Shoshone on the trail excused herself, saying she would quickly catch up with the party. An hour later she returned, carrying her newborn child.

Although the Shoshone in Idaho resisted encroachment on the Oregon Trail and fought several bloody battles with whites—including the infamous massacre at Bear River—one large Shoshone band escaped the warfare that pervaded the West. Led by their great chief, Washakie, the Wind River Shoshone lived in relative isolation in the Wind River Basin of central Wyoming, protected by the Rocky Mountains on the west and the Bighorn Mountains on the east. Washakie was so committed to peace that when one of his

sons prepared to join a war party, he warned him, "My son, rather than see you take up arms against the white man, I will strike you dead." ■

Opposite: As a child, Naiche, younger son of Cochise, is said to have accompanied his mother and father to the fateful meeting with Lieutenant Bascom at Apache Pass. Later Naiche fought with Geronimo.

claiming that he had tried to escape. A soldier scalped the dead Indian in the morning, keeping his long, black hair as a souvenir, while the rest of his body was thrown into a shallow grave—only to be dug up so that the post surgeon could cut off Mangas's massive head for scientific research. The head was boiled down in a big black pot and sent off to the East, where a phrenologist proclaimed that the cranial capacity of the giant warrior was larger than that of Daniel Webster. The skull was later used as a lecture exhibit.

Angered by the murder of their greatest leader, the Apache were even more incensed by what had been done to his body. "To an Apache," one chief explained, "the mutilation of the body is much worse than death, because the body must go though eternity in the mutilated condition." For more than 20 years, the Southwest would bleed and suffer for the mutilation of Mangas and the hanging of Cochise's relatives, until the very word "Apache" became a symbol for the darkest fears of the American frontier. The war cry would be sounded by Cochise himself, then by Victorio, and others whose names and powers would only gradually be revealed, including a ruthless, resolute warrior who called the death of Mangas Coloradas, "perhaps the greatest wrong ever done to the Indians."

His name was Geronimo.

ALL THINGS IN NATURE

On January 29, 1863, 11 days after Mangas met his death at the hands of California Volunteers in New Mexico, a large band of Northwest Shoshone encountered another column of California Volunteers in southern Idaho. Like the Apache, the Shoshone were a wide-ranging people; this particular band, led by Sagwitch, the older political chief, and Bear Hunter, the younger war chief, occupied a central territory among the Shoshone lands. Many years later, Sagwitch's granddaughter, Mae T. Parry, described her people's life in those times:

The Northwestern Shoshones traveled with the changing seasons. They looked upon the earth not just as a place to live, but they called the earth their mother. She was the provider of their livelihood. The mountains, streams and plains stood forever they said, but the seasons walked around annually. All things in nature were fixed with the Indian.

In the early fall the Northwesterns moved into the general area of Salmon, Idaho, to fish. After the fishing was over and the fish had been prepared for winter use, they moved into Wyoming to hunt buffalo, elk, moose and antelope. It was very important to get the big game for it meant food, clothing and shelter to them.

In the spring and summer most of their time was spent traveling about Utah. Here they gathered seeds, berries, roots and also hunted smaller game. In late October a move was made into western Utah and parts of Nevada for the gathering of pine nuts. Most of the food was gathered and dried for their winter camping site, an area near Franklin, Idaho. Little did they realize that in 1863 this area would be a bloodbath for them.

Sagwitch and Bear Hunter had watched the Mormon entry into the Great Salt Lake valley in 1847, and for more than a decade they had enjoyed peaceful relations with the pioneers, who followed Brigham Young's policy "to feed and clothe [the Indians]…and treat them in all respects as you would like to be treated." By 1862, however, new gold strikes in what are now the states of Idaho and Montana brought a steady stream of prospectors north through Shoshone territory, adding to the well-established traffic on the Oregon-California Trail and depleting the already sparse resources of the semiarid land. Whereas other tribes had treaties and annuities to help them through such times of transition, the Shoshone were starving, forced to raid along the trails and test the generosity of the Mormons.

Tensions became acute in the Cache Valley, just northeast of the valley of Great Salt Lake, where resourceful Mormon pioneers had dug an irrigation canal to turn a dry land of sagebrush and wild grass into fertile fields. Although the settlers tried to follow Young's instructions, they began to resent the increasingly aggressive demands of the native people. "I rec'd your letter an have given the Indians a beef critter as directed," one settler reported to the Mormon leader, adding that he and his neighbors had also delivered 205 bushels of wheat and 2,000 pounds of flour besides "what they get at our houses." Around the same time, Peter Maughan, the first Mormon bishop in the valley, wrote to Young, "It does seem to me that the Indians on the North are determined to drive us to hostile measures. I suppose they have taken 100 horses in three weeks...I have never seen them so bold and daring in the Brethrens houses insulting the woman etc...."

THE PRIVILEGE OF AGETTING SHOT

At Fort Douglas, built on a mountain bench high above Salt Lake City, Col. Patrick Connor knew the troubles of the Cache Valley settlers, but he was not particularly concerned with the problems of the Mormons, whom he regarded as "traitors, murderers, fanatics, and whores." Connor's column of 850 California volunteers had marched across the Nevada desert that summer to set up a U.S. military presence in Utah Territory. His mission was two-fold: To keep an eye on the Mormons, whom many Americans mistakenly regarded as sympathetic to the Confederacy, and to protect the trails for emigrants, miners, and the overland mail. From the beginning, Connor had operated with ruthless efficiency, ordering one of his officers to "destroy every male Indian whom you may encounter in the vicinity of the late massacres."

By January 1863, the colonel was convinced that the Northwest Shoshone were responsible for a series of murderous attacks that had left scores of travelers dead along the trails. In fact, many of these attacks were carried out by other Shoshone bands, perhaps by other tribes, but Connor knew that the band under Sagwitch and Bear Hunter were camped for the winter along the Bear River, just north of the Cache Valley. "I determined," he wrote to his superiors, "although the season was unfavorable to an expedition in consequence of cold weather

The Mormons' arrival at the Great Salt Lake (above) in 1847 followed a 17-year 2,000 mile odyssey. Joseph Smith had founded the religion with six followers in 1830, in Fayette, New York. But incessant persecution forced the Mormons to relocate first to Ohio, then Missouri, and then Nauvoo, Illinois, where Smith was killed by an angry mob. Brigham Young assumed leadership, and in 1846 he led 147 followers westward to the Great Salt Lake. The U.S. refused to recognize their self-proclaimed state of Deseret and made it part of Utah Territory in 1850, though Young was appointed governor. Conflicts escalated, until 1857 when President James Buchanan sent troops to seize Salt Lake City and remove Young from office.

and deep snow, to chastise them if possible."

Connor had other reasons for "chastising" the Shoshone as well. His patriotic California Volunteers itched to fight the rebels in the East, so much so that they had collected over $25,000 for the war effort—at a time when they were paid $13 a month— and made a formal written proposal to the War Department to allow them to pay their own passage from San Francisco to Panama, "for the privilege of going to the Potomac and agetting shot." When the proposal was turned down, the men chafed at the prospect of spending their enlistments in the desert wastelands, where they blistered under the summer sun and froze around winter sagebrush fires. Morale was low, desertion high; Connor needed a good fight to satisfy his men. And on a personal level, the ambitious colonel wanted a successful battle to earn himself a general's star, just as his fellow Californian James Carleton had earned his fighting Indians in New Mexico.

Afraid the Shoshone might escape if they noticed large troop movements, Connor sent an advance detachment of 70 men, mostly infantry, with 15 supply wagons and 2 howitzers, perpetrating the illusion that a routine wagon train was moving north along the trail. Two days later, Connor himself followed with the cavalry, riding all night through snow and cold that froze the riders feet in their stirrups and left their whiskers and moustaches "chained together by ice." Before the expedition was over, almost 75 men—a fourth of Connor's command—would be lost to frostbitten feet.

CARNAGE IN THE RAVINE

In the early morning darkness of January 29, 1863, the forces met near the Shoshone camp, nestled along a willow-lined creek on the other side of the Bear River. Not counting those who were lost to the cold or detailed to watch the wagons, Colonel Connor had close to 200 fighting men to face an equal number of Shoshone warriors sleeping in the quiet village with their families. The howitzers had been left behind, mired in drifting snow.

The attack began in the hazy light of dawn, when Major

James McGarry led two companies of cavalry across the swift, half-frozen river. The Shoshone, roused from slumber by Chief Sagwitch, fired their rifles from the protection of the willows and natural embankments, and at first the troopers caught the worst of it, with 7 to 14 men falling dead in the snow while 20 more were wounded. Connor followed with the infantry, who struggled so desperately to cross the icy river that the cavalry had to ferry them on horseback. Once the full force was across, the soldiers flanked and swarmed upon the village, fighting for two hours from lodge to lodge, hand-to-hand, man-to-man. In close quarters, the army pistols and ready ammunition supply turned the once-even battle into a slaughter. While the soldiers carried 16,000 rounds, the Shoshone women and old men molded bullets in the midst of battle.

"Every Indian captured… during the present war who has been engaged in hostilities against whites…will be hanged on the spot, women and children in all cases being spared."

DEPARTMENT OF THE PACIFIC, APRIL 7, 1862

"The carnage presented in the ravine was horrible," wrote a reporter on the scene. "Warrior piled on warrior, horses mangled and wounded in every conceivable form, with here and there a squaw and papoose, who had been accidentally killed…." Chief Sagwitch escaped when he tumbled into the cold river and hid under the brush. His 12-year-old son played dead—on orders from his grandmother—and though a soldier discovered he was still alive, the man refused to shoot, a moment of mercy in the killing fields. Bear Hunter was not so fortunate. According to Shoshone tradition, he was wounded by soldiers, who "whipped him, kicked him and tried several means of torture...." When the stoic war chief refused to cry out for mercy, an enraged soldier thrust a red-hot bayonet through his ears.

It was over by ten o'clock in the morning, four hours after it had begun. Connor's losses were substantial by the standards of the time: 14 dead on the field and 9 who later died of their wounds. The Shoshone losses were staggering. Out of some 450 people in the village, at least 250 died that cold morning, including as many as 90 women and children. In all the battles west of the Mississippi, it may have been the largest single slaughter of Indian people by the United States Army.

Patrick Connor won his general's star for the Battle of Bear River, and was praised by his superior as "a man of observation, undaunted firmness, and self-possession under all circumstances." The Mormons of the Cache Valley offered even higher praise, calling his bold strike "an intervention of the Almighty." Yet the bloody battle failed in Connor's stated goal to chastise the Indians. Instead the Shoshone vowed to "kill every white man they could find," and the following months saw a rash of attacks and raids from the Cache Valley to the gold fields of Idaho and Montana. It was not until the summer of 1863, when the U.S. government finally made treaties with the Shoshone bands and offered meager dispersals of food and supplies, that a measure of peace came to the region.

PANNING GOLD OUT OF SAGEBRUSH

As the threat of Indian attack abated, miners in what is now Montana created a chaotic world of Wild West violence all their own. Though never as large as the rushes to California and Colorado, the Montana excitement had a unique intensity, coming as it did in the midst of the Civil War, when gold was desperately needed, while many western mining men had

temporarily given up the chase to fight for the blue or the gray. Nonetheless, there were plenty of adventurers, scoundrels, and hard-core prospectors ready to follow the cry of gold, and it was in the rich placers of Montana that they came closest to their dream of finding a new California.

In July 1862—the same month Connor's volunteers marched across Nevada—a group of Colorado miners on their way to the gold fields of Idaho stopped to prospect under the vast, arching sky northeast of the continental divide, amid broad mountain basins draining toward the Missouri. In a glistening creek that ran into the Beaverhead River, a miner named John White found enough "color" to cause considerable excitement. Unaware that Lewis and Clark had named the stream almost 60 years earlier, White and his companions dubbed it Grasshopper Creek for the pests that dogged their every footstep. Drawing miners already in the area, a town quickly rose along the creek, in the higher country about 12 miles up from White's initial find. They called it Bannack, a misspelled tribute to the local Bannock Indians, who were culturally related to the Paiute and Shoshone.

At first the banks of Grasshopper Creek were so rich that a man could find a dollar's worth of gold by pulling up a sagebrush and shaking the dirt from its roots into a pan, and "panning gold out of sagebrush" became a running joke among the excited prospectors. By the following spring, however, the golden sand and gravel had begun to play out, and a group of men organized a prospecting party up the Yellowstone River.

The main party men left Bannack on April 9, but seven others who had intended to join them missed their connection—and it was these men who would ultimately find the gold. Trying to catch up to the larger group, the seven prospectors were captured by Crow Indians, who considered killing them, until one of the prospectors, a tall prankster from New Brunswick named Bill Fairweather, pulled live rattlesnakes out of his shirt and hit a medicine man with a bush. Another prospector, a half-breed who acted as interpreter, explained that the Indians thought Fairweather was crazy, and that harming him would release the evil spirit that made him so. The half-breed decided it would be safer to stay behind with the Crow, while the other six

The Long Walk

CARLETON, CARSON, AND THE NAVAJO

By the time Gen. James Carleton and his California Column reached Santa Fe in the fall of 1862, Confederate forces had already been driven from New Mexico by volunteers from Colorado. So the Californians turned to fighting Indians instead. As field commander, Carleton chose the famous Indian scout, Colonel Christopher "Kit" Carson, ordering him to force the Mescalero Apache onto a reservation in the Pecos River Valley. "There is to be no council held with the Indians, nor any talks," Carleton told Carson. "The men are to be slain whenever and wherever they can be found."

Although Carson didn't take Carleton's command seriously, one of his officers ordered soldiers to fire directly into a gathering of Mescalero leaders, killing 11 and wounding 20 others. By the time Carson arrived, the resistance had been broken, and Carson quickly forced some 400 Mescalero onto a reservation called Bosque Redondo or "Circle of Trees," for a circular grove of cottonwood trees. It was a dry, barren place, so isolated that Carleton decided it would be perfect for the troublesome Navajo tribe—then some 12,000 strong—ranging over the spectacular canyonlands of the Colorado Plateau.

Carleton, in fact, underestimated the number of Navajo and the suitability of Bosque Redondo. He was simply carrying out the vision of his predecessor, Col. Edward Canby, who, after several frustrating campaigns, had concluded that the Navajo would either have to be exterminated or removed to "points so remote from the settlements as to isolate them entirely from the inhabitants of the territory."

Carleton issued an ultimatum, giving the Navajo until July 20, 1863, to surrender or be considered hostile. Anxious for victory, he ordered Carson into the field three weeks before the ultimatum expired, with a force of almost 1,000 men, including Mexican, Ute, and Zuni volunteers, all traditional Navajo enemies eager for plunder and Navajo slaves. Carson—who understood the Indians as well as any white man in the West—attacked their sources of livelihood, burning Navajo fields and orchards, stealing flocks and herds, destroying hogans. Although he treated individual Indians well, Carson's soldiers killed over 300 Navajo in 1863 alone, capturing some 700 more. Army losses were relatively minor.

The greatest blow of all came in January 1864, when Carson and a smaller column of 375 men penetrated the ancient Navajo stronghold of Canyon de Chelly, not only a place of refuge for their flocks, but a place of spiritual refuge as well, where the "ancient ones," the Anasazi, had built their cliff cities in the chocolate-streaked canyon walls. By the end of the year, over 8,000 Navajo had made the 300-mile "long walk" to join the Mescalero Apache at Bosque Redondo. "People were shot down on the spot if they complained about being tired or sick," wrote one chronicler, "or if they stopped to help someone. If a woman became in labor with a baby, she was killed. There was absolutely no mercy."

Life on the reservation was as bad as the march to get there. The Mescalero escaped in 1865; but the Navajo—ravaged by starvation, disease, and homesickness—remained until 1868, when they were allowed to return to a large, new reservation that included their homelands around Canyon de Chelly. Back in their sacred world, they never fought the whites again; today the Navajo are the largest American Indian tribe. ∎

Called "Little Chief" by the Indians, five-foot-six Kit Carson mapped trails with John C. Fremont before fighting in the Mexican War. During the Civil War he organized the 1st New Mexico Volunteers and reluctantly forced the Navajo from their sacred homeland in Canyon de Chelly (right).

men headed back for Bannack, fighting off another Crow attack along the way, near the present site of Bozeman.

Fearing further Indian troubles, they decided to leave the regular trail and follow the course of the Madison River until they turned west and cut across the Tobacco Root mountain range, finally reaching a creek in a narrow gulch lined with alder. On the evening of May 26, four of the men went up the creek to prospect, while Bill Fairweather and Henry Edgar watched the horses and decided to do a little prospecting of their own. Edgar described the moment in his diary:

> Bill went across to a [gravel] bar to see or look for a place to stake the horses. When he came back to camp he said, "There is a piece of rimrock sticking out of the bar over there. Get the tools and we will go and prospect it." Bill got the pick and shovel and I the pan and went over. Bill dug the dirt and filled the pan. "Now go," he says, "and wash that pan and see if you can get enough to buy some tobacco when we get back to town."

To the men's delight, there was more than enough to buy tobacco; as it turned out, there was enough in that gulch to buy whatever their hearts desired. By the time the other four prospectors returned, Fairweather and Edgar had over $12 worth of gold, finding as much as $5 in a single pan. Over the next two days, the men staked claims and panned almost $200 worth before heading back to Bannack. Though they tried to keep the find a secret, the signs were obvious: The men ate an expensive meal of bacon and eggs, bought new suits of clothes, and replenished the supplies they had lost to the Crow. When they tried to slip out of town on the morning of June 2, a crowd of 200 prospectors followed them down the Beaverhead.

Alder Gulch, as Edgar named it, quickly developed into one of the richest mining districts in history. By 1900, this single gulch would yield over $85 million worth of gold, with at least $30 million coming in the first few years. By late summer 1863, there were some 10,000 men working for 17 miles along the creek, harvesting gold faster and easier than anyone had harvested it since the halcyon days of California. It was an irresistible magnet for mayhem, according to one contemporary chronicler, attracting "the greatest aggregation of toughs and criminals that ever got together in the west....deserters from the Union and Rebel armies, river pirates and professional gamblers and sharpers." He didn't mention stagecoach robbers and cold-blooded murderers, but they came, too.

I Am Innocent

By October 1863, the prospect of a long, cold winter was already tangible in the crisp mountain air. Some of the Alder Gulch prospectors decided to return to the "states" with their new-found riches. One of them was "Bummer Dan" McFadden, a colorful character who, depending upon the story, received his nickname for his lazy habit of "bumming" handouts from fellow miners or because he had been an officer's aide, or "bummer," in the army. In any case, Dan had struck one of the richest claims in the gulch, and he was nervous about the rough characters who were filtering into Virginia City. He took every precaution he could to protect his gold, suspending the sacks of dust on leather thongs and hanging them inside his pants, while stuffing more sacks into his pockets. Fearful lest he be noticed leaving Virginia City on the stage, Dan walked 20 miles to a remote station before finally boarding the stagecoach for Bannack, from there to Salt Lake City and the states.

It was all for naught—as the tired horses pulled the stage through a narrow defile, two men wrapped in blankets with hoods over their heads stopped the stage and forced the driver to search the passengers. When he came to Dan, the driver found the sacks in his pockets and moved on, but one of the masked men ordered him to take the sacks under Dan's pants as well. The outlaws knew what they were looking for and they got it.

Bummer Dan's was the first stage robbed between Virginia City and Bannack, but it wasn't the last. The true extent of the great Montana "crime spree" remains in doubt. "One hundred and two people had been certainly killed by those miscreants...," wrote one imaginative writer of the time. "All that was known was that they started for various places and were never heard of again." Modern historians point out, however, that during a 14-month period before and after the founding of Alder Gulch, there were 18 documented murders and 11 robberies, and most of the murders had more to do with whiskey, Indians, or women than with stealing gold. Yet, whatever the numbers, the citizens of Alder Gulch were clearly troubled. They had no local government—the town of Virginia City would not be incorporated until January, while the Territory of Montana would be formed the following spring—and the only local law was a branch office of Sheriff Henry Plummer, who worked and lived in Bannack, over 80 miles away.

In December, a young German immigrant named Nicholas Tbalt was found near the Bannack road, frozen stiff with a bullet in his head and lariat marks around his neck. The man who found him, William Palmer, owned a saloon in Nevada City, just down the gulch from Virginia City; he brought the body back in a wagon and displayed it in front of his saloon—which proved good for business and bad for the outlaws. That afternoon, Palmer led two dozen horsemen back down the road, and they returned with several suspects, including a tall, blonde fellow named George Ives, who was already suspected in the robbery of a mail coach bound for Salt Lake City.

Now the citizens galvanized their resistance and the man who led the charge was a young lawyer named Wilbur Sanders who didn't drink and sang too loudly in church, both suspect behaviors on the hard-scrabble frontier, but who proved a brave, if bombastic prosecutor. The trial of George Ives was held in the snowy streets of Nevada City, with two wagons providing seats for the prisoners, their lawyers, and witnesses, while a semicircle of benches formed a jury box and a big bonfire provided heat for participants and onlookers alike.

After three days of long orations, a 24-man jury convicted Ives of the murder of Nicholas Tbalt. One juror believed that he was innocent of the murder, but Sanders jumped up on a wagon and made a motion that the crowd ignore the dissenting vote and accept the verdict of the majority. When the crowd roared its approval, Sanders made a second motion that Ives be hung right

During the early evening of May 26, 1863, itinerant prospectors found gold in Montana's Alder Gulch (above). Although they had originally hoped for "enough to buy some tobacco," the gulch proved to be one of the richest strikes in the West, yielding some $85 million in gold by 1900. Within a few months of the discovery, an estimated 10,000 miners were working up and down the gulch, giving rise to a string of boomtowns, including wild and rollicking Virginia City.

then and there. Again the crowd approved. After a third motion to take Ives's property in order to pay the expenses of trying and killing him, the condemned man was led over to a wooden box where a noose dangled from the beam of an unfinished building. With the noose around his neck, just before the box was kicked out from under him, Ives said, "I am innocent of this crime; Alex Carter killed the Dutchman."

George Ives's death by hanging marked the beginning of Montana vigilante justice. Wilbur Sanders and five others formed a secret Vigilance Committee, swearing to rid the mining regions of the criminal element, unfettered by the constraints of due legal process. Others quickly joined them, and on December 23, two days after the hanging of George Ives, a self-appointed posse of 24 men rode out of Virginia City to apprehend Alex Carter, the man Ives had named as the killer. When they couldn't find Carter, they seized a good-natured cook named Red Yeager, who had given Carter a letter of warning; Yeager admitted delivering the letter, but said a local bartender had actually written it, so the vigilantes decided to hang them both for interfering with "justice."

GOOD-BYE, BOYS

If the stories are true, Red Yeager faced his demise with extraordinary good humor, shaking the vigilantes' hands with the noose around his neck, saying "Good-bye, boys; God bless you, you are on a good undertaking." Moments earlier, however, before he stepped into the noose, Red allegedly decided to spill the beans, describing a well-organized, secret criminal organization in which the members recognized each other by several signs, including the password, "I am innocent." He supposedly provided a detailed list of men, including himself, who belonged to the organization. The chief and criminal mastermind was none other than Henry Plummer, the duly elected sheriff of both Bannack and Virginia City.

Despite the freezing weather, four men rode to Bannack and organized the locals into a committee to hang the sheriff and two of his deputies. By the cold evening of Sunday, January 10,

1864, over fifty men had joined the vigilante movement. They took the deputies first, one from the cabin he shared with his wife, the other passed out on a gambling table. Then they went for Plummer, who was sick and resting at the home of his sister-in-law. Under the pretense of discussing another criminal, the vigilantes drew the sheriff outside, where Plummer was herded toward a gallows he had built himself on the edge of town. Wilbur Sanders drove the men on, shouting, "Company! Forward march!"

"Indians are coming! Indians are advancing on the town to burn and massacre! Hurry our wives and children to places of safety!"

A COLORADO RANCHER GALLOPING THROUGH DENVER, JUNE 1864

All three men claimed their innocence, but as far as the vigilantes were concerned, the time for innocence was passed. Under the gallows, Plummer spoke of his beloved wife, who was away in the East, and asked to see his sister-in-law. He asked for a jury trial, for time to settle his affairs, for time to pray. But the night was freezing cold, and the men who surrounded him were in a hurry. So after watching his two deputies hanging in curse-filled agony, he made one last request: "Give me a high drop, boys." This they did, "as high as circumstances permitted," according to one account, "by hoisting him up as far as possible in their arms, and letting him fall suddenly. He died quickly and without much struggle."

The next morning, a mob went after the only Mexican in town, Joe Pizanthia, who they called "the Greaser." Although he had not been named as one of the gang, they were interested in "investigating his career in the Territory," and when he defended himself by killing one of the men in the mob, they hauled out a howitzer and blasted his cabin until it exploded in flames. Then they dragged Pizanthia, still half-alive, out in the street, strung him up from a pole and riddled his body with bullets. After hanging another man in Bannack, the vigilantes returned to the Virginia City area, where they hung five suspects on January 14. By early February, nine more had been strung up in the surrounding area, bringing the total to 22 executions in less than six weeks.

Though the pace of vigilante justice slowed after this initial onslaught, the vigilantes remained an organized force for several years. In late 1864, they hung a man in Bannack who had committed the "crime" of saying the "strangling" vigilantes had hung some "good men." In time, however, as the territorial government became established and a measure of civilization came to the Montana frontier, the citizens began to regard the vigilantes as being as dangerous as the alleged gang of criminals they had originally formed to combat. One disgusted citizens group posted a notice that any future hangings would be punished at a rate of five to one, a warning that tended to have a chilling effect on further vigilante activities.

All Citizens of Colorado

During the winter of 1863-1864, as the vigilantes of Montana pursued what they believed to be a vast criminal conspiracy, the Governor of Colorado Territory, John Evans, contemplated a more frightening conspiracy on the plains: A secret agreement among the Sioux, Cheyenne, Arapaho, Comanche, and Kiowa to unite in a massive force "capable of sweeping off white settlers" from Texas to the Canadian border. Evans' source was a disreputable trader named Robert North, "who had been loafing around Arapaho camps and living off the Indians for years." Many disputed North's story then, as they do today; the half-breed Cheyenne trader George Bent, who often lived among his mother's people, called it "a lie from beginning to end."

Yet there may have been something behind it—not the grand conspiracy North described—but a growing united front, with the elect Cheyenne warrior society, the Dog Soldiers, at the heart of it. Raids on the western trails did increase during the Civil War, and history had taught the Americans that the native people often banded together when whites fought among themselves. It had happened in the Ohio River Valley during the War of 1812, when the British aided the united forces of Tecumseh; why could it not happen in the Platte Valley during the Civil War?

In the end, however, what really mattered was not so much the conspiracy itself—whether real or imagined—but the fact that John Evans believed in it, and trumpeted the idea in frantic telegrams and letters to the East. A physician, businessman, and friend of Lincoln, Evans had already made his mark in Illinois, where he founded Northwestern University in the town of Evanston, named in his honor. Now he had even bigger dreams for Colorado. "No other land offers such opportunities for the vast accumulation of wealth," he proclaimed. As a commissioner of the newly formed Union Pacific Railroad corporation, he dreamed of routing iron rails through Colorado, dreamed of leading the territory to statehood and representing her in the United States Senate. These dreams depended on gaining clear title to Indian lands and protecting the growing settlements from attack; the conspiracy theory fed both his darkest fears and his deepest pragmatic needs.

That summer, after a series of escalating incidents, it seemed that Evans' obsession with an Indian war had become a self-fulfilling prophecy. Hostile warriors raided wagon trains and isolated settlements, leaving a trail of mutilated bodies, kidnapping women and children, stealing livestock and whatever plunder they could find. By mid-August the flow of freight stopped on the Platte Road, and mail from the East had to be shipped to Denver by way of Panama and San Francisco. On August 11, with most of his regular fighting force occupied against the Confederates on the Missouri frontier, Evans issued a proclamation authorizing "all citizens of Colorado, either individually or in such parties as they may organize,...to go in pursuit of all hostile Indians on the plains,...to kill and destroy

Henry Plummer

RUMOR VS. REALITY IN THE WEST

*T*HE LAWMAN WHO teeters on the edge of the law is a classic archetype of the Wild West, embodied most famously in the careers of Wild Bill Hickok and Wyatt Earp. Before these, however, there was Henry Plummer, an even darker archetype of a frightening breed: the bad sheriff.

The Plummer legend arises out of the complex, confusing period of vigilante justice during the early gold rush days of Bannack and Virginia City, Montana. The suave, smooth-talking sheriff of both towns, so quick with his revolver that "he could draw the pistol and discharge the five loads in three seconds," Henry Plummer allegedly led a sophisticated band of road agents, who knew each other by secret signs and tracked every shipment of gold, killing and robbing at least 102 men in a "reign of terror" that could be stopped only by the quick and final justice of the hangman's noose.

This story has been passed down for a century and a quarter; yet the original chronicler of the Plummer saga, a mining camp intellectual named Thomas J. Dimsdale, was an unabashed apologist for the vigilantes and didn't witness the events he described. It's only recently that two modern scholars, R.E. Mather and F.E. Boswell, have reexamined the evidence with a more objective eye.

While Dimsdale portrayed Plummer as a "wily seducer" and "a very demon," Mather and Boswell see him as an effective law officer and "gifted leader" who could never live down his unfortunate past. Originally, from Maine, Plummer had first come west in the rush to California, where as town marshal of Nevada City he gained a reputation as a "prompt and energetic" public officer, who "when opposed in the performance of his official duties,…became as bold and determined as a lion." While performing these duties, Plummer shot a man in what appeared to be self-defense; yet after a lurid, emotionally-charged case that went twice to the California Supreme Court, he was sentenced to San Quentin for second degree murder.

Suffering from tuberculosis, Plummer was released after six months; while he recovered from his illness, he never recovered his reputation. Rumors of his questionable character set several prominent Bannack citizens against him, notably Sidney Edgerton, who would become the first governor of Montana Territory, and his nephew, Wilbur Sanders, the crusading lawyer who became the driving force behind the vigilantes. The conflict was exacerbated by political differences in the overheated atmosphere of the Civil War.

The evidence against Plummer was minimal at best: A teenage boy saw a flash of red when a hooded man opened his coat, a fact that seemed to match the bright red lining of Plummer's coat. And Red Yeager, one of the first men hung, supposedly identified Plummer as the outlaw leader before he died—though no one but the vigilantes heard Yeager's "confession." As for the gang itself, there were relatively few documented murders and robberies during Plummer's term of office, and crime in the mining region seems to have increased and become better organized after Plummer and the alleged gang members were executed.

Although they stop short of exonerating Plummer, Mather and Boswell make a strong case for the dangers of vigilante justice. "I don't know if Plummer was guilty or not," Mather says, "but the vigilantes didn't know, either." ∎

Nevada City, Montana, (above) was the site of the trial of George Ives, the first act in the drama of vigilante justice that led to the hanging of Sheriff Henry Plummer in Bannack, set in the shadow of the Bitterroot Range (right). Plummer was one of 22 men hanged by vigilantes during the winter of 1863-64.

as enemies of the country wherever they may be found, all such hostile Indians." Four days later, he received authorization to raise a special force, the Third Colorado Regiment, for a period of a hundred days in order to fight the Indians.

In mid-September, while Cheyenne warriors still controlled the Platte Road, the people of Colorado Territory voted on the question of statehood. By this point, Evans' popularity had dipped so low that he withdrew his own candidacy for the Senate in hopes of saving the issue of statehood. It didn't help; the voters rejected statehood by an overwhelming margin—a clear personal defeat for Evans, as well as for his right-hand man, Col. John Chivington, the Colorado military commander who had run for the House of Representatives. Chivington, a former Methodist preacher they called the Fighting Parson, was a huge, belligerent, bear of a man who had made his reputation battling Confederates at Glorieta Pass in New Mexico. But that was two years past, and as far as the citizens of Colorado were concerned, he hadn't done much against the Indians.

Like Coming through the Fire

While Evans and Chivington licked their wounds, a peace movement had already begun on the Pplains, led by the great Cheyenne "peace-chief," Black Kettle, along with his brother White Antelope, the ancient One-Eye, and the English-speaking Arapaho chief, Left Hand. In a hastily arranged conference at their camp on the Smoky Hill River, the Indians met with Maj. Edward Wynkoop, the commander of an American outpost in southeastern Colorado called Fort Lyon. To show their good faith, they returned several white captives—ransomed from hostile warriors—and made it clear that they wanted nothing but peace. Wynkoop, the tall, handsome scion of a wealthy Philadelphia family, made a powerful impression on these men, not only for his polite manners and striking appearance, but because he came to see them on their terms, in the middle of the plains, where his soldiers were outnumbered eight to one. He told them honestly that he wasn't powerful enough to negotiate, but he promised a hearing with Governor Evans, who was also

the Indian agent for the territory. In late September the people of Denver watched in fascination as the Indian leaders entered the city in two wagons."

For John Evans, the peace conference was nothing but an annoyance, and he made his feelings quite clear to Major Wynkoop. His new Third Regiment was ready for action, and the action he had in mind could hardly take place in an atmosphere of peaceful negotiation. "What shall I do with the Third Regiment, if I make peace?" he asked Wynkoop more than once. "What shall I do with the Third?"

For the chiefs, however, the conference was deadly serious. Their only concern was the survival of their people, and they saw very clearly that there could be no survival in war with the whites. After the other leaders had spoken, Black Kettle eloquently expressed his feelings:

> I followed Major Wynkoop to Fort Lyon, and Major Wynkoop proposed that we come to see you. We have come with our eyes shut, following his handful of men, like coming through the fire. All we ask is that we may have peace with the whites. We have been traveling through a cloud. The sky has been dark ever since the war began. These braves with me are all willing to do what I say. We want to take good tidings home to our people, that they may sleep in peace.

Although both Evans and Chivington remained combative throughout the conference, the Cheyenne and Arapaho leaders returned to Fort Lyon with the clear understanding that they had been ordered to do so as a condition of remaining at peace with the whites. This was a continuation of a policy that Evans had established early in the summer, when he ordered "all friendly Indians" to "go to places of safety." But when Major Wynkoop tried to feed the Indians at the fort, he was summarily relieved of command and replaced by Maj. Scott Anthony—who sent the Indians away, telling them to camp on a meandering, half-dry stream called the Big Sandy or Sand Creek, about 40 miles from the fort. It was a barren, gameless area, but the hungry and desperate Indians camped there anyway, believing they were under the protection of the United States Army.

On November 14, Brig. Gen. Patrick Connor arrived in Denver to tumultuous acclaim. He had been ordered there to secure the Platte Road "without regard to department lines," which meant that he could operate freely within Chivington's Colorado Territory. Governor Evans, who always wanted more troops, was happy to see him, but for John Chivington this was the final straw. The brief enlistment of his vaunted "hundred dazers" was about to expire and he hadn't accomplished much of anything. He determined to destroy an Indian village, just as Connor had done in Idaho, and he had to do it soon. Evans apparently concurred, conveniently leaving the territory for Washington, D.C., satisfied that all would be well in Colorado.

> ## "Scalps are what we are after.... I long to be wading in gore."
>
> COLONEL JOHN CHIVINGTON

On the cold morning of November 29, 1864, Colonel Chivington and his men approached Sand Creek from Fort Lyon, where they had picked up Major Anthony and another 125 soldiers. The total force was probably around 700 men, while there were perhaps 600 Indians sleeping in the camp, including about 550 Cheyenne under Black Kettle and White Antelope and around 50 Arapaho under Left Hand. At least two-thirds of them were women and children.

"Men, strip for action," Chivington shouted, ordering the soldiers to take off their coats. "Take no prisoners....I don't tell you to kill all ages and sex, but look back on the plains of the Platte where your mothers, fathers, brothers, sisters have been slain, and their blood saturating the sand of the Platte." It wasn't precisely an invitation to massacre, but it had the desired effect.

When a group of Cheyenne and Arapaho women first sounded the alarm, the still-sleepy Indians were understandably confused. They believed they were camping where they had been ordered to camp, believed they were under the protection of the soldiers at Fort Lyon. Black Kettle hauled out a big American flag and a white flag of truce, both of which he been given several years earlier when he signed a treaty giving away his lands. Now he frantically tied them to a lodge pole and lifted it upright, waving the flags back and forth, calling for women and children to gather around him. Chivington's men fired on them anyway, and as the battle raged, it was the women and children who took the brunt of the soldiers' fury. A white interpreter later described the horror:

> They were scalped, their brains knocked out; the men used their knives, ripped open women, clubbed little children, knocked them in the head with their guns,... mutilated their bodies in every sense of the word.

By late afternoon, there were almost 70 mutilated Indian bodies, at least two-thirds women and children, lying in the sand and scattered pools of the streambed, and on the banks and hills beyond. Among the dead were White Antelope and One-Eye, who had stood beside Black Kettle in trying to lead the Cheyenne on the peaceful road. Many others, including Left Hand, escaped the battlefield only to die of their wounds. As much as any Indian leader, with his knowledge of the white man's language and way of life, Left Hand had irrevocably dedicated himself to the cause of peace, once saying that "the whites might murder their men and do anything they pleased to them, but they would never fight."

EMBLEMS OF JUSTICE AND HUMANITY

Chivington and his men marched through the streets of Denver triumphantly bearing Indian scalps. "A high old time there was last night," crowed the *Rocky Mountain News*. "Our streets,

The Minnesota Uprising

FROM THE WHITE point of view, the worst slaughter in the history of the West occurred in August 1862, in southern Minnesota. There the Santee Sioux or Dakota—eastern relatives of the Lakota—faced starvation on their small reservation along the Minnesota River, where unscrupulous government agents and traders were more concerned with lining their own pockets than feeding the Indians. "If they are hungry," one trader suggested, "let them eat grass or their own dung."

On August 17, four young warriors dared each other to kill a white man,

and the resentment exploded in violence. By the time the warriors arrived at their village, they had killed five whites, and the Santee convinced their chief, Little Crow—formerly a staunch proponent of peace—to lead them in a war against the intruders.

What followed was the worst nightmare of every pioneer. For a week, Santee war parties ravaged the settlements and attacked the forts, killing, raping, and torturing their victims. When it was over, between 500 and 800 whites were dead, including men and women, young and old, regular soldiers and volunteers. The callous trader was found with his mouth stuffed full of blood-soaked grass.

The uprising ended in late September, when U.S. troops defeated the Sioux at Wood Lake. After 303 warriors were sentenced to death in a hurried series of military trials, President Abraham Lincoln spared all but 38, who hung together on a cold December day in the public square of Mankato, Minnesota. It was the largest mass hanging in U.S. history. ■

hotels, saloons and stores today were thronged with strangers, chiefly Indian killers." Some days later, soldiers of the "Bloody Third" displayed their scalps on a Denver stage to the roar of an approving crowd.

For John Chivington, however, the glory was short-lived. On January 4, 1865, five weeks after the massacre, he resigned his commission under pressure from his commanding officer. Three days later, more than a thousand Cheyenne, Arapaho, and Lakota warriors—the largest Indian force yet assembled on the plains—attacked the town of Julesburg, Colorado, and went on to terrorize the Platte Road. It was the beginning of the united war that Governor Evans had long imagined. The statements of Indian leaders suggest that Sand Creek was an important factor in turning peaceful or ambivalent men onto the path of war. "What do we want to live for?" asked one Cheyenne chief during this time. "The white man has taken our country, killed all our game; was not satisfied with that, but killed our wives and children. Now no peace. We want to go and meet our families in the spirit land....We have raised the battle-ax until death."

Three separate inquiries were held into the Sand Creek incident, each collecting testimony that shocked and sickened those who heard it. In Washington, D.C., the joint congressional committee charged with investigating the conduct of the Civil War chastised Colonel John Chivington and his soldiers in the strongest possible words:

It is difficult to believe that beings in the form of men, and disgracing the uniform of United States soldiers and officers, could commit or countenance the commission of such acts of cruelty and barbarity as are detailed in the testimony, but which your committee will not specify in their report....

As to Colonel Chivington, your committee can hardly find fitting words to describe his conduct. Wearing the uniform of the United States, which should be the emblem of justice and humanity; holding the important position of commander of a military district, and therefore having the honor of the government to that extent in his keeping, he deliberately planned and executed a foul and dastardly massacre which would have disgraced the veriest savage among those who were the victims of his cruelty.

John Evans also faced considerable criticism for his part in the tragedy, and after the assassination of Abraham Lincoln, he was asked to resign as governor by new President Andrew Johnson. Unlike Chivington, however, who spent the rest of his life defending his actions, Evans was able to put Sand Creek behind him, going on to make a fortune in Colorado real estate.

Supporters of Evans and Chivington pointed to the atrocities committed along the Platte that summer, as well as the alleged presence of fresh white scalps in the Indian camp, an indication that hostile warriors were given refuge with Black Kettle's peaceful people. One woman, living in Denver at the time of the attack, clearly expressed the feelings of the Colorado pioneers: "Had you been living at that time, as we were, in a constant state of fear and anxiety, almost daily seeing the bodies of friends or acquaintances that had been mutilated by the Indians, you would have found no censure in your heart for Colonel Chivington's act."

From the beginning, Americans had convinced themselves that the relentless westward march was the march of civilization. Certain aspects of native culture, reinforced by the whites' own religious and cultural prejudices, had blinded the newcomers to the sophisticated social and spiritual lives of the native people. And so the idea persisted, allowing even the most humane white thinkers to justify the taking of Indian lands as a necessary step for the greater good. Sand Creek shook this idea to its very roots. Other incidents in the West during the Civil War—the murder of Mangas, the slaughter at Bear River, even the vigilante movement of Montana—might have shaken it as well, had they been better reported and understood at the time, but it was Sand Creek that forced America to confront the hard edge of the frontier—or as one senator called it, the "boundary line between savage and civilized life."

A gathering of dazed and frightened refugees from the Minnesota Uprising gaze balefully into the camera. The Dakota chief, Little Crow, who led the uprising against his better judgment, was apalled at the carnage, for he knew Federal reprisals would be swift and severe. "Kill one—two—ten, and ten times ten will come to kill you," he admonished his warriors. "Count your fingers all day long and white men with guns in their hands will come faster than you can count....They will all turn on you and devour you and your women and little children just as the locusts in their time fall on the trees and devour all the leaves in one day."

THE INDIANS

Fighting for Their Homes

MAKING IT DIFFICULT for Indians to accept reservation life was the fact that the reservations were unsuitable for maintaining their traditional culture. The understandable reluctance of Indian leaders to live in these places led to countless battles with federal troops. The Modoc War led by Captain Jack, for example, might have been avoided if the tribe had been granted a reserve in their ancestral home along the Lost River of northern California. Instead, they were forced onto a reservation in Oregon where the Modoc chafed under the domination

Wovoka, Paiute

of the larger Klamath tribe.

A similar problem arose with the Apache after the death of Cochise. The powerful leader had negotiated an acceptable reservation that included the Chiricahua and Dragoon mountains of southeastern Arizona, but after his death Cochise's people were moved to the miserable, malarial flats near the San Carlos agency to the north, a place they came to hate so much that leaders like Geronimo broke out again and again, leaving a trail of terror in their wake.

Victorio led another Apache band that lived happily for a time in their ancestral mountains of New Mexico. Pleading not to be transferred to San Carlos, Victorio turned belligerent when his pleas fell on deaf ears. "You can take our women and children in your wagons," he warned, "but my men will not go." In the end, Victorio led a brilliant, though doomed guerrilla campaign that left a legacy of blood along the border.

The Navajo were luckier. While over 8,000 surrendered to Kit Carson and Gen. James Carleton in 1864, a group led by Manuelito lived as guerrillas in the mountains of Arizona for two years until starvation brought them to the Bosque Redondo Reservation in New Mexico, where they joined the rest of their sick and starving people. The conditions were so appalling that in 1868, the Navajo were

Captain Jack, Modoc

Cochise, Apache

Victorio, Apache

Cheyenne at the Pine Ridge Reservation

Oglala Sioux delegation with Red Cloud at center

given a reservation on their ancestral lands around Canyon de Chelly in Arizona. "We told the drivers to whip the mules, we were in such a hurry," Manuelito recalled. "When we saw the top of the mountain…we felt like talking to the ground, we loved it so, and some of the old men and women cried with joy when they reached their homes."

As hard as this transition was, it was peaceful compared to the ordeals of the Lakota and Cheyenne, who fought after the Civil War under great warriors like Red Cloud and Roman Nose. "If the Great Father kept white men out of my country, peace would last forever," said Red Cloud in 1867, "but if they disturb me, there will be no peace." Red Cloud won a hard-fought victory the following

White Man Runs Him, Crow

year, but the peace proved illusory and the battle continued under Crazy Horse and Sitting Bull, who defeated George Custer's Seventh Cavalry at the Little Bighorn.

Custer himself relied on the advice of Indian scouts, believing it necessary to "fight the devil with fire." His favorite scout was an Arikara named Bloody Knife, whom he called "my brother." Before he marched in search of the great encampment under Sitting Bull, however, Custer borrowed a number of Crow scouts, including White Man Runs Him, from another command. The scouts told Custer that there were too many Lakota and Cheyenne to fight: He ignored their advice and paid the price. Bloody Knife died in battle, but White Man Runs Him lived to tell the tale.

The Indian victory at the Little Bighorn only postponed the inevitable, and the Lakota and Cheyenne were eventually forced onto reservations as well. In 1890, desperate and despairing, the Lakota embraced the Ghost Dance religion, founded in Nevada by Wovoka, a young Paiute shaman. Wovoka's religion preached peace above all, but the Lakota developed their own interpretations, including the Ghost Shirt, which was supposedly impervious to bullets—a belief that made their Federal guards nervous and led to the massacre at Wounded Knee. ■

Roman Nose, Cheyenne

Manuelito, Navajo

IRON RAILS

"*Let us resolve to have a railroad to the Pacific—
to have it soon. It will add more to the strength and wealth of
our country than would the acquisition of a dozen Cubas.*"

HORACE GREELY, 1859

IRON RAILS

*L*ONG BEFORE THE DISCOVERY OF CALIFORNIA GOLD, A HANDFUL OF MEN ENVISIONED THE DAY WHEN IRON RAILS WOULD SPAN THE CONTINENT. AMONG THE FIRST WAS A RESTLESS WELSHMAN NAMED JOHN PLUMBE, WHO PETITIONED CONGRESS TO BUILD A TRANSCONTINENTAL RAILROAD IN 1838 AND WAS TOLD HE MIGHT AS WELL ASK "TO BUILD A RAILROAD TO THE MOON." • EAST COAST MERCHANT ASA WHITNEY SAW THE WESTERN RAILROAD AS A FAST ROUTE TO THE ORIENT. IN 1845, HE ASKED CONGRESS FOR A STRIP OF LAND SIXTY MILES WIDE FROM LAKE MICHIGAN TO THE PACIFIC OCEAN, REASONING THAT HE COULD SELL THE LAND TO PAY THE EXPENSES OF BUILDING THE RAILROAD. HE WAS REFUSED, BUT THE IDEA OF BARTERING LAND FOR CONSTRUCTION WOULD RETURN. • THE RUSH TO CALIFORNIA UPPED THE ANTE CONSIDERABLY. THERE WAS NOW GOLD ON THE "MOON," AND THAT GOLD REQUIRED TRANSPORT AND PROTECTION IN THE EVENT OF WAR. IN 1852, THE CALIFORNIA LEGISLATURE PROCLAIMED THAT "THE INTERESTS OF THIS STATE, AS WELL AS THOSE OF THE WHOLE UNION, REQUIRE THE IMMEDIATE ACTION OF THE GOVERNMENT

It took a handful of visionaries, some shady financiers, and a legion of laborers (above) to build a railroad across the seemingly impassable Sierra Nevada (opposite and previous page). In seven years, they managed to do what many thought impossible—build a railroad across the continent.

of the United States for the construction of a national thoroughfare connecting the navigable waters of the Atlantic and Pacific oceans...."

The following year, Congress ordered the Army Corps of Topographical Engineers to survey possible routes. Their final reports, issued at great expense beginning in 1856, contained engravings of breathtaking scenery and details about flora, fauna, and native people, but little information that would be useful in building a railroad. Moreover, the reports only heightened the growing debate: Southern politicians favored the southernmost route, which the army engineers considered the cheapest; yet northern legislators feared they would lose a southern railroad— and California—in the looming battle over slavery. The route that was ultimately chosen, along the Platte River, was not actually surveyed, but some knowledgeable men banked on it anyway. One of them was a raw-boned Illinois congressman named Abraham Lincoln, who acquired land near Council Bluffs, Iowa, a logical starting point for a railroad line along the Platte.

Asa Whitney had once said that if a Pacific railroad were to be built, "some one's whole efforts, energies, and life must be devoted to it." Although Whitney tried to be that someone, another Easterner named Theodore Judah grabbed the reins. Humorless, driven, and intensely practical, Judah had come to California as chief engineer of the Sacramento Valley Railroad, completed in 1856, which connected Sacramento with the gold fields. Even as he built this short line, he dreamed of the "most magnificent project ever conceived," extending the rails across the continent. After examining the early army reports, Judah offered Congress a proposal in 1857, pointing out that financial backers would require solid details before investing their money:

> When a Boston capitalist is invited to invest in a railroad project,...he does not care to be informed that there are 999 different varieties and species of plants and herbs, or that grass is abundant....He says, let me see your map and profile, that I may judge of its alignment and grades....Have you any tunnels and what are their circumstances?...How many bridges, river crossings,

culverts,...how about timber and fuel? Where is the estimate of the cost of your road?

Despite the practicality of Judah's approach, Congress was too torn by sectionalism and slavery to act. Aided by a friend, Dr. Daniel Strong, Judah explored a route through Dutch Flat, an area north of the American River, then up over the Sierras through the pass where the Donner Party had met with disaster. While investigating the route in October 1860, Judah and Strong barely escaped a similar fate, racing down from the mountains in the middle of the night when they were caught in the first snowstorm of the season. Convinced that they had found the route, the two men drew up an agreement to elicit stock subscriptions for the Central Pacific Railroad.

CRAZY JUDAH AND THE BIG FOUR

They found no takers in San Francisco, where the moneyed men had lost investments in the ill-fated Sacramento Valley Railroad and weren't about to risk more cash with "Crazy Judah." Undeterred, Judah moved on to Sacramento, where he met with a group of local businessmen, persuading seven of them to join with him in financing a proper survey of the proposed route. "You will have control of business interests that will make your fortune in trade," Judah promised. "Why, you can have a wagon road if not a railroad."

Among Judah's new partners were the gold-rush merchants who would become famous as the "Big Four." First among equals was Collis P. Huntington, a strapping six-footer who would become the driving force behind the railroad's business deals. Though initially skeptical of Judah's railroad, Huntington saw enough potential to convince his partner, Mark Hopkins, a thoughtful man of careful judgment and integrity. "I never thought anything finished until Hopkins looked at it," he once said, "which is praise enough." Huntington also brought in Leland Stanford, rising star in the California Republican party, and Charles Crocker, a bull of a man whom Huntington counted as "one of the best businessmen in California."

At the time they joined with Judah in the Central Pacific Railroad, the Big Four had combined assets of less than $1.5 million, but they were destined to make fortunes beyond belief. "We were successful, we four," Huntington later explained, "because of our teamwork. Each complimented the other.... There was Stanford, for instance, a man elected senator and governor, a man who loved to deal with people....There was Mark Hopkins. He was a fine accountant and understood the value of everything....Then, there was Crocker, the organizer, the executive, the driver of men." And there was Huntington, the glue who held them all together, a man who refused to take "no" for an answer.

Despite the formidable talents of Theodore Judah and the Big Four, it took a war to jump-start the railroad. When Confederate guns fired on Fort Sumter in April 1861, the need for the railroad became more apparent than ever, while the resistance of southern legislators was no longer an issue. The Central Pacific Rail Road of California was incorporated two months later, on June 28, 1861. Judah completed his survey in early August and set sail for the East Coast that fall. It was his fourth visit to Washington to lobby for the railroad, but now, with his detailed survey in hand and war raging throughout the land, he was confident of success.

Though it took time to push the legislation through Congress and to defeat another powerful lobby that wanted to build west from Missouri, President Lincoln finally signed the Pacific Railroad Bill on July 1, 1862, creating the Union Pacific Railroad Company to build "a single line of railroad and telegraph from a point on the western boundary of the State of Iowa to be fixed by the President of the United States." At the same time, the already established Central Pacific would build "from the navigable waters of the Sacramento River to the eastern boundary of California" and meet the tracks from the east. Not surprisingly, the starting point for the Union Pacific was later fixed at Council Bluffs, where the President of the United States happened to own some land.

Both companies received the same compensation: Alternate sections of land on either side of the track, equaling ten sections

State and territory borders as of 1869
Present-day state names in gray

The route of the first transcontinental railroad was a compromise between conflicting interests; Southern politicians favored a route through the southwest while others wanted a railroad through the far north. Over the next 25 years four more transcontinental lines crossed the nation. The Atchison, Topeka, and Santa Fe met the Southern Pacific at Deming, New Mexico in 1881, forming the nation's second transcontinental route. The storied Santa Fe then obtained other lines to the east and west, becoming the only 19th century railroad to run on its own tracks from Chicago to the Pacific Coast. The Southern Pacific—run by the same "Big Four" who built the Central Pacific—developed its own line between Los Angeles and New Orleans. Far to the north, the Northern Pacific had reached Bismarck, South Dakota, in 1873, but it was not until 1883 that it became a transcontinental railroad, connecting Duluth, Minnesota, and Tacoma, Washington. The last of the transcontinental lines was the Great Northern, which connected St. Paul and Seattle in 1893.

Making Ends Meet

PARTICULARLY FRUSTRATING to the Union and Central Pacific was the requirement that tracks had to be laid *continuously* in order for the railroads to receive their land grants. So to save time, they cut corners. Many bridges like the one below were hastily-assembled with timbers and only later replaced with stronger masonry structures. These temporary structures would, in the words of one reporter, "shake the nerves of the stoutest hearts when they see what is expected to uphold a train in motion."

Then there were the tunnels. Particularly daunting was the 1,659 foot-long Summit Tunnel, at more than 7,000 feet above sea level the highest of the six tunnels needed to cross the Sierras. The rock was exceptionally difficult to drill, and even with the hundreds of kegs of blasting powder Charlie Crocker was shipping in daily, only about eight inches of granite yielded per day. Though construction supervisor James Strobridge eventually switched to more powerful nitroglycerin, it took the better part of a year to complete the tunnel, working from both sides.

On the Central Pacific, Chinese laborers did the most dangerous blasting.

To cut a roadbed across the sheer face of a mountain, they were lowered in baskets from the mountaintop to the proper height, where they would drill holes and fill them with blasting powder. Then, in a carefully choreographed maneuver, they would light the fuses as their coworkers furiously raised the baskets. This practice gave rise to the term "Chinaman's chance," a euphemism for very poor odds indeed. ▪

or 6,400 acres per mile, and government bonds issued at a rate that depended upon the topography: $16,000 per mile in the flat regions, $32,000 in the desert basin between the Sierras and the Rockies, and $48,000 in the mountains. Although the terms may sound generous, the land would be worth little until the railroad was actually built, and even then the dry western soil would require large-scale irrigation before it could be profitably farmed and settled. The government bonds would pay perhaps half the construction costs, but since they constituted a first mortgage, the railroads would find it difficult to raise additional funds with their own bonds. Moreover, they had to complete 40 miles of track before collecting the bonds. To actually pay for labor and supplies, they would then have to convert most of the government securities into paper "greenbacks," often at a reduced rate—reduced much further in California, where everything had to paid for in gold and greenbacks brought at best 65 cents on a dollar.

Despite the daunting financial situation, the Central Pacific held a gala groundbreaking ceremony in Sacramento on January 8, 1863, featuring speechmaking and shovel-turning by Leland Stanford, who was now not only the president of the railroad but the governor of California. "This work will go on from this side to completion as rapidly as possible," Stanford promised. "There will be no delay, no backing, no uncertainty in the continued progress. We may now look forward with confidence to the day, not far distant, when the Pacific Coast will be bound to the Atlantic Coast by iron bonds." Optimistic words at a time when the company owned no rails, no locomotives, and no rolling stock—all of which would have to be purchased in the East at inflated wartime prices and shipped around Cape Horn.

Theodore Judah returned shortly after the ceremony and immediately locked horns with the Big Four over how to build their railroad. The conflict was in essence a battle between a technically proficient dreamer who had lived and breathed "his railroad" for years and a group of hard-nosed merchants who were more concerned with the balance sheet than with connecting the continent. By the fall of 1863, the conflict had grown so bitter that the Big Four bought out Judah, yet leaving the door open for Judah to buy them out. Hoping to tap the deep pockets of eastern capitalists, Judah and his wife set sail for the East, but he contracted yellow fever while crossing the Isthmus of Panama, and died two days after his arrival in New York. If the railroad he envisioned had existed, Theodore Judah would have lived, and the entire history of western railroading might have been different. As it was, the Central Pacific was now firmly in the hands of the Big Four.

Quick Work, You Say

At a stockholder's meeting in New York City on October 30, 1863—the day before Theodore Judah arrived in New York in the throes of death—a medical school graduate named Thomas C. Durant seized control of the Union Pacific Railroad Company. A master of stock manipulation who had honed his skills on eastern railroads, Dr. Durant was obsessed with making money. His partner was a wealthy eccentric, George Francis Train, who, unlike Durant, was driven more by the grandeur of the project than by the potential for profit. On December 2, Train spoke passionately at the groundbreaking ceremony in Omaha, across the muddy Missouri from Council Bluffs: "The Pacific railroad is the nation and the nation is the Pacific railway.…This is the grandest enterprise under God!"

Despite such high-flown sentiments, no real work began on the Union Pacific until the end of the Civil War, when a ready labor force became instantly available. In the interim, Durant angled for leverage that made it possible, according to historian Dee Brown, "for him and his close associates to enter upon a colossal looting of the people's treasury and plundering of national land resources."

Realizing that profits in railroad building went to construction contractors, Durant and Train set up a company they named Crédit Mobilier of America which would contract services with the Union Pacific at prices they would determine. At the same time, the two men worked with Collis P. Huntington to change the terms of their government agreement, bribing legislators to pass a new Pacific Railway Act which awarded them

In a sign of changing times, horse-drawn wagons cross paths with an iron horse near Promontory Summit, Utah. President Grant forced the Union and Central Pacific lines to meet here after the railroad directors, greedy for the profit to be made with each mile of track laid, had worked past each other for nearly 200 miles—a senseless competition that cost many workers their lives while wasting the tax-payers' money. Promontory itself, a high, barren, sagebrush-dotted basin near the northern rim of the Great Salt Lake, enjoyed a brief period of fame as the point where East met West, but soon faded into relative obscurity as Ogden became the main station in the area.

twice as much land per mile, all mineral rights, and converted the government bonds to a second mortgage, allowing them to sell first-mortgage bonds to the public. A dissenting congressman labeled their maneuvering "the greatest legislative crime in history."

The Big Four built 18 miles of track under the old act, stretching their personal credit so thin that Charles Crocker later admitted, "I would have been glad…to have got a clean shirt and absolution from my debts." Though financial difficulties lingered under the new law, the company pushed on toward the Sierra Nevada while Durant continued to maneuver in the East— ordering his chief engineer to raise construction estimates from the real cost of between $20,000 and $30,000 per mile to an inflated cost of $50,000, assuring Durant and his partners in Crédit Mobilier a tidy profit of $20,000 to $30,000 for every mile of track. Although the chief engineer did as he was told, he resigned in disgust. Undaunted, Durant put a more malleable "consulting engineer" named Silas Seymour in charge, who was so incompetent that he wanted to lay the iron rails on parallel timbers rather than cross ties.

Beginning in July 1865, the Union Pacific inched westward from Omaha at a rate of a mile per week. The snail's pace might have continued indefinitely were it not for the energetic efforts of another railroad company owned by famed explorer John C. Fremont, which had begun to build west across Kansas, calling itself the Union Pacific Railway, Eastern Division. Although it was originally intended as a branch line, the Pacific Railroad Bill contained a unique provision: If the Kansas railroad beat the Union Pacific to their junction point—planned at the 100th meridian on the western Nebraska plains—it could then continue building westward to California. Faced with the possibility of losing his carefully orchestrated profits, Durant decided to get serious about building a railroad.

On the advice of Gen. William T. Sherman, hero of the Civil War and staunch supporter of the railroad, Durant convinced a 35-year-old general named Grenville Dodge to work for him as chief engineer. Dodge had rebuilt southern railroads and bridges for the Union army during Sherman's march on Atlanta, and he knew the difference between parallel timbers and cross ties.

Durant also hired another young general named John S. Casement and his brother Dan as construction contractors. The Casement brothers were tiny, bearded men, "about the size of twelve-year-old boys but wearing larger hats," yet they were powerful motivators who led by example, reward, and sheer force of character. While Dodge brought practical vision and administrative skills, the Casement brothers—along with construction superintendent Samuel B. Reed—infused the Union Pacific with military-style organization and discipline in the spring of 1866.

"We have drawn the elephant. Now let us see if we can harness him up."

Theodore Judah, on passage of the Pacific Railroad Bill

According to a newspaperman who watched the work process, the surveyors and locators were "the advance guard" laying out the line, followed by graders who built the roadbed, blasting through gorges and building bridges as necessary. "Then comes the main body of the army, placing the ties, laying the track, spiking down the rails, perfecting the alignment, ballasting and dressing up and completing the road for immediate use." As the rails advanced, trains kept pushing forward carrying all the materials necessary to keep on building, "thirty seconds to the rail for each gang, four rails to the minute…Three strokes to the spike, ten spikes to the rail, four hundred rails to the mile. Quick work, you say—but the fellows on the Union Pacific are tremendously in earnest."

By October, the earnest fellows of the Union Pacific had easily won the race to the 100th meridian, 247 miles from

Omaha. Durant and Train celebrated with a grand excursion for 200 invited dignitaries that included a Pawnee war dance and mock battle, a gourmet dinner washed down with champagne, a lecture on phrenology, a fireworks display and a prearranged prairie fire—all in the heart of the Nebraska plains.

In late November, the Casement brothers and some 2,000 workers established winter quarters 43 miles beyond the meridian, where the broad Platte branches to the north and south. They called it North Platte—at first a sea of canvas tents, within weeks a booming town of a hundred buildings, a good percentage of them saloons and bordellos. It was like the great wild days of the gold rushes: Hordes of young men with money to spend and time on their hands; only now, with iron rails connecting the boomtown to the East, and gamblers and "soiled doves" already mobilized after following the troops during the war, the rush came faster than it had ever come before. Newspaper reporter Henry M. Stanley, who would soon be famous for finding Dr. Livingstone, described the scene:

> Every gambler in the Union seems to have steered his course for North Platte, and every known game under the sun is played here. The days of Pike's Peak and California are revived. Every house is a saloon and every saloon is a gambling den. Revolvers are in great requisition….Old gamblers who revelled in the glorious days of "flush times" in the gold districts declare that this town outstrips them all.

The Best In The World

Building from the east, the Union Pacific had a ready supply of laborers. A good percentage were brawny Irish immigrants, but there were also American-born men of various ethnic backgrounds including former slaves. Grenville Dodge had suggested forcing captured Indians to work under army guard, but the idea never took hold; by the end of the Civil War there was a huge reservoir of men who needed work and the railroad could easily transport them to the job site on the rails.

On the other side of the continent, the Central Pacific—which began construction during the war—faced a chronic labor shortage. Although the great days of the gold rush were over, men could still earn more money in the mines of California or Nevada than they could earn on the railroad, and those who did agree to work were always threatening to strike. In 1865, Charles Crocker suggested the idea of hiring Chinese laborers. He was impressed with the work habits of his own Chinese houseman, as well as with the way the Chinese had worked gold claims abandoned by whites. Not only that, the Chinese would work for less: $30 to $35 a month rather than $2 or $3 a day.

Crocker's tall, glowering construction superintendent, James H. Strobridge, resisted the idea. "I will not boss Chinese," he said simply. "From what I've seen of them, they're not fit laborers anyway. I don't think they could build a railroad." Strobridge's biggest objection was that the Chinese were physically weak and not masons.

Huge Charlie Crocker refused to back down, bellowing, "Did they not build the Chinese Wall, the biggest piece of masonry in the world?"

Reluctantly, Strobridge agreed to hire 50 Chinese as an experiment; after working them for a single 12-hour shift he asked for 50 more. Soon the Central Pacific was hiring every available Chinese worker in California, and Leland Stanford—who had railed against these "dregs of Asia" in his inaugural speech as governor—was trying to import 15,000 laborers direct from China. "As a class they are quiet, peaceable, patient, industrious and economical," Stanford wrote to President Andrew Johnson. "Ready and apt to learn all the different kinds of work required in railroad building, they soon become as efficient as white laborers. More prudent and economical, they are contented with less wages."

For Stanford and his partners, "less wages" was the salient point, but for the men on the front lines, the steady skill of the Chinese laborers provided a unique lesson in racial tolerance. Chief construction engineer Samuel S. Montague admitted that "Some distrust was at first felt regarding capacity of this class for the services required, but the experiment has proved eminently

ALTHOUGH THE construction of the Union Pacific provoked its share of Indian resistance, it was the parallel railroad through Kansas that bore the full fury of Indian attack. While the main line of the Union Pacific followed the Platte River, where whites had traveled for decades, the Kansas railroad followed a less-traveled route along the Smoky Hill River, through the heart of Cheyenne buffalo hunting territory.

In June 1869, "when the grass and flowers on the plains of Kansas and Colorado were nearly knee high," a Kansas Pacific surveyor named Howard Schuyler found himself surrounded on three sides by Indians with "half a mile of broken ground cut by deep narrow ravines" behind him, according to Schuyler's younger brother, James, who was with the rest of the surveying party several miles to the rear.

Schuyler spurred his horse across the ravines only to find himself encircled by another 40 Indians on the other side. Armed with a 12-shot Winchester carbine, Schuyler killed one man, burst through the circle and killed another, whose blood "spurted over Howard's buckskin leggings, saddle and horse." Though Schuyler was unharmed, his horse had

Our Miraculous Escape
ATTACK ON THE KANSAS PACIFIC

been wounded, and one of the warriors caught up to them:

"Thus they rode, nose to tail, for a mile or two, the Indian occupying the time in shooting at Howard. Three pistols, six-shooters, he emptied, and bullets flew all around poor Howard on every side. Four more entered the poor horse, already so badly wounded; a bullet pierced Howard's clothes at his side; another cut the strap of his field glass,...another cut off his spur,...a fourth

pierced the wooden breech of his rifle...others struck the saddle, and in short they seemed to strike everywhere but where they were aimed."

In an official report, Howard himself told the story in more laconic terms. "He emptied his revolver at me, but without other effect than to tear my clothes, then striking me on the head with his lance-staff told me in good English to 'come off,' which, under the circumstances, I did not feel justified in

doing. Having him in good range, I placed my gun against his side and fired...." According to James, Howard's shot blew "a hole through that seemed as large as one's arm."

When his horse collapsed, Schuyler fired from behind its prostrate body, killing another warrior and driving the attackers away before joining the rest of his men, who were fighting their own battle near the supply wagon. The Indian attack "was most terrifying to me" admitted James, "a boy fresh from school, who had never experienced any sort of warfare...but Howard, who had gone through four years of the War of the Rebellion, and seen three or more years of border warfare with the Indians, was quite exhilarated by the excitement," so exhilarated in fact that, as they fought their way back to camp, he stepped out alone, several hundred yards from the others, firing from the open prairie until the Indians retreated.

Only James was wounded in the attack, and he recovered fully, as did Howard's horse. "Our miraculous escape was long the subject of wonder on the frontier," James remembered. "It always excites me to think or tell of it." ◾

Though the Union Pacific had its troubles with Indians, it was the Kansas Pacific working further south, that bore the brunt of Indian hostilities. Beginning in 1868, the Atchison, Topeka and Santa Fe (above) built a second railroad through Kansas (opposite), cutting southwest from the Kansas Pacific line.

successful....Many of them are becoming very expert in drilling, blasting and other departments of rock work." James Strobridge was the biggest convert, crowing that his Chinese workers were quite simply "the best in the world." Before the project was finished, over 12,000 Chinese would be employed by the Central Pacific Railroad.

By the end of 1866, while the Union Pacific workers enjoyed their wild winter at North Platte, Nebraska, the Sacramento *Union* proudly announced:

> The Central Pacific is now completed and in daily operation from Sacramento to Cisco...reaching within twelve miles of the summit of the Sierra Nevada mountains and 5,911 feet above the level of the sea—a higher altitude that is attained by any other railroad in America....Twelve tunnels, varying from 800 to 1,650 feet in length, are in process of construction along the snow belt...employing in these tunnels an aggregate of 8,000 laborers.

Although the paper expressed confidence that "during the year 1867 the road will be completed and in operation to the eastern line of the state," the high Sierras proved a more daunting barrier than anyone expected. Like the proverbial tortoise and the hare, the slow-starting Union Pacific would continue streaking across the Plains and up over the relatively easy passes through the Rockies while the Central Pacific would struggle with the Sierras for two long winters.

HELL ON WHEELS

In the spring of 1867, the Casement brothers established an advance camp near Julesburg, Colorado; when the tracks reached the camp in midsummer, the gamblers, prostitutes, and saloon-keepers of North Platte boarded trains for "sinful Julesburg," draining the earlier settlement from its one-time population of 5,000 to 300. The ever-observant Stanley wrote of the new town, "There appears to be plenty of money here, and plenty of fools to squander it....These women are expensive articles, and

come in for a large share of the money wasted. In broad daylight they may be seen gliding through the sandy streets...carrying fancy derringers slung to their waists, with which tools they are dangerously expert."

As the men pushed the rails westward, at least a mile a day, sometimes as many as four miles, they were increasingly exposed to Indian attack. For the Plains Indians, the iron horse was an abomination, belching fire, scaring the game way, and bisecting the buffalo range. Grenville Dodge, who had a tendency to exaggerate his dealings with the Indians, later claimed, "Every mile had to be run within range of musket and there was not a moment's security. In making surveys, numbers of our men, some of them the ablest and most promising, were killed."

The greatest resistance actually occurred to the south, where Cheyenne Dog Soldiers harassed the Union Pacific, Eastern Division as it built through the heart of their Kansas hunting grounds. In 1867, however, a military campaign aimed at protecting the Kansas road drove some raiders north into Nebraska and Colorado, making it a dangerous summer along the Platte. The most spectacular attack came far behind the track-layers, when a Cheyenne raiding party approached the already functioning railroad near Plum Creek, Nebraska, in early August 1867. A young warrior named Porcupine remembered:

> We saw the first train of cars that any of us had seen. We looked at it from a high ridge. Far off it was very small, but it kept coming and growing larger all the time, puffing out smoke and steam, and as it came on we said to each other that it looked like a white man's pipe when he was smoking....Not long after this, as we talked of our troubles, we said among ourselves: "Now the white people have taken all we had and have made us poor and we ought to do something."

Near dusk, the Cheyenne cut the telegraph wire that ran along the rails and used it to attach a railroad tie to the track. When a group of five repairmen set out to investigate the break, their handcar hit the railroad tie and they found themselves surrounded by Indians. Four of the men were killed, but the fifth, an Englishman named William Thompson who had been shot in the arm, played dead while one of the Cheyenne scalped him. "I can't describe it to you," he later said. "It just felt as if the whole head was taken right off."

The Indian dropped the scalp as he galloped away, and Thompson managed to recover it, lying in agony in the tall grass for an hour and a half until he heard the "low rumbling" of the oncoming train. "I might have been able to flag it off had I dared," he admitted, but he didn't dare, and the engine jumped the rails—where the Cheyenne had piled up more obstructions— taking several freight cars with it, killing the engineer and mortally injuring the fireman. The conductor and several other men in the caboose escaped and warned another approaching freight train, while the Cheyenne looted the cars of "whatever might be useful," including bolts of calico, which they tied to their horses' tails, and a barrel of whiskey, which they drank.

In the confusion, Thompson escaped with his scalp and made it to a station, where his wounds were dressed and his scalp placed in a pail of water that he carried all the way back to Omaha. There he ran into fellow Briton, Henry Stanley, who seemed to be everywhere along the Union Pacific in those days. "The scalp was about nine inches in length and four in width," Stanley reported, "somewhat resembling a drowned rat as it floated, curled up, on the water." A local doctor was unable to reattach the scalp to Thompson's head. He later donated the scalp to the Omaha Public Library, where it was displayed under a glass jar for many years.

Despite the threat of Indian attacks, the rails reached into Wyoming by the end of 1867, and another wild winter camp was established, named—with some irony—Cheyenne. Once again, all the gamblers and dance-hall girls boarded the first passenger train out of Julesburg for the new, trackside town, soon followed by a freight train loaded with buildings, tents, and dance floors. According to one story, when the heavily laden flat cars pulled up to Cheyenne, a brakeman shouted, "Gentlemen, here's Julesburg!" The ease with which these wild boomtowns could be moved along the tracks gave rise to a

The "Big Four," (clockwise from top left) Collis Huntington, Mark Hopkins, Leland Stanford, and Charlie Crocker were the prime movers of the Central Pacific Railroad, driving their workers hard and lobbying Congress even harder for land grants and favorable financing. Huntington, Stanford and Crocker were large men of boundless energy, while Hopkins, the group's gaunt accountant, was "a bloodless creature who would would sip half a cup of tea while his partners plowed through a six-course meal."

classic American descriptive phrase: Hell on Wheels.

While the Union Pacific kept pushing westward, the Central Pacific was still stuck in the Sierras. By this time Congress had removed legal restrictions on the endpoint of the California line—it was every railroad for itself—so the Big Four decided to lay track on the eastern side of the mountains even as they continued to blast tunnels through the hard granite. It was one thing to move the men, but something else to move the huge, heavy work trains. "We hauled locomotives over," big Charlie Crocker later remembered, "and when I say we, I mean myself. We hauled them on sleighs....We hauled some of them over on logs, because we could not get a sleigh big enough." In November 1867, Summit Tunnel was completed at an elevation of more than 7,000 feet, but it wasn't until the snows melted in June that the line over the Sierras could be connected with the track already laid in Nevada. At the same time, other Central Pacific crews rushed to build expensive snowsheds back in the mountains to keep the tracks open the next winter.

Now the race with the Union Pacific took on daily urgency, and with the urgency came wasteful absurdity. At stake were some of the most lucrative miles of the whole project—built through the desert basins at double the rate of the plains—as well as control of the equally lucrative trade with the booming Mormon metropolis of Salt Lake City. Brigham Young, an astute businessman as well as a booster of the railroad, signed contracts with both companies to employ Mormon workers as graders in the Salt Lake City area. Some 200 miles were double-graded by the Mormons, a completely unnecessary expense ultimately paid for by the people of the United States.

At the end of 1868, the two lines were less than 400 miles apart. Both companies worked through the winter, with the Union Pacific getting a taste of the snow-covered hardships in the Wasatch Range that the Central Pacific had experienced in the Sierras. Grenville Dodge later estimated that it cost four times as much to build through the mountains during the winter than it would have cost during the summer, but Charlie Crocker's Chinese were moving at a steady mile a day through the relatively balmy Nevada desert, so the ever-greedy

Dr. Durant ordered Dodge to push on anyway.

By late March 1869, the blue-clad Chinese workers of the Central Pacific and the predominantly Irish workers of the Union Pacific were working side-by-side on the slopes of the Promontory Range, just northwest of the Great Salt Lake. Here was some of the most difficult and wasteful double grading of all, not only in money and man-hours, but in human life. Whereas the competing Mormon crews had labored in peace, the brawling Irish didn't like working so close to the Chinese—at one point the rival crews were a hundred feet apart—and rock- and dirt-throwing incidents soon gave way to explosive "accidents."

"The Union's powdermen sometimes laid blasts rather far to the right of their own line," wrote one historian, "and a thousand graders looked on in innocent wonderment as the earth parted and the Chinese and scrapers, horses and wheelbarrows and picks fountained upward. The Orientals regathered their forces, buried their dead, and continued placidly about their business until another blast brought another temporary pause. But the sport ended when a section of the Union's line mysteriously shot upward and it became the Irishmen's turn to take time out for grave-digging." After several incidents, the crews agreed to notify each other before each blast.

Faced with the possibility that the two greedy railroads might blithely pass in the night, the government of new President Ulysses S. Grant ordered them to set a meeting point. In early April, Collis P. Huntington hashed it out with representatives of the Union Pacific in Washington, agreeing that the tracks would meet at Promontory Summit, but that the Union Pacific would then sell its tracks into the key junction town of Ogden, north of Salt Lake City, thus giving both railroads access to the rich trade of the Great Salt Lake valley. With the agreement and the coming of spring, the battle—between grasping railroads, between rugged men and rugged land—was essentially over. On April 28, the men of the Central Pacific put on a show in honor of their hard-driving boss, big, bellowing Charlie Crocker, who, according to legend, had once bet Thomas Durant ten thousand dollars that his men could lay ten miles of track in a single day. Although Crocker and James Strobridge used their now-respected Chinese workers in moving materials up and down the line, they chose eight muscular Irishmen to actually carry the rails. It was a full-speed, 12-hour marathon, with a civilized one-hour break for lunch, and when it was over the Central Pacific had laid ten miles and 56 feet of track, a record that still stands today.

> *"I say to the Congress…*
> *'Hurry up, hasten the work.*
> *We want to hear the iron horse*
> *puffing through the valley.'*
> *What for? To bring*
> *our brothers and sisters here."*

BRIGHAM YOUNG

Dr. Durant wasn't there to see the impressive display, and he almost missed the joining of the rails—an event that newspapers called second only to the signing of the Declaration of Independence. The great moment was originally scheduled for Saturday, May 8, but when a trainful of Californians, led by Leland Stanford, arrived on the afternoon of the 7th, they were informed that heavy rains had washed out the tracks east of Ogden, blocking the train carrying Durant and other Union Pacific dignitaries. In fact, the miserable weather was only part of the story; several hundred angry railroad workers had hijacked Durant's private car and chained it to a sidetrack, making it clear that he wasn't going anywhere until they received their back wages. Although the details are vague, Durant was apparently able to obtain enough money—a California paper reported it was $253,000—by the morning of May 8, and the men released him to continue on his way. Disgruntled workers were actually the least of Durant's problems; he was in the midst of losing a long and bitter battle with men as avaricious as himself for control of the railroad and his precious Crédit Mobilier.

After a weekend of rain, the morning of May 10, 1869, dawned clear and cool in the broad basin of Promontory Summit, almost a mile above sea level. Despite the name, the "summit" was imperceptible, the iron bands stretching across a dry, flat, circular valley under the shadow of the heavily eroded Promontory Range. Fourteen tents advertising rotgut potations with names like Red Cloud and Blue Run fluttered in the steady breeze.

At 8:45 a.m. the Central Pacific train arrived to the cheers of the growing crowd. Governor Stanford's car, decked in red, blue, and gold bunting, was left on a siding to wait for the noontime celebration. Two Union Pacific trains arrived after ten, carrying Durant—his head aching from drowning his sorrows in champagne—and various dignitaries in the first train, while four companies of infantry and two brass bands followed behind. At 11:15, Stanford's train pulled forward, and the Central Pacific party went over to shake hands with their competitors. Although the handshakes looked cordial enough to the crowd, the two groups argued vehemently for the next 40 minutes over who would drive the final spike. The sticking point was Grenville Dodge, who felt the Union Pacific was by far the superior line—almost twice as long—and he was the obvious man to drive the spike. Finally, at five minutes to the scheduled hour of twelve, with the temperature rising to 69 degrees and Durant's head throbbing in the Utah sun, the Union Pacific men agreed to follow Stanford's program.

The ceremony began with the construction superintendents carrying out a polished laurel-wood tie, while two work gangs, one from each railroad, carried the final rails. According to one onlooker, as the rails were about to be laid someone shouted to photographer Charles R. Savage, "Now's the time, Charlie! Take a shot!" whereupon the Central Pacific's Chinese work gang, who knew only the more violent meaning of the word "shot," dropped their rail and headed for cover—to the general hilarity of the

A Ride On The Rails

IN THE EARLY days, all transcon ti-nental railroad travelers from the East connected through Chicago, where they chose one of several routes to Council Bluffs, Iowa. There passengers and luggage were loaded onto a "rickety old ferry" to cross the muddy Missouri to Omaha, where the Union Pacific tracks began. They changed trains at Promontory, or at Ogden, for the ride on the Central Pacific.

First-class fare from Omaha to Sacramento cost $100, with an additional $4 per day for a sleeping berth on a luxurious Pullman Palace car. Although $100 was a good month's wages, demand for the Pullman cars was overwhelming. Second class tickets cost $75, while $40 bought a cramped seat on hard wooden benches.

A journey that once lasted months now took four to seven days, and though they complained of bad food and unexpected delays, most early train travelers appreciated the difference. "Inch by inch, they *climbed* down the rugged passes," wrote one passenger contemplating the trials of early wagon trains; "*now* in luxurious coaches, with horses of iron,...we are carried along in comfort." ■

Opposite: An estimated 550,000 emigrants passed Independence Rock in Wyoming during the great overland migrations, a chapter in the American West that effectively ended with the completion of the transcontinental railroad.

drunken crowd—and returned only after lengthy explanations.

With the rails in place, the telegraph operator signaled stations across the country to clear their lines in anticipation of the great moment. First, a minister from Massachusetts offered a prayer, rejoicing in "the human mind with its powers of invention, its capacity of expansion." Then, a representative of Sacramento presented Stanford with the golden spike, forged from California mines, the symbolic last spike of the transcontinental railroad. "Never since history commenced her record of human events," the representative said, "has man been called upon to meet the completion of a work so magnificent in contemplation, and so marvelous in execution."

At least three other special spikes were used: Silver from the Comstock Lode, a gold-silver-iron alloy from Arizona, and another golden spike from California. In his booming speech, Stanford conjured a vision of cheap freight rates and enough traffic to require two more sets of rails. "Now, gentlemen," he finished, "with your assistance we will proceed to lay the last tie and last rail, and drive the last spike."

Grenville Dodge came forward and spoke briefly in lieu of Thomas Durant. "Gentlemen, the great [Sen. Thomas] Benton proposed that some day a giant statue of Columbus be erected on the highest peak of the Rocky Mountains, pointing westward, denoting that as the great route across the continent. You have made that prophecy today a fact. This is the way to India!"

After the crowd cheered Dodge's stirring words, the laurel tie was placed beneath the rails, and the four special spikes were slipped into predrilled holes, tapped into place with a silver-plated maul by various dignitaries. Now came the moment that all America awaited, the completion of the mightiest work of man, the great transcontinental railroad. After all the glittering symbolism, the true "last spike" would be of common iron in a common tie, hammered by an iron maul, with the spike and maul attached to telegraph wires so the blows could be transmitted from coast to coast. Even the drunken revelers in the dazzling Utah sun hushed in reverence as Stanford lifted the maul above his head, ready to strike the monumental blow, to be heard "the farthest of any by mortal man." Half-tangled in wires, the nervous railroad president—who hadn't pounded too many spikes of late—brought the hammer down weakly and completely missed the golden spike. Red-faced, Stanford handed the hammer to Durant, who missed the spike as well, while the raucous crowd "yelled like to bust."

It didn't matter. The telegraph operator tapped out, "Done!" and jubilant crowds celebrated coast-to-coast. In San Francisco the surging electricity rang the fire bells and shot a 15-inch cannon at a nearby fort. Mormons prayed in Salt Lake City, a parade began in Chicago, and citizens sang the Star Spangled Banner in the streets of Buffalo. The Liberty Bell rang in Philadelphia, one hundred guns fired in Omaha and in New York, and a magnetic ball fell from the Capitol dome in Washington, D.C. And behind her locked door in Greenfield, Massachusetts, the widow of Theodore Judah felt a strange presence. "It seemed to me," she later wrote, "as though the spirit of my brave husband descended upon me, and together we were there [at Promontory] unseen, unheard of men."

In the visible world, the laurel tie and precious spikes were replaced by standard materials so the two engines—Jupiter of the Central Pacific and Number 119 of the Union Pacific—could pull forward and meet on the final rails, their cowcatchers touching in a champagne-drenched kiss that San Francisco newspaperman Bret Harte immortalized in verse:

> What was it the Engines said
> Pilots touching,—head to head
> Facing on the single track,
> Half a world behind each back?

Stanford, Durant, and the other dignitaries retired for a long afternoon of champagne toasts, which either eased Durant's headache or gave him another one, while the giddy workers converged on the rotgut tents. Many of them were now unemployed, but they were justly proud of what they'd accomplished. In a few short years, they had done the impossible, spanned the vast land with iron rails, changing America forever. They had built "a railroad to the moon."

BUFFALO WARS

"Fathers, if I went into your country to kill your animals, what would you say? Should I not be wrong, and would you not make war on me?"

BEAR TOOTH, CROW, NOVEMBER 1867

BUFFALO WARS

In June 1865, Gen. John Pope—the outspoken commander of the Plains from Texas to Canada—advised General in Chief Ulysses S. Grant that "the Government will find it true economy to finish this Indian war this season, so that it will stay finished." • The Civil War was over, and the nation was moving west again—on roads, railroads, and rivers. Pope knew that Indians would continue to resist encroachment, just as he knew that army ranks would soon be depleted as decommissioned soldiers returned home. Something had to be done about the "Indian problem," and now was the time to do it. Six thousand soldiers took the field that summer, the largest force ever sent against the Plains Indians. The unsuccessful campaign was an expensive disaster, costing the people of the United States almost $20 million dollars in supplies alone. One field commander groused that placing a bounty on Indian scalps "would be cheaper and more effective than sending large bodies of troops, who can never be successful in hunting small bodies of Indians in their broken, mountainous terrain."

The Lakota warrior Red Cloud led a confederation of Lakota, Cheyenne (above), and Arapaho against white encroachment on their hunting grounds in Montana and Wyoming (opposite), only to be forced onto a reservation in South Dakota, where buffalo graze today in Custer State Park (preceding page).

The most expensive and disastrous operation was an expedition into the undulating grasslands drained by the Powder River, a glittering tributary of the Yellowstone in what is now Wyoming and Montana. The grasslands were the prime hunting grounds of the Lakota, the last remaining area north of the Platte where free-ranging Indians could still exist on the buffalo herds. Dry, rough, and desolate, the region held little appeal for white settlers, but it lay in the path of the Bozeman Trail, a new and shorter route to the rich Montana gold fields. Having witnessed the destruction of the buffalo along the Platte, the Lakota fought to defend against white encroachment along the Bozeman Trail so violently that the route became known as the Bloody Bozeman.

The leader of the Indian resistance was a hardened, hawk-nosed warrior named Red Cloud. A decade earlier, he had been one of the young Oglala circling the camp of Conquering Bear as he died with Lieutenant Grattan near Fort Laramie. Now in his early forties, Red Cloud was a man the warriors followed, not a chief, but a war leader who fought without mercy. "The Great Spirit raised both the white man and the Indian," Red Cloud said. "He raised me in this land and it belongs to me. The white man was raised over the great waters, and his land is over there. Since they crossed the sea, I have given them room. There are now white people all about me. I have but a small spot of land left. The Great Spirit told me to keep it."

In 1865, the Powder River country was an uncharted wilderness, falling vaguely under the command of Gen. Grenville Dodge, who would leave the army the following year to build the Union Pacific Railroad. To lead the troops into the field, Dodge chose Patrick Connor, the aggressive officer who the Indians called "Star Chief" because of the coveted general's star he had won destroying the Shoshone village at Bear River. Connor divided his 2,500-man force into three columns: The first two would march toward the Black Hills while Connor himself would lead the third column up the Bozeman Trail. "You will not receive overtures of peace or submission from Indians," Connor ordered his column commanders, "but will attack and kill every male Indian over twelve years of age."

When Connor's orders reached the divisional headquarters in St. Louis, General Pope was angered and alarmed. Although a firm believer in military force, Pope was not without conscience, and he did not want another Sand Creek on his hands. "These instructions are atrocious," he informed Dodge. "If any such orders as General Connor's are carried out it will be disgraceful to the Government and will cost him his commission, if not worse." Connor was already in the field when he received word to change his orders, and it's unlikely that he notified his column commanders, as they had all but disappeared in the northern plains. Wandering through hostile, unknown territory without competent guides, accurate maps, or adequate supplies, the two Black Hills columns barely made it back alive. By late August, after a month in the field, the troops were so short of rations that they began slaughtering their mules, and scurvy broke out among the men. Lakota and Cheyenne war parties shadowed the slow-moving troops, skirmishing when they could, taunting them when they couldn't, while a freak September sleet storm froze their half-starved horses, forcing the soldiers to leave hundreds of carcasses behind. Finally, barefoot and dressed in rags, the men were reduced to eating their remaining horses raw because they were too afraid of Indian attack to stop and build a fire.

Connor's own column fared somewhat better. Moving up the Bozeman Trail, he built a fort on the Powder River which he named after himself. Leaving a cavalry company to defend the fort, Connor marched across the broken plains to the Tongue River, another tributary of the Yellowstone. Ironically, had he continued up the Powder, he would have encountered Red Cloud's warriors who were eager to fight; instead, Connor attacked a peaceful Arapaho village, killing over 60 Indians, including women and children, destroying tons of food and supplies, making enemies of those who survived. After failing to rendezvous with his other columns, Connor sent out a search party of Pawnee scouts under Maj. Luther North, who tracked down the lost command and escorted them back to Fort Connor—where the general arrived a few days later to find "as completely disgusted and discouraged an outfit of men as I ever saw." He also found new orders which abolished his command on the plains and called for his return to Utah. Patrick Connor left the army the following year.

IN THIS AND THE GREAT SPIRIT

The Powder River expedition marked the end of the belligerent approach to the Indians that had characterized the Civil War years. Even tough-minded Gen. William T. Sherman—who had replaced Pope as commander on the plains—saw the benefits of peace, if for no other reason than it would give him time to prepare for a new military assault. "All I ask is comparative quiet this year," he wrote to Grant's chief of staff in 1866, "for by next year we can have the new cavalry enlisted, equipped, and mounted, ready to go and visit these Indians where they live."

In early June 1866, peace commissioners E.B. Taylor and Col. Henry Maynadier met with Lakota leaders at Fort Laramie in an attempt to resolve the issue of travel on the Bozeman Trail. Though men of good will, Taylor and Maynadier underestimated the complexity of the situation. While there were always Indians willing to sign a peace agreement in return for gifts, those who signed were not necessarily those who could ensure that the conditions of the agreement were upheld. On the Bozeman Trail, the man who was key to the success of any treaty was Red Cloud, and he left the council three days after it began, placing his hand on his rifle according to one account and saying, "In this and the Great Spirit I trust for the right."

The exact circumstances of Red Cloud's departure are unclear, but a few days after he left, a caravan led by Col. Henry B. Carrington arrived near the fort with 700 soldiers, including a well-armed brass band, as well as a contingent of officers' wives and children, two howitzers, and an assortment of machines, building supplies, and furniture. Dubbed "Carrington's Overland Circus" by the soldiers, the expedition had been ordered to establish a series of forts along the Bozeman Trail. Though the whites failed to see the absurdity of the situation, the Indians were astounded that while Maynadier and Taylor were negotiating peace, Carrington was busy trying

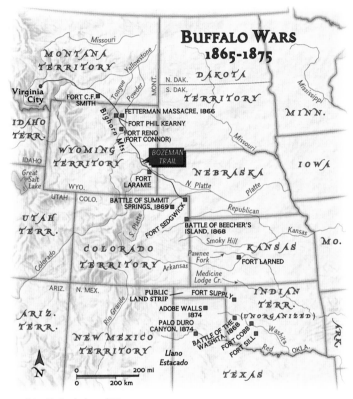

State and territory borders as of 1872
Present-day state borders and names in gray

To protect settlers and prospectors headed toward the gold mines of Montana, the army built a series of forts along the Bozeman Trail. This construction was the spark that ignited Red Cloud's War, which ended with the army abandoning the forts in 1868. Though Red Cloud and his warriors joyously burned two of the forts to the ground, their victory was a hollow one. They were ultimately forced onto reservations, as were tribes like the Kiowa and Comanche on the southern plains.

to establish a military presence along the trail. Those who did not care signed the treaty anyway and took their presents. But others—the Oglala who followed Red Cloud—expressed their disgust as they stormed away. "Great Father sends us presents and wants new road," said one leader, "but white chief goes with soldiers to steal road before Indian say yes or no."

Moving into the Powder River country, Carrington's column relieved the beleaguered troops at Fort Connor, renamed Fort Reno, where the men had been pinned down that winter and spring by Red Cloud's warriors. Leaving one-quarter of his soldiers behind, Carrington continued northward and established his main post at the forks of Little and Big Piney Creeks, a gentle grassland benath the majestic Bighorn Mountains. On the morning of July 17, four days after Carrington arrived, Red Cloud's warriors ran off 175 government horses and mules and killed two soldiers who came in pursuit. The same day, six whites were killed in nearby Peno Valley, while a small party of Montana emigrants were massacred on the Bozeman Trail. The skirmishes marked the beginning of a bloody and resolute guerrilla resistance that became known as Red Cloud's War.

Although an intelligent and capable administrator, Colonel Carrington had no battlefield experience; he had come to Fort Laramie with women, children, and a big brass band—he wasn't expecting a war. In the wake of Red Cloud's attacks, the colonel became obsessed with building a secure stockade to protect his command. His source of lumber, the Pinery, was located on the slopes of the mountains about five miles away, and wood trains became a prime target of Indian attack. Nonetheless, Carrington ultimately built an impressive fortress, with a wall 8 feet high and almost 1,500 feet around. In early August, while construction continued, he sent 150 men north to establish yet another post on the Bozeman Trail called Fort C.F. Smith.

By late summer, 3,000 warriors had joined Red Cloud, including Lakota, Cheyenne, and Arapaho, all fighting against the newly established forts on the trail. In less than five months, Fort Phil Kearney alone faced over 50 hostile actions and "nearly every train and person that attempted to pass over the Montana road" was attacked. "The usual order of the day," one soldier reported, "was to make a forced march to the relief of some immigrant or freight train. In most cases the Indians had taken their toll and gone before we arrived."

Through it all, Colonel Carrington remained unwilling to take decisive action, angering many of his officers, including several men who arrived in early November. One of them was Capt. William J. Fetterman, a muttonchopped Civil War hero who carried the "brevet" or honorary rank of lieutenant colonel. "We are afflicted with an incompetent commanding officer," Fetterman wrote three weeks after his arrival, "but shall be relieved of him in the re-organization." Like many men who had proven themselves under fire in the South, the 31-year-old Fetterman had little respect for the fighting ability of the Indians. Carrington's wife, Margaret, later wrote that the officer boasted: "A company of regulars could whip a thousand [Indians], and a regiment could whip the whole array of hostile tribes."

On the morning of December 21, 1866, sparkling snow dotted the ridges surrounding the fort. The wood train left for the Pinery about 10 a.m. and within an hour, Carrington received the signal that the Indians had attacked. Around the same time, ten warriors, led by a young Oglala named Crazy Horse, appeared at the crossing of the Bozeman Trail and Big Piney, shouting taunts at the soldiers in English: "You sons of bitches, come out and fight us!"

Carrington fired his howitzer at the Indians and ordered Capt. James W. Powell to lead a relief party for the wood train. Although often critical of Carrington, Powell had capably handled a similar assignment two days earlier, escorting the wagons back to the fort and chasing the Indians across Big Piney, while obeying Carrington's explicit orders not to follow the warriors over Lodge Trail Ridge—a high hump of land that separated the valley of the Piney from the rough broken country of the Peno Valley beyond. Carrington himself had been caught by the Indians on the other side of the ridge two weeks earlier, and he understood the dangers of the wild, undulating land.

On this day, however, Captain Fetterman claimed the right

of command based on his brevet rank, and Carrington yielded. Fetterman left the fort with a company of 80 men, including 2 other officers, 2 civilians, 49 infantrymen, and 27 cavalry soldiers. Carrington gave Fetterman much the same orders he had given Powell: "Support the wood-train, relieve it, and report to me. Do not engage or pursue Indians at its expense; under no circumstances pursue over the Ridge, namely, Lodge Trail Ridge, as per map in your possession." Just to make sure they got it right, Carrington had his adjutant repeat the orders and then repeated them himself.

From the fort, Carrington watched through his field glasses as Fetterman led his command along the Big Piney where it ran beneath Lodge Trail Ridge. It wasn't the direct road to the wood train—Carrington suspected they were trying to outflank the attackers—but the Indians fled across Big Piney when they noticed the approaching troops. The command then doubled back to follow the warriors led by Crazy Horse, and moved north on the Bozeman Trail, up over a low saddle on the edge of Lodge Trail Ridge, before finally disappearing from sight.

Amid the rough hills and creek beds on the other side of the ridge, over 1,500 warriors waited in ambush. Swarming on Fetterman's command with bows and lances, war clubs, knives, and old guns, the attackers surprised the infantry on a rocky knoll that became known as Massacre Hill, where soldiers— armed with single-shot, muzzle-loading muskets—were so overwhelmed that charging warriors hit each other with arrows as they closed in. The better-armed cavalry were caught a mile ahead, where the knoll sloped down toward the valley. Most were cut down in retreat, but the two civilians and several veterans offered tougher resistance, dismounting and surprising the Indians with the firepower of their repeating rifles. They died anyway—as did Capt. William J. Fetterman, his throat slit from ear to ear by an Oglala named American Horse. It was over in half an hour.

As the Indians finished off the wounded and began to mutilate the bodies—so they might suffer in the afterlife—one of the soldiers' pet dogs came running and barking through the bloodstained grass. "All are dead but the dog," shouted a

Although the Lakota resolutely defended their hunting grounds along the Powder River, the region was a recent acquisition, the Lakota having driven the Crow out of the area in the mid-19th century. During the Indian Wars, most of the Crow lived among the eastern Rocky Mountains of what is now Montana; a smaller group, however, called the River Crow, ranged among the plains and buttes (above) near the upper Missouri River. Though the Crow disdained white culture, they eagerly traded with the whites and later served as scouts against the Lakota, as well as in the army's campaign against the Nez Perce, who fled from Oregon through Idaho and Montana in 1877.

Lakota warrior. "Let him carry the news to the fort."

"No," replied a Cheyenne. "Do not let the dog go." And so another warrior killed it with an arrow.

When he heard shots from the other side of the ridge, Colonel Carrington sent out a relief force of 30 men under Capt. Tenodor Ten Eyck, who was soon reinforced by another 40 men and wagons to carry the dead. Many years later, Ten Eyck described what he witnessed that day, an account still chilling in its details:

> The firing ceased shortly after we left the post and was not heard again. After a hurried march of four miles, I ascended the Ridge with my men which overlooked the Valley. We saw many Indians...but no sign of Fetterman's command....A rocky knoll rose in the valley about a ½ mi. away and about this, 4 Indians were riding, waveing their bonnets and shouting challenge to come down. I ordered my best marks-men to fire upon these, hoping to bring them down, but they were unable to reach them. They returned and joined the others gathered in great number further away.
>
> ...I descended, with part of my men, in the direction of the rocky knoll. One of the skirmishers in advance came back, saying that what we supposed to be a heap of cottonwood logs, was the bodies of Fetterman's men. This was true, and all were killed. Within a small space, most were found, horribly mutilated. I loaded the wagons with as many of the bodies as they could contain, being myself obligated to handle the greater part of them, the soldiers being so overcome with horror, as almost unable to obey orders. It was after dark when we returned to the Post.

The Fetterman Massacre shocked the nation just as the Grattan Massacre had shocked it in 1854. Two separate inquiries were inconclusive. The army tended to blame Colonel Carrington, rather than the brashly heroic Captain Fetterman, while the civilian commission suggested that the army's entire reading of the situation on the Bozeman Trail was misguided. "The difficulty...was, that the commanding officer of the district was furnished no more troops or supplies for this state of war than had been provided and furnished him for a state of profound peace." It was General Sherman himself who had suggested to Carrington that he take his officers' wives and children to the Powder River, as if the whole expedition would be as pleasant as a walk through the park.

"The Indians are very hostile and barbarous, and annoy us in everyway they can."

Captain William J. Fetterman, November 26, 1866

While Red Cloud may not have been present at the time of the Fetterman attack, he continued to be the driving force behind the Powder River resistance. Although peace commissions made three trips to Fort Laramie in 1867 and 1868, Red Cloud refused to negotiate as long as the whites remained in his country. "We are on the mountains looking down on the soldiers and the forts," he said in one message. "When we see the soldiers moving away and the forts abandoned, then I will come down and talk." Finally, beginning in late July 1868, the army withdrew, and the Indians burned Fort Phil Kearney and Fort C.F. Smith to the ground. Red Cloud rode into Fort Laramie that November, a triumphant general surrounded by his warriors, ready to negotiate.

Red Cloud's War was the only prolonged conflict ever won by the native people against U.S. forces. But the nature of the victory was transitory, if not illusory. By the time the forts were abandoned, the railroad had pushed beyond the Rocky

Mountains, providing an even faster route to the Montana gold fields that completely bypassed the Bozeman Trail. It was the gold that mattered, not the trail itself, and by the summer of 1868 the trail was no longer worth defending.

The Fort Laramie Treaty of 1868 officially ended the hostilities. For Red Cloud and his fellow warriors, the most important victory was the treaty provision that called for the removal of whites from the Powder River country. Yet, whether they realized it or not—and several Lakota leaders, including Red Cloud, would later dispute this—those who signed the treaty were also agreeing to live on a reservation to the east of the great buffalo range, a huge tract of land comprising most of what is now western South Dakota, including the sacred Black Hills. Although they retained vaguely defined hunting rights in the Powder River country and along the Republican River to the south, "so long as the buffalo may range thereon in such numbers as to justify the chase," confinement on the reservation would ultimately mean an end to the Lakota tradition of living off the buffalo, a fundamental change in the Lakota way of life. For Red Cloud himself, the hard-won pact marked the difficult transition from warrior leader to the more complex and ill-defined role of statesman and peacekeeper. Though he battled over many issues, Red Cloud never fought the United States again.

THE MAGIC OF ROMAN NOSE

In the summer of 1866, as Carrington faced Red Cloud along the Bozeman Trail, a similar resistance formed in western Kansas, on the gently rolling plains of the Smoky Hill River. At the heart of the movement were the Cheyenne Dog Soldiers, along with some Arapaho and southern Lakota. Many of them had joined Red Cloud in the north, but though they respected all the Oglala was trying to do, they longed for their own country and the relatives they had left behind; so they returned to Kansas and decided to fight for their land, just as Red Cloud was fighting for his.

The man who led them was much like Red Cloud: Not a chief, but a warrior who fought without fear. His name was Roman Nose. A handsome man with steady gaze and powerful magic, he had led one of the attacks on the lost columns of "Star Chief" Connor, riding his white pony along the line of soldiers taunting the bluecoats until they emptied their guns. His horse was killed, but Roman Nose was unharmed.

In November 1866, Roman Nose informed an agent of the Overland Stage Company that he would attack the stages if they continued to roll along the Smoky Hill Road. Though early snowstorms had closed the road for the winter, General Sherman mobilized a force of 1,400 men on the Kansas plains the following spring, under the leadership of Gen. Winfield S. Hancock, a tall handsome hero of the Civil War, who "presented an appearance that would attract the attention of an army as he passed." Along with infantry and artillery, Hancock's command included the Seventh Cavalry, led by an equally dashing officer named George Armstrong Custer, a famous "boy-general" of the Civil War, now reduced to the post-war rank of lieutenant colonel.

At Fort Larned, on the Pawnee Fork of the Arkansas River in central Kansas, General Hancock met the Indians at night—though the Cheyenne always held peaceful councils during the day—and fired his artillery to emphasize his readiness to fight, earning the Indian nickname "Old Man of the Thunder." "The white man is coming out here so fast that nothing can stop him," Hancock boasted about the railroad building rapidly across the plains toward the Smoky Hill. "Coming from the East, and coming from the West, like a prairie on fire in a high wind....You must not let your young men stop them; you must keep your men off the roads."

Although the assembled chiefs expressed a willingness to keep the peace, Roman Nose had not attended the council meetings with Hancock, for only chiefs had been invited. Consequently Hancock resolved to march on the Cheyenne camp, about 35 miles up the Pawnee Fork, and confront Roman Nose directly. Edward Wynkoop, the former army officer who had befriended the Cheyenne before Sand Creek and now served as their agent, warned Hancock that such a belligerent display would be unwise, but the general nevertheless marched on the Indian village with an army which, in Wynkoop's words, "presented as warlike an appearance as any that ever marched to meet an enemy on a battlefield."

As Wynkoop had predicted, the blustering show of force ended in disaster. Women and children fled from the approaching army, while Roman Nose and several chiefs rode out to meet Hancock. Answering Hancock's questions, Roman Nose whispered to Chief Bull Bear that he planned to kill the general right then and there. Fearful of the consequences, the chief led the warrior away, and the conference ended with Hancock ordering the Cheyenne to bring back their women and children. Instead, the Cheyenne disappeared onto the plains, and Hancock angrily ordered his men to destroy their village, after counting its contents: 251 teepees, 962 buffalo robes, 436 saddles, tons of meat, and everything else the Indians needed for their daily life.

In rage and retribution, Indian warriors terrorized the central plains, raiding stage stations and railroad camps, running off stock, ripping down telegraph wires, skirmishing with soldiers, and closing the road along the Smoky Hill. Custer and his cavalry chased them for roughly a thousand miles, up to the Platte and the Republican River, back to the Smoky Hill, accomplishing little, but so impressing the Indians with his stamina that they called him "Hard Backsides."

"The operations of General Hancock," wrote peace commissioner John B. Sanborn, "have been so disastrous to the public interests, and at the same time seem to me to be so inhuman, that I deem it proper to communicate my views.... For a mighty nation like us to be carrying on a war with a few straggling nomads, under such circumstances, is a spectacle most humiliating, an injustice unparalleled, a national crime most revolting, that must, sooner or later, bring down upon us or our posterity the judgment of Heaven."

By October, Hancock had been removed from the plains, while a new peace commission was established at Medicine Lodge Creek, a tree-shaded stream south of Fort Larned. General Sherman sent the commission grudgingly into the field,

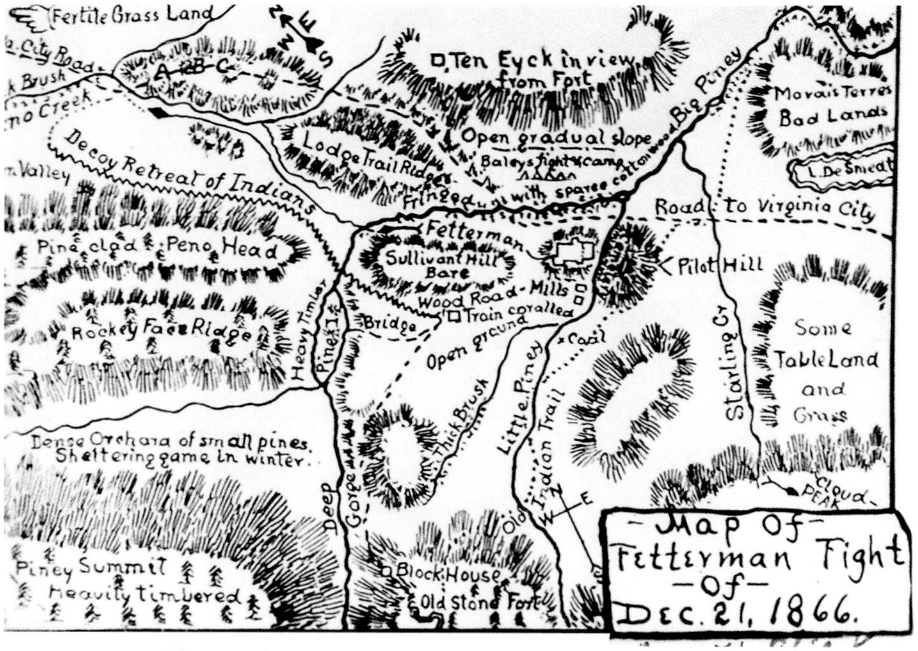

Fertile Grass Land
City Road
Brush
Creek
A B C
N E S
Ten Eyck in view from Fort
Big Piney
Morais Terres Bad Lands
Open gradual slope
Baley's fight & camp
Lodge Trail Ridge
Decoy Retreat of Indians
Valley
L. De Smeat
Fringed with sparse cottonwood
Road to Virginia City
Fetterman
Pine clad
Peno Head
Sullivant Hill Bare
Pilot Hill
Wood Road - Mills
Train corralled
Bridge
Rockey Face Ridge
Heavy Timber
Pines
Open ground
Coal
Starling Cr
Some Table Land and Grass
Thick Brush
Little Piney
Indian Trail
Old
Dense Orchard of small pines. Sheltering game in winter.
Deep Gorge
Cloud Peak
Piney Summit
Heavily timbered
Block House
Old Stone Fort
Map Of Fetterman Fight Of Dec. 21, 1866.

To the end of his long life, Colonel Henry B. Carrington claimed that William J. Fetterman disobeyed his orders not to pursue the Indians over Lodge Trail Ridge. Yet in this map, drawn 38 years after the event, Carrington confused the issue—correctly indicating Fetterman's initial pursuit of the Indians who had attacked the wood train (arrow from center of map), but failing to indicate Fetterman's reverse maneuver to follow the warriors under Crazy Horse, which took him along the Bozeman Trail ("Road to Virginia City") over a low saddle beside Lodge Trail Ridge and into the valley of Peno Creek, where he and his command met disaster on a long, sloping hill (marked "A B C").

believing that when it came to hostile Indians, "it makes little difference whether they be coaxed out by Indian commissioners or killed." In exchange for presents—particularly the precious ammunition they needed to hunt the diminishing buffalo—the Indian leaders agreed to accept two separate reservations in what is now western Oklahoma, where they would receive specified supplies for a period of 30 years while trained to be farmers. With the end of the Civil War, railroad expansion, and the renewed hunger for western lands, it had become apparent that the Indians would have to be removed from the path of the whites, who, as General Hancock had rightly observed, were coming "like a prairie on fire in a high wind."

One leader who would not be coaxed onto the reservation was Roman Nose, who watched the conference from a distance, but refused to sign the treaty. Without the assent of Roman Nose, the Medicine Lodge Treaty was doomed from the start. Congress was slow in appropriating money to provide food and ammunition for those Indians who retreated to the south, and by the following spring, hungry warriors and their families rode north across the Arkansas River to hunt along the Smoky Hill and the Republican rivers. At the same time, northern warriors filtered down from the Powder River country, until by late summer there were perhaps a thousand lodges of hostile Cheyenne, Arapaho, and Lakota on the high plains of western Kansas and eastern Colorado—hunting and living their traditional life, while raiding the ever-encroaching white settlements. Gen. Phil Sheridan, who replaced Hancock on the central and southern plains, reported 79 settlers killed from August through mid-October.

Profane and brutally competent, Sheridan sent three regiments of cavalry into the field, while commissioning a special unit of fifty scouts, all "first class hardy frontiersmen" with experience on the plains. In mid-September, the scouts tracked the Indians up the Arikara Fork of the Republican River, just across the Colorado border. A hunting party discovered the scouts, and at dawn on September 17, the hardy frontiersmen awoke to find themselves surrounded by more than 600 warriors. A handful of eager young warriors charged the camp,

William J. Fetterman

William J. Fetterman *(below)* desperately wanted to be a military officer. His father, a West Point graduate, resigned his commission when his wife died shortly after William was born. William was nine when his father died as well, and he was raised by his mother's brother, a West Point officer who distinguished himself in the Mexican War. In 1853, 18-year-old William Fetterman, employed as an assistant bank teller in Rochester, New York, called on his family connections when he wrote to the commandant of West Point: "I am very anxious to procure an appointment to the Military Academy." He was turned down, and it wasn't until the Civil War broke out in 1861 that William J. Fetterman got his chance to be a soldier.

By all accounts, he was a good one, quickly promoted from lieutenant to captain, later receiving brevet promotions to major and lieutenant colonel for "great gallantry and good conduct" in a series of bloody battles that took him from the siege of Corinth, Mississippi, to Sherman's destruction of Atlanta, Georgia. When he arrived at Fort Phil Kearney in November 1866, Fetterman was welcomed as an able officer who had "earned the reputation of

being a brave soldier," wrote Margaret Carrington, Colonel Carrington's wife, who also praised "his gentlemanly manners and adaptation to social life." He cared for his men as well, according to one of his soldiers, "always looking out for them, seeing to their needs, and saving all unnecessary suffering." Yet he chafed under Carrington's passive leadership and had no respect for the fighting ability of the American Indians—a fatal misjudgment that caused William J. Fetterman and his men the ultimate "unnecessary suffering." ■

ALTHOUGH NATIONAL attention generally focused on the plains during the Indian conflicts after the Civil War, the new "Peace Policy" instituted by President Ullysses S. Grant faced one of its greatest tests in northern California. The trouble dated to 1864, when a small tribe called the Modoc were forced onto a reservation in southern Oregon, where they found themselves in conflict with the larger Klamath tribe. The next year 60 or 70 families followed a young leader named Kintpuash—known to whites as Captain Jack—off the reservation, back to their homeland along the Lost River, just south of the California-Oregon border.

Tensions between Indians and settlers rose for seven years, until finally, on November 29, 1872, a troop of cavalry tried to drive the Indians back to the reservation. Instead, the Modoc fled toward the south, taking refuge among the fissures and caves of black-rock lava beds that the Indians called Land of Burnt-Out Fires. To the frustrated whites, it became Captain Jack's Stronghold, where Jack and some 50 warriors held off government forces that ultimately approached a thousand men.

In mid-January 1873, over 300 soldiers, supported by artillery and citizen

The Modoc War

BATTLE ON THE LAVA BEDS

volunteers, advanced across the lava beds, only to be enshrouded in fog and pinned down by Indian sharpshooters when the fog lifted. The troops retreated with 9 killed and 28 wounded—never having seen a single Modoc.

Failing in warfare, the government sent a peace commission led by Gen. Edward R. S. Canby, a Civil War hero who commanded the Department of the Pacific. When Captain Jack asked for a reservation that would include his

homeland, Canby demanded unconditional surrender—an impasse that created conflict among the Modoc leaders. While Jack wanted to wait for better terms, militants led by a medicine man called Curly Headed Doctor pressured him into violent action. On Good Friday, April 11, 1873, Captain Jack shot Canby in the face and finished him off with a knife, while his comrades killed another commissioner and wounded yet another.

The death of Canby—the only

regular army general killed during the Indian Wars—led to a relentless campaign against the Modoc, who now faced hunger, thirst, and internal dissent. Yet the Indians managed one last impressive victory. On April 26, a band of 22 Modocs under a war leader known as Scarfaced Charley ambushed a detachment of soldiers on the lava beds, killing 25 men before Charley called out to the survivors: "All you fellows that ain't dead had better go home. We don't want to kill you all in one day."

Over the following month, most of the Modoc surrendered, worn out by their grueling life on the run. On June 1, Captain Jack and his family emerged from a cave and surrendered as well, Jack saying simply that his "legs had given out." Jack and three other leaders were hung that October; their heads were later cut off and sent to the Army Medical Museum in Washington D.C. That same month, 155 Modoc people were exiled to the Indian Territory, 1,500 miles from their home, in response to General Sherman's angry desire that "the tribe of Modocs would disappear." It didn't, and in 1909 the remaining 51 Modocs returned to the Klamath Reservation. ◼

The deep crevices within northern California's lava beds (right) offered the Modoc a nearly impregnable stronghold from which they repulsed repeated attacks from federal troops (above). When brute force failed, it took negotiation and treachery to subdue the tribe.

allowing the scouts to take defensive positions on a sandy, brush-covered island in the middle of the dry stream bed. There they held the Indians off with their rapid-firing Spencer carbines, deflecting massive Indian charges which collapsed under their steady fire.

Roman Nose was not among the attackers. The magic he was convinced made him invincible on the battlefield had been broken at a recent feast, when he unknowingly ate fried bread cooked by a Lakota woman using an iron fork. While his followers attacked, he remained behind in his lodge, believing he would die in battle without his protective medicine. But he would not stay away for long. That afternoon, not yet painted for war, he surveyed the scene from a high hill as all eyes turned to see what he would do. "Here is Roman Nose," chided an old curmudgeon named White Contrary, "the man we depend upon, sitting behind this hill." Roman Nose laughed at the insult, as if he were already resigned to his fate, and prepared for battle. Wearing war paint and a long, flowing warbonnet, he led a charge against the island, just as he had led so many charges before, but now the magic was gone, and a bullet tore into his spine. He died around sundown.

The scouts held out for eight days. Six were killed and fifteen wounded. Reduced to eating dead horses, they were relieved by a column of black "Buffalo Soldiers" from the Tenth Cavalry, summoned by two scouts who had managed to slip away. By the time the cavalry arrived the Indians were ready to leave, tired of the stench of rotting flesh that came from the island and deeply disheartened by the loss of their great war leader. Although the whites referred to this grim encounter as the Battle of Beecher's Island, after one of the scouts who was killed, the Cheyenne remembered it as the Fight Where Roman Nose Was Killed.

The Only Good Indians

That winter, General Sheridan launched a massive, three-pronged offensive across the central and southern plains. The most devastating strike came at the hands of Custer and the Seventh Cavalry, who rode through wet, ever deepening snow to attack a Cheyenne village on the Washita River, near the Antelope Hills of western Oklahoma. The village belonged to Black Kettle, the peaceful chief who had seen his people slaughtered at Sand Creek just four years earlier; but though Black Kettle had never wavered in his commitment to peace, he admitted that he could not control his young warriors, and it was their trail that led Custer to the village.

Attacking at dawn on the cold, hazy morning of November 27, 1868, Custer's men seemed to come out of nowhere, riding, slashing, and firing at the Cheyenne from every direction as the metallic strains of Custer's favorite song, "Garryowen," played in the background. To Black Kettle, who rose early and sounded the alarm, it must have seemed as if the four long years since Sand Creek had passed in an instant. The horror was happening again. But whereas he and his wife survived the earlier attack—only to remember it in shame—on this day they were cut down in the first wave, riding together on a single pony.

Custer claimed that he killed 103 warriors, while capturing 53 women and children, but Indian sources dispute this, saying most of the dead were noncombatants. Custer's own losses were substantial: 21 killed, including 2 officers, and 14 wounded; most of Custer's dead were from a detachment he abandoned in the middle of battle—a military decision he had to defend for the rest of his brief life. Despite the large casualties Custer sustained, the Battle of the Washita made his reputation as an Indian fighter. Attacking aggressively under winter conditions, he "destroyed everything of value to them," according to his own report, including their food, their supplies, and their pony herd. Patrick Connor had slaughtered the Shoshone in winter five years earlier, but it made little impression on the other side of the mountains; now Hard-Backsides Custer had made it depressingly clear that there was nowhere the Indians could hide from the bluecoats.

A parade of chiefs surrendered that winter, bringing their people to old Fort Cobb, about a hundred miles down the Washita from Black Kettle's ill-fated village. There they would live peaceably on white man's rations, as some had done before in different winters, under different circumstances, at different forts. But now the conditions had changed. "You cannot make peace now," Sheridan told them, "and commence killing whites again in the spring. If you are not willing to make a complete peace, you can go back and we will fight this thing out."

The first Comanche leader to come in was sad-faced Tosawi, or Silver Knife, who gazed optimistically at the husky little general and introduced himself in broken English: "Tosawi, good Indian."

"The only good Indians I ever saw were dead," Sheridan gruffly replied.

> "...either the Indian must give way, or we must abandon all west of the Missouri River, and confess...that forty million whites are cowed by a few thousand savages."
>
> GENERAL WILLIAM T. SHERMAN, SEPT. 24, 1868

In the spring of 1869, the Kiowa and Comanche were forced to settle around Fort Sill, about 40 miles to the south of Fort Cobb, while the Cheyenne and Arapaho were moved north to Fort Supply, which Custer had established during his winter campaign. The Dog Soldiers remained defiant; that summer, warriors under Tall Bull terrorized Kansas, Nebraska, and Colorado—ripping out two miles of railroad track, raiding white settlements, killing settlers, and kidnapping two women along

the way. Maj. Eugene Carr and the Fifth Cavalry pursued the marauding Cheyenne with a force of 500 men, including 3 companies of Pawnee scouts under Maj. Frank North—who had also commanded the Pawnee on Connor's Powder River expedition—as well as a white scout named William F. Cody, who had earned the nickname "Buffalo Bill" for his prowess in providing buffalo meat for workers on the Kansas railroad.

On July 11, Carr found Tall Bull's camp at Summit Springs, where a little stream runs beneath a gently elevated ravine on the high plains of northeastern Colorado. The Indians were resting on a warm and pleasant day, waiting for the South Platte waters to go down, so they could cross and join their northern relatives along the Powder River. A little after noon, Carr's men—led by Frank North and the Pawnee scouts—swept through the camp, catching the Indians by surprise, killing over 50 and taking 18 prisoners. Tall Bull took up a defensive position in the rough ravine, where he was killed with a single shot to the forehead as he poked his head above the rocks. Although Buffalo Bill took credit for the shot and later turned the Battle of Summit Springs into a grand spectacle in his Wild West show, the perfect shot was probably fired by Frank North. Sixty years later, Frank's brother, Luther, remembered a moment when the true horror of the battle became clear:

I will never forget that little creek. When we came up to the village after the fight was over, I sat down on the east bank and dipped a cup of water and drank it. There was a storm coming up. This must have been about five or six o'clock, and just as I was drinking, the sun shone through the clouds straight in my face. I dipped another cup full, when one of my Pawnee boys said, "Don't drink that," and pointed up the stream to my left and there, about ten feet above me lay a dead Indian. His head was crushed in and the water was running through the wound and down to where I was dipping it up. If you ever saw a sick man I was one.

"I Love to Roam"

IN THE MID-19TH CENTURY, the Kiowa ranged across the broad grasslands of what is now Oklahoma *(far right)* and northern Texas, following the buffalo over the southern plains. Like their close allies, the Comanche, they were expert horsemen and fearless raiders who preyed on Indian enemies as well as frontier settlements and wagon trains. Unlike the Comanche, the Kiowa regularly held the sun dance and shared other cultural traits with northern Plains tribes like the Cheyenne, Arapaho, and Lakota.

During the early 1870s, as they struggled with the difficult adjustment to reservation life, the Kiowa followed a trio of dynamic leaders, including Lone Wolf and Kicking Bird—who fought for their people's allegiance in a conflict typical of the time, with Lone Wolf calling for war just as firmly as Kicking Bird preached peace. The most colorful Kiowa leader of all, however, was Satanta *(below)*, a broad-chested, arrogant and energetic man with a booming voice that earned him the sobriquet "Orator of the Plains."

Although just as intransigent as Lone Wolf when it came to the whites, Satanta was less concerned with tribal leadership, living in a bright red teepee and following his own individualistic instincts. "I love to roam the wide prairie," he once said, "and when I do it, I feel free and happy, but when we settle down, we grow pale and die." The words proved prophetic, for when Satanta was returned to prison after the Red River War, he despaired so deeply at confinement that he committed suicide by jumping out a second-story window of the prison hospital. ■

The Battle of Summit Springs broke the back of the Dog Soldiers, bringing peace to the settlements of Kansas and Colorado after almost a decade of conflict. Though the peace had been won by brutal warfare, a new nonviolent "peace policy" now marked Indian relations throughout the West. The idea of a more humane approach toward the Indians had been gaining prominence since the atrocities of Sand Creek and the end of the Civil War, but the policy became official with the inauguration of Ulysses S. Grant in March 1869. Influenced by his old friend and Civil War aide, Ely S. Parker, a full-blooded Seneca who was the first Indian to serve as Commissioner of Indian Affairs, Grant surprised his fellow military comrades by extending the olive branch to the Indian "enemy."

Defined as "the hitherto untried policy in connection with Indians, of endeavoring to conquer by kindness," Grant's peace policy followed the Medicine Lodge and Fort Laramie treaties, which had established reservations for the Plains Indians. The reservation system ultimately proved a failure, and it may be difficult to imagine that it was conceived as an act of "kindness," yet the reservations were considered a humane alternative by many in the 1860s, particularly when compared with the military alternative of extermination. Grant took control of administering the distribution of food and supplies from the military and assigned it to missionaries, awarding responsibility for specific Indian agencies to specific religious groups, a system that ultimately included every major Christian denomination.

Among the first agents in the field was Lawrey Tatum, a husky, balding Quaker who was assigned to the Comanche and Kiowa agency at Fort Sill in 1869. "Bald Head" Tatum, as the Indians called him, struggled mightily to turn the fundamentally warlike Comanche and Kiowa into peaceful farmers—a losing battle that sorely tested his Christian beliefs. The Indians camped far from the agency, coming in only on weekly ration days, while scoffing at those who tilled the hard, western soil. "I don't like corn," one Kiowa complained. "It hurts my teeth."

The Kiowa and Comanche wanted to hunt buffalo, and

there were still large herds running free to the west, in the wild, seemingly endless expanses of the Texas Panhandle—an area that the Spanish had named the Llano Estacado, or Staked Plains. Some Comanche bands refused to come into the reservation, including the Quahada or Antelope Eaters. They insisted on living their traditional life in the Llano Estacado, offering a tempting alternative to those who remained under Tatum's charge. In the spring of 1870, with the first meager production of corn depleted and the Indians facing starvation, Tatum was forced to grant permission for a buffalo hunt, which not only provided much needed food but also served to remind the Comanche and Kiowa of their life as free men.

Of more concern to the government, however, was the engrained Comanche and Kiowa habit of raiding settlements and wagon trains. The Texans had been complaining to the government for decades, and neither the complaints nor the raids stopped now that the Indians were settled on the reservation. Tatum recognized the problem, but wasn't sure that the Indians under his charge were at fault, suspecting instead that the Quahada Comanche on the Staked Plains were responsible. Then, in May 1871, the truth became clear, when a hundred Kiowa raiders slipped off the reservation and ambushed a wagon train on the Salt Creek Prairie along the old Butterfield Trail. Although the party included several prominent Kiowa war leaders, the raid was reportedly led by a medicine man named Mamanti, who urged that a smaller wagon train be allowed to pass, predicting that richer prey would follow. Ironically, the first wagon train carried General Sherman who was touring the Texas frontier to determine the true nature of the Indian problem. Mamanti's prediction saved Sherman's life, and it proved accurate when a large train of ten freight wagons followed Sherman along the trail. The warriors killed seven teamsters and stole forty-one mules, but were disgusted to discover that the wagons contained nothing but corn.

Five days later, Sherman arrived at Fort Sill, his ears ringing with the complaints of Texas settlers. Sherman was still at the fort on May 27 when the Kiowa came for their weekly rations,

and Tatum asked about the attack at Salt Creek. To his amazement and disappointment, a big, effusive war leader named Satanta proudly admitted responsibility for the raid. "If any other Indian claims the honor of leading that party he will be lying to you," Satanta boasted. "I led it myself." Pouring out a long list of grievances—the lack of arms and ammunition for hunting, the approaching railroad, the rough treatment at the hands of Texans and bluecoats—Satanta made it clear that the Indians intended to continue raiding in Texas that summer.

His pacifist convictions deeply shaken, Tatum sent word to the Fort Sill commander, Colonel Grierson, requesting that Satanta and other leaders be arrested—setting the stage for one of the most dramatic personal confrontations in the Wild West. On the porch of the commanding officer's quarters, General Sherman, who had succeeded Grant as General in Chief of the U.S. Army, faced the Kiowa leaders. He ordered the arrest of Satanta, another war leader, Big Tree, and the grizzled chief, Satank. When Sherman told them they would be taken to Texas to be tried by a civilian court, Satanta flung his blanket open and reached for his pistol. Sherman shouted an order and the shutters of the commanding officer's house flew open as Colonel Grierson's Buffalo Soldiers trained their carbines on the Indians. Satanta backed down, and the conference continued until anger flared again. Two Indians attacked Sherman simultaneously: One launched an arrow that was knocked off course by a fellow tribesman; another was wrestled to the floor by Colonel Grierson as he aimed his rifle.

A week later, the three Kiowa leaders were handcuffed, chained, and loaded into wagons. Old Satank began to sing his death song as he left Fort Sill: "O sun, you remain forever, but we Kaitsenko must die. O earth, you remain forever, but we Kaitsenko must die." Ripping his flesh, he pulled out of his handcuffs and attacked his guard with a hidden knife before he was shot down and killed. Satanta and Big Tree were both found guilty and sentenced to death by the Texas jury, only to have the sentences commuted to life imprisonment by the governor of Texas, who feared their executions might incite

further violence. They were released in two years, largely through the efforts of Lone Wolf, who now led the war faction among the Kiowa and proved himself a brilliant diplomat during an official visit to Washington, D.C. "Bald Head" Lawrie Tatum, who had come to the Fort Sill agency as a firmly committed pacifist, was so disgusted by the government's leniency with Satanta and Big Tree that he resigned his position. General Sherman was angered as well, and his concerns proved well-founded as Comanche and Kiowa raiders ravaged the Texas frontier through the winter of 1873.

THE LEADER'S ROAD

While Satanta, Big Tree, and Lone Wolf led the Kiowa resistance, a new young war chief rose among the Quahada Comanche who still roamed the Llano Estacado. Quanah Parker was the handsome, charismatic half-breed son of a Comanche chief and a captured white woman. In memory of his mother, who had been recaptured by Texas Rangers when he was a boy, Quanah treated white captives more humanely than most Comanche and claimed that he never harmed women or children. White men were another matter; these he killed with passion—especially the hated hunters who slaughtered his sacred buffalo for their valuable hides, leaving the carcasses to rot in the hot Texas sun. From 1872 to 1874, just as Quanah gained power, 3.7 million buffalo were killed on the Plains, only 150,000 of them by the Indians—a harvest of greed that shocked the Indian people. "The buffalo is our money," explained one Kiowa leader. "…Just as it makes a white man's heart feel to have his money carried away, so it makes us feel to see others killing and stealing our buffaloes, which are our cattle given to us by the Great Father above to provide us meat to eat and means to get things to wear."

In June 1874, the Quahada Comanche held a sun dance, the great religious ceremony of the Plains Indians. The Comanche did not normally practice the sun dance ritual, though they had often visited Kiowa dances as spectators. Now, however, inspired by a young medicine man named Esa-tai, they felt the need for tribal renewal and solidarity; other Comanche joined them, as did their Kiowa allies and their former enemies, the Cheyenne and Arapaho. At the dance, Esa-tai claimed that he had been taken up to see "the Great Father of the Indians, who is greater and higher than the white man's God," who had given him powerful medicine. "He told me how to make paint that will turn away bullets," the young visionary explained. "...the Great Father will give you power. You shall drive out the white men and the Great Father will bring the buffalo back again."

When the dance was over, Quanah Parker, with Esa-tai riding beside him, led hundreds of warriors—Comanche, Kiowa, Cheyenne, and Arapaho—to attack a camp of 28 buffalo hunters at an old abandoned fort called Adobe Walls in the Llano Estacado. One of the hunters, young Billy Dixon, later described the sight of the Indians attacking in the morning sun:

There was never a more splendidly barbaric sight.... Hundreds of warriors, the flower of the fighting men of the southwestern Plains tribes, mounted upon their finest horses, armed with guns and lances, and carrying heavy shields of thick buffalo hide, were coming like the wind. Over all was splashed the rich colors of red, vermilion and ochre, on the bodies of the men, on the bodies of the running horses. Scalps dangled from bridles, gorgeous warbonnets fluttered their plumes, bright feathers dangled from the tails and manes of the horses, and the bronzed, half-naked bodies of the riders glittered with ornaments of silver and brass. Behind this head-long charging host stretched the Plains, on whose horizon the rising sun was lifting its morning fires. The warriors seemed to emerge from this glowing background.

After losing three men who were caught outside the protective walls, the buffalo hunters held off the three-day attack with their high-powered, telescopic rifles. Despite Esa-tai's promises, the white men's bullets killed at least 13 warriors and wounded many others—including Quanah Parker, who took a bullet in the side that would have killed him had it not

General Phil Sheridan (above) was a pugnacious bulldog who prosecuted the army campaign on the Plains with relentless efficiency. Like General Sherman, his mentor and commander, Sheridan believed in total war and had no sympathy for those who criticized his attacks on Indian villages. "If a village is attacked and women and children are killed," he said, "the responsibility is not with the soldiers but with the people whose crimes necessitated the attack. During the [Civil] war did any one hesitate to attack a village or town occupied by the enemy because women or children were within its limits? Did we cease to throw shells into Vicksburg or Atlanta because women and children were there?"

The Fate of the Buffalo

REACHING PRESENT-DAY South Dakota in 1806, Lewis and Clark encountered the seemingly endless herds of buffalo that roamed the plains. "The moving multitude...darkened the whole plains," they wrote of their experience. There were at least 30 million buffalo in America at the time, providing both physical and spiritual sustenance to the Indians of the plains.

Such a supply would have been inexhaustible had the animals been killed only as needed, which is what the Indians did for most of their history. But problems arose when the demand for buffalo hides skyrocketed, fed by the invention of a new tanning method and by the transcontinental railroad, which could quickly move the hides to market. Armed with high-powered rifles that could fell a buffalo from 600 yards, hunters bagged a staggering one million animals per year through the 1870s. Some 40,000 hides a day were shipped east from Dodge City. The railroads also disrupted herd migration patterns and deprived the buffalo of grazing land.

Alarmed by the slaughter in 1874, Congress presented President Grant with a bill restricting buffalo hunting on federal land. Smarting from the appalling losses the Indians were inflicting on his army, the old general vetoed it. The bill reappeared in 1876 only to die again. "I believe it would be a great step forward in the civilization of the Indians and the preservation of peace on the border if there was not a buffalo in existence," argued Congressman James Throckmorton. He very nearly got his way; by 1889 there were fewer than a thousand buffalo scattered around the country. It ultimately took breeding stock transplanted from New York's Bronx Zoo to help repopulate the species. Today there are some 200,000 buffalo in the West. ∎

Opposite: Born of an Indian father and white mother, Quanah Parker proved an able leader in war and peace. He was a leading proponent of the peyote religion, a unique synthesis of Christian and Indian traditions.

deflected off his buffalo powder horn. Esa-tai defended his medicine, saying some warriors had disobeyed his orders by killing a skunk along the way, and it was this taboo that broke the medicine. Yet even as he spoke, a bullet struck the medicine man's horse despite its coating of magic paint. A Cheyenne warrior turned on Esa-tai, threatening to beat him, but was restrained by the assembled chiefs. "The Cheyennes were pretty mad at Esati," Quanah later explained in his clear but idiomatic English. "What's the matter you medicine?...'pole cat medicine'...." It is said that Quanah never trusted a medicine man again.

The attack on Adobe Walls was the opening battle in a conflict that became known as the Buffalo War or the Red River War. Using much the same concept he had employed in his winter offensive of 1868, General Sheridan sent five converging forces into the wild Texas Panhandle, weathering heat and drought so severe that the soldiers in one unit were forced to cut their veins and drink their own blood to moisten their lips. Though there were few battles or casualties, the relentless pursuit of the bluecoats in wild, uncharted territory wore down the Indians' resistance, while a new law allowed the army to pursue "hostiles" across reservation boundaries. There was nowhere left to hide. The turning point in the war came in late September, when troops under the command of swashbuckling Ranald Mackenzie swept through a large Comanche-Kiowa-Cheyenne village in Palo Duro Canyon, a jagged, well-watered oasis cut into the Llano Estacado. Though only three warriors were killed in the attack, Mackenzie captured the pony herd, almost 1,500 horses, taking the best for his men and killing a thousand others, leaving them to rot on the featureless plains.

The dogged pursuit of the Indians continued into the winter, when a cold norther' blew down from Canada, whipping wind and snow across the southern plains, forcing soldiers and Indians alike to take refuge from the storm. By early spring, most of the warriors had surrendered. Quanah Parker and the Quahada held out the longest, riding into Fort Sill with quiet dignity on June 2, 1875.

"A leader's road is a hard road," Quanah later said. Yet with his mixed blood and ability to speak English, Quanah Parker walked that road more easily than most, making a rapid and remarkable adjustment from war chief on the wild plains to statesman on the reservation. Others did not fare so well. Satanta was sent back to the Texas prison, where he killed himself in despair, jumping out of a second-story window. Over 70 other Indians were shipped to the damp cells of Fort Marion, off the coast of St. Augustine, Florida, far from the open spaces of their beloved plains. Kicking Bird, a Kiowa "peace chief" who identified the ringleaders among his tribesmen, died mysteriously two days after the prisoners departed; Mamanti, the medicine man who apparently poisoned him, died at Fort Marion— willing his own death, the Kiowa believed, because he had used his dark powers on one of his own tribe.

In the end, however, it was neither poison nor suicide, neither imprisonment nor military action that brought final defeat to the Plains Indians. It was the slaughter of the buffalo, the precious resource that afforded them food, clothing and shelter—a slaughter that continued even after the Indians surrendered, first wiping out the southern herds, then the northern herds as well.

Although some white Americans questioned the extermination of the buffalo, others saw it as the most effective and permanent way to subjugate the Indian people. In 1875, Gen. Phil Sheridan testified before a joint session of the Texas legislature, suggesting that the lawmakers give each buffalo hunter a bronze medal with a dead buffalo on one side and a discouraged Indian on the other. "Those men have done more in the last two years and will do more in the next year to settle the vexed Indian question than the entire regular army has done in the last 30 years," Sheridan admitted. "They are destroying the Indians' commissary; and it is a well-known fact that an army losing its base of supplies is placed at a great disadvantage. Send them powder and lead, if you will, and for the sake of lasting peace, let them kill, skin, and sell until they have exterminated the buffalo. Then your prairies will be covered with speckled cattle and the festive cowboy, who follows the hunter as a second forerunner of civilization."

THE CATTLE TRADE

"No animal of the cow kind will shift and take care of itself under all conditions as will the Longhorns."

CHARLES GOODNIGHT

THE CATTLE TRADE

WHEN CONFEDERATE VETERANS RETURNED TO TEXAS AFTER THE CIVIL WAR, THEY FOUND FARMS AND RANCHES ABANDONED OR FALLEN INTO DISREPAIR. TRAILS HAD TURNED TO RUTS AND FIELDS TO WEEDS; FENCES WERE BROKEN AND BARNS COLLAPSED. UNTENDED DOMESTIC ANIMALS ROAMED THE OPEN PLAINS. CONFEDERATE CURRENCY WAS WORTHLESS. • AS THE MEN RODE FURTHER WEST, BEYOND THE RED RIVER, ACROSS THE SABINE AND TRINITY, THEY DISCOVERED A NEW KIND OF CURRENCY: CATTLE—FIVE MILLION HALF-WILD LONGHORNS, ROAMING THE GRASSLANDS AND THICKETS FROM THE BRAZOS TO THE RIO GRANDE. • DESCENDED FROM SPANISH CATTLE FIRST BROUGHT TO TEXAS BY EXPLORERS AND MISSIONARIES, LATER MIXED WITH BRITISH BREEDS BROUGHT BY AMERICAN SETTLERS, THE LONGHORNS WERE AS TOUGH AND WELL-ADAPTED TO THE LAND AS WERE THE TEXANS THEMSELVES. MUSCULAR AND LEAN, WITH DEEP-SET CRAZY EYES, LEATHERY SKIN, AND SPREADING SHARP-TIPPED HORNS, THEY SURVIVED DROUGHTS AND BLIZZARDS, AND LIVED ON ALMOST NOTHING—ROUGH GRASS, SPINY MESQUITE, AND WATER THAT WASN'T FIT FOR HUMAN CONSUMPTION. LONGHORN MEAT

Previous page: It was across Kansas prairies like this that Texas ranchers drove thundering herds of cattle to market.
Opposite: Cattle drives gave rise to the West's most famous icon—the cowboy (above).

was tougher than corn-fed eastern cattle, but it would feed the hunger of the North, where industrial cities exploded with postwar masses. A longhorn steer that sold for three or four dollars in Texas—if it sold at all—might bring forty dollars in Chicago, even more in New York. "The big Texas problem," as historian Wayne Gard defined it, "was to link a four-dollar steer to a forty-dollar market."

Texans had done it before the war, driving cattle as far as California in the West, to New Orleans and Chicago in the East, where the longhorn could be shipped even further by river or rail. Many early drives headed for Missouri—first St. Louis, later Kansas City and St. Joseph—following a wide, well-traveled route that became known as the Shawnee Trail. Although it provided the most direct connection with northern markets, drovers on the Shawnee Trail faced mounting resistance from Missouri and Kansas farmers, who feared the longhorns would infect their domestic cattle with a tick-borne disease known as Spanish or Texas fever. Though the tough longhorns had developed an immunity to the fever, they carried the ticks, causing sporadic yet devastating outbreaks among the local herds.

THE MOST DANGEROUS WILD ANIMAL IN AMERICA

In order to drive their cattle, the Texans had to gather a herd. Later called a roundup, herd-gathering was called a "cow hunt" in the early days, a term that reflected the wild nature of the beasts. Some cattle had never been domesticated at all, while others had run off from ranches or been born in the wild during the war. Millions were unbranded mavericks, named after lawyer Samuel Maverick who lost most of his unbranded herd in the 1850s. As the cattle industry developed, the herding of unbranded cattle, or "mavericking," would be considered a crime, a small step down from outright theft or rustling; but in the chaos after the war, mavericks were free for the taking— though the taking took courage, skill, and a well-trained horse. One early observer described the longhorns as "fifty times more dangerous to footmen than the fiercest buffalo," while Theodore

Roosevelt, who knew the West well, observed that a "mean Texas longhorn could be the most dangerous wild animal in America."

A few cattlemen made drives in 1865, but most returned from the war too late in the season to put together a herd, and set their sights on 1866. Over 200,000 longhorns walked out of Texas that year, heading for far-flung markets from New Mexico and Colorado to Iowa, Illinois, and Louisiana. Those who traveled up the old Shawnee Trail, into eastern Kansas and Missouri, faced legal restrictions against transporting diseased cattle across state and territory borders. These restrictions were often enforced by armed mobs who turned the trail drivers away, fearing the spread of Texas fever—or so they said. In fact, much of the resistance reflected the still simmering hostilities of the Civil War, and many men in the border region were more interested in killing the Texans and stealing their cattle than they were in preventing the spread of fever.

A young Texas cattleman named Jim Daugherty—driving his own herd before the age of 20—met up with a band of former Kansas guerrillas called Jayhawkers along the Kansas-Missouri border. When one of Daugherty's cowhands reached for his gun, a Kansan shot him dead, sending the herd into a wild stampede. "The Jayhawkers took me to Cow Creek which was nearby," Daugherty later remembered, "and there tried me for driving cattle into their country, which they claimed were infested with ticks which would kill their cattle. I was found guilty without any evidence….Then they began to argue among themselves what to do with me. Some wanted to hang me while others wanted to whip me to death." Fortunately for Daugherty, "one of the big Jayhawkers" was touched by his youth and convinced the others to let him go. The young cattleman lost about 150 steers, almost a third of his herd, but after burying his dead trail hand he drove the rest of the herd to market and made a profit anyway, selling the steers for 35 dollars a head.

Daugherty's encounter and the similar experiences of other cattlemen threw the rebuilding cattle trade into confusion. The rewards were great, particularly if herds were driven north, but the dangers and restrictions were daunting. In early 1867, six states passed new laws barring Texas cattle from their lands: Colorado, Kansas, Nebraska, Missouri, Illinois, and Kentucky. The Kansas law offered a loophole for enterprising cattlemen; longhorns would be allowed into the southwestern quarter of the state, and, with certain restrictions, Texans could drive them further north to be shipped out of state on the Union Pacific Railway, Eastern Division (later called the Kansas Pacific).

In March 1867, a livestock company in the capital city of Topeka informed Texas cattlemen of the new Kansas law, offering to lead them through Kansas safely and purchase Texas cattle at stockyards to be built at an unnamed point along the railroad, somewhere to the west. Nothing came of the offer; the Texans were skeptical of northern promises, and the Topeka company never built their stockyards.

Around the same time, Joseph G. McCoy, born into the cattle business near Springfield, Illinois, began to wrestle with the same problem. Just 29 years old, McCoy had recently joined his two older brothers in their prospering livestock firm, fattening cattle on Illinois corn and shipping them to market. Spurred by reports of huge Texas herds and the difficulties of driving them north, McCoy became obsessed with finding a solution until it became, he said, "a waking thought, a sleeping dream."

At first, McCoy considered shipping the longhorns on barges down the Arkansas River, then up the Mississippi to Cairo, Illinois. Before acting on this idea, he took a trip on the railroad, which then reached almost halfway across Kansas. At the tiny town of Abilene, not far from the end of the track, the train happened to be delayed for an hour while a bridge was repaired—just enough time to allow McCoy to look around and talk to the local people. Abilene was "a very small, dead place," he later wrote, "consisting of about one dozen log huts, low, small, rude affairs, four-fifths of which were covered with dirt for roofing...." Nevertheless, Abilene had much to recommend it: rich grasslands, good water, and sparse population. Though the local citizens McCoy spoke to didn't know it at the time, Abilene wouldn't be a small, dead place for long.

On his return trip to Springfield, McCoy presented his idea

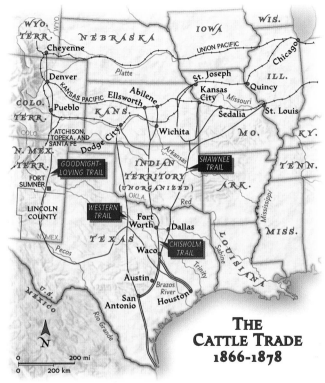

THE CATTLE TRADE 1866-1878

State and territory borders as of 1872
Present-day state names in gray

Before the Civil War, the main route for taking Texas cattle to market was the Shawnee Trail, which led to St. Louis, Sedalia, and Kansas City, Missouri. But when Missouri and eastern

Kansas imposed a quarantine on Texas longhorns, the Chisholm Trail became the route of choice. Ranchers used two other trails to take their cattle further north: The Western Trail through

Dodge City up to Montana and the Dakotas; and the Goodnight-Loving Trail through New Mexico, Colorado, and Wyoming.

On the Trail

DESPITE THE COWBOY'S hallowed place in American folklore, the number of men who actually participated in the long drives were relatively small, perhaps 35,000 between 1866 and 1896. Most were young—in their late teens or twenties—and poorly paid; in the early days an average cowboy earned $30 per month, while an older, experienced hand might make 10 dollars more.

More than 5,000 cowboys were black and another 5,000 were Mexicans. The blacks were mostly ex-slaves, many of whom had worked with cattle in Texas before the Civil War; while the Mexican vaqueros were the original cowboys who taught the Texans techniques of riding and roping. There were also Indian cowboys and a surprising number of Europeans, including the "black sheep" of British noble families.

A typical trail herd of 3,000 longhorns would be controlled by 12 to 18 cowhands, who drove the cattle an average of 10 or 12 miles each day. The trail boss, or drover, rode ahead of the herd, finding the best places for water and fresh grass, while the cook followed behind, driving the rattling chuckwagon. The wrangler, usually a young fellow just learning the ropes, looked after the spare horses, perhaps three or four for every cowhand.

The rest of the men controlled the cattle—a pair of cowboys riding in the lead, the others strung out on either side of the long, snaking line of longhorns, and a final pair riding "drag" behind the herd, breathing the dust of 12,000 hooves. One man who went up the trail in 1868 later recalled that riding drag was the best place to learn cusswords.

The trail was a good place to learn songs, too—songs to quiet the restless herd, songs just to pass the time. "A cowboy's life is a wearisome thing," went one ballad. "It's rope and brand and ride and sing....We ride the range from sun to sun, For a cowboy's work, Lord, is never done." ∎

Opposite: Wildflowers like these Texas bluebonnets added color to the long, dusty trail.

of using the railroad to transport cattle to the president of the Union Pacific, Eastern Division in St. Louis, who reacted with a good-natured skepticism that reflected the wild, speculative nature of his own business—building across the Kansas prairie, beyond the edge of white settlement and into the hunting grounds of hostile Cheyenne warriors. "I do not believe that you can, to any extent, establish or build up a cattle trade on our road," he said. "It looks too visionary, too chimerical, too speculative; and it would be altogether too good a thing to happen to us or to our road." Still, the railroad promised a switch and sidings for the proposed stockyards and a payment of five dollars for every carload of cattle that McCoy managed to ship on the rails.

Looking for the best route across Missouri, McCoy next visited the president of the more established Missouri Pacific railroad. McCoy later recalled the president's reaction when he asked for freight rates to St. Louis in his autobiography, *Historic Sketches of the Cattle Trade*:

> ...the railroad official, tipping his cigar up at right angles with his nose, and striking the attitude of indescribable greatness, when stooping to notice an infinitesimal object, and with an air bordering on immensity, said:
> "It occurs to me that you haven't any cattle to ship and never did have any, and I, sir, have no evidence that you ever will have any, and I think you are talking about rates of freight for speculative purposes; therefore, you get out of this office, and let me not be troubled by any more of your style."

McCoy walked out of the president's office, wondering at "the inscrutable purposes of Jehovah in creating and suffering such a great being to remain on earth, instead of appointing him to manage the universe," and within twelve hours had a better deal with another railroad, having negotiated rates from the Missouri River to Quincy, Illinois, and on to Chicago.

In June 1867, Joseph McCoy bought 250 acres of land in Abilene and immediately set to work building stockyards, as well

would tell me a lot of stuff about how they got started, and how in Chicago and those eastern cities they wasn't allowed on the streets, how their clothes would be taken away from them, only what they needed in the house, so it was like being in prison.

"They could do as they pleased out here. And they were human, too. They always had money and they would lend it to fellows that were broke."

For the people of Abilene, the most frightening aspect of cowboy culture was not the drinking, gambling, or whoring, but the favorite Texas prerogative of shooting up the town. "Every cowboy that came into town had to pass my office door," recalled Thelphilus Little, who owned a lumberyard in the heart of Texas Abilene. "There were hundreds of them every day and every 'son of a gun' had *two* guns and I thought every gun was as long as an Ohio fence rail. These boys came into town and did not leave Texas Street, would drink and gamble, get rip-roaring crazy drunk and towards evening jump their Texas ponies and then begin to shoot hundreds of shots, yelling like a million Indians, ponies on the dead run. Every boy passed my office and by the time they got there the air was lurid as they shot upwards. At first I would run to the door to see the show, but I soon learned to crawl into a hole and pull the hole in after me or pull a pile of lumber over on to me."

Realizing the need to control the wild cattle trade, the citizens incorporated Abilene as a city in September 1869, and appointed five men as trustees until elections could be held—including Joseph G. McCoy, the man who put Abilene on the map. Yet even as he took his place among the town fathers, McCoy was in the process of going bankrupt. McCoy had been forced to sell his Great Western Stockyards in the spring of 1870 after the Kansas Pacific Railroad refused to pay him a promised bonus for each car he had shipped. McCoy ultimately won a settlement of over $5,000 in a case that went all the way to the Kansas Supreme Court, but the ruling came too late to salvage his Abilene livestock business.

Among its first actions, the city government issued a statute banning firearms in town. When the council posted notices announcing the ban, the cowboys promptly shot them to

The Kid

HE WAS A VIOLENT boy in a violent world, a slight, bucktoothed gunslinger with cold blue eyes and a ready grin. His real name was probably Henry McCarty—or it might have been William H. Bonney—but for the last months of his short, explosive life they called him Billy the Kid *(opposite)*.

The Kid's criminal career began a year after his mother died, in 1875, when he was 15. He stole some clothes from a laundry in Silver City, New Mexico, was imprisoned, and escaped through the jail chimney. Fleeing to Arizona, he learned how to handle a gun and killed a drunken bully in a barroom brawl. The serious killing began in 1878, when 18-year-old Billy became a staunch soldier in the "Lincoln County War," a battle for control of the cattle industry in southeastern New Mexico. Fighting for a cause he believed in, the Kid participated in several killings, including the ambush of county sheriff William Brady. When the war was over, he turned to cattle rustling, counterfeiting, and mail robbery.

In late 1880, Billy was captured by the new Lincoln County sheriff, a tall, tough, ex-buffalo hunter named Pat

Garrett. Brought to trial for the murder of Brady and another man, the Kid took it all in stride. "What's the use of looking on the gloomy side of everything?" he asked. "The laugh's on me this time." The laugh was on Garrett when the Kid escaped, killing both his guards. But Garrett laughed last. On the night of July 14, 1881, after tracking him down to the small settlement of Fort Sumner, Pat Garrett killed Billy the Kid—just 21 years old—with two blind shots in a darkened bedroom. ■

REWARD
($5,000.00)
Reward for the capture, dead or alive, of one Wm. Wright, better known as

"BILLY THE KID"

Age, 18. Height, 5 feet, 3 inches. Weight, 125 lbs. Light hair, blue eyes and even features. He is the leader of the worst band of desperadoes the Territory has ever had to deal with. The above reward will be paid for his capture or positive proof of his death.

JIM DALTON, Sheriff.

DEAD OR ALIVE!
"BILLY THE KID"

By 1884, THERE were 1.5 million head of cattle in Wyoming, worth over $45 million dollars. Cattle was a big business dominated by big companies and "cattle kings" who grew rich grazing their animals on unclaimed government land. The potential for profits drew many "small cattlemen" as well, creating a conflict between what a Laramie newspaper called "big thieves [and] small thieves." The bone of contention between them was mavericking—branding unbranded cattle on the open range. In the early years, mavericks were free for the taking, but in 1884, the big cattlemen tried to exercise control of unbranded range cattle through the powerful Wyoming Stock Growers Association. Small ranchers who didn't play by their rules were "branded" as rustlers.

The conflict exploded in violence on July 20, 1889, when alleged rustlers Jim Averill and Ella "Cattle Kate" Watson were hanged near Independence Rock. Although some said Kate was a prostitute who accepted stolen cattle for her favors, the hanging of a woman outraged most Wyoming citizens. The coming of statehood in 1890 didn't temper the violence, and another alleged rustler was hanged the following year.

The focus of the cattle conflict shifted

Johnson County War

BLOOD ON THE RANGE

to Johnson County, a rolling rangeland drained by the Powder River. In late 1891, two small ranchers were ambushed and murdered near the county seat of Buffalo, while another suspected rustler, Nate Champion, survived an attack along the Powder. Events came to a head in early April 1892, when a six-car special train left Cheyenne for Casper, the closest railhead to Johnson County. It carried 52 vigilantes: a contingent of armed cattlemen reinforced by more than 20 hired Texas gunmen,

2 reporters, and a doctor. Financed by the big cattle interests the "Invaders" or "Regulators" headed for Johnson County with a list of alleged rustlers they planned to drive out of the county, or kill.

Their plans went awry at the KC Ranch, on the middle fork of the Powder River, where they gunned down a suspected rustler named Nick Ray and then spent the entire day battling Nate Champion—who single-handedly held them off while keeping a remarkable diary of the events:

"They are still shooting and are all around the house. Boys, there is bullets coming in like hail." Unable to drive him out, the Invaders set fire to the house and shot Champion as he tried to escape.

As the Invaders moved north toward Buffalo, they received a report that a citizens' army awaited them. Fortifying themselves at another ranch called the TA, the hunters became the hunted when over 200 armed men attacked on April 11. The hapless Invaders were saved on the morning of the third day when federal soldiers arrived to arrest them, apparently on the behest of two Wyoming senators who had awakened President Benjamin Harrison in the middle of the night. The only fatalities among the Invaders were two Texans who accidentally shot themselves and later died of gangrene.

The trial of the Invaders degenerated into a farce, fed by the rich cattlemen's political clout and the fact that Johnson County was too broke to pay for proper incarceration and prosecution. Although bitterness continued for years, the failure of the Invaders and the brave resistance of the small cattlemen ultimately led to greater cooperation on the rangelands of Wyoming. ■

They called themselves the Regulators (above), but to the people of Johnson County these cattlemen and gunslingers were the Invaders. Opposite: Along with an estimated ten million longhorns that trailed north from Texas came a million horses, including perhaps the forebearers of this Montana herd.

shreds—just as they tore down the small stone jail while still under construction. When county lawmen proved ineffective, the council decided to hire a marshal, turning to local men who fared no better than the posters or the jail.

Finally, on May 30, 1870, the city of Abilene hired a broad-shouldered, steely-eyed Irishman named Thomas Smith, who had grown up in New York City and come west to work on the railroad. Smith headed straight for the wild streets of Texas Abilene on a Saturday night, where he faced down a rowdy bully named Big Hank, knocking him flat with a powerful punch to the jaw and taking Big Hank's guns away from him before he knew what hit him. The next morning, Smith had a similar encounter with a tough character named Wyoming Frank. In both instances he relied on nothing but his quick fists and courage. "After that, all went off serenely, so far as shooting promiscuously went," wrote J.B. Edwards, who arrived in Abilene just before the new marshal. "Smith was alert and watchful, seemed to have a magnetic way and a bold, but manly style and very little shooting took place during his reign in 1870." In August, the city raised Smith's salary from $150 to the princely sum of $225 a month, retroactive to the Fourth of July.

Late that fall, after the Texans had headed back down the Chisholm Trail, Smith and another law officer went to arrest a homesteader named Andrew McConnell, who had killed a man in a quarrel over cattle that had crossed his land. In this case, Smith's personal bravery proved foolhardy, as he stormed into McConnell's rude dug-out while the officer who accompanied him waited outside with one of McConnell's neighbors. Shots echoed from within, and Smith and McConnell tumbled out into the yard, where the neighbor attacked Smith with an ax while the other lawman fled across the Kansas prairie. When a well-armed posse returned to the site, "they found Smith's body lying some ten yards from the dugout with his head severed from his body, excepting the skin on the back of his neck."

In April 1871, Joseph McCoy was elected the first mayor of Abilene. His first order of business was to find a new marshal to replace Tom Smith. On the recommendation of an old friend, he hired James Butler Hickok, "Wild Bill" to many who knew him and to most of those who didn't. McCoy and Hickok made an interesting pair—both born on Illinois farms in 1837, both flamboyant and charismatic men. But whereas McCoy made his reputation with cattle, Hickok made his with a gun.

A DEAD SHOT WITH A PISTOL

By the time Hickok arrived in Abilene, his reputation was well-established through a blend of truth and fiction: The truth from his experiences as a wagon driver, Union sharpshooter and spy, frontier army scout, gambler, and peace officer; the fiction from a fanciful "interview" that appeared in *Harper's New Monthly Magazine* in 1867, portraying Wild Bill as a frontier superman who "with his own hands has killed hundreds of men." Bill had killed his share, but it was hardly hundreds—closer to half a dozen before he came to Abilene, not counting his military experiences. Yet even those who disputed the exaggerated tales agreed that Wild Bill was "a dead shot with a pistol."

Standing over six feet, "straight as a man could be formed," with long flowing hair and piercing blue-gray eyes, Hickok was the first of the famous Wild West gunfighters, and like those who followed, his reputation as a "fast gun" drew a long parade of drunken fools who wanted to test his mettle. His exploits in the Union army brought additional conflict with the Texas cowboys, most of whom had fought for the South. And his storied success with the ladies added to the stew. "He was more or less annoyed by jealous-natured, hard characters," remembered J.B. Edwards. "He was very careful in his movements not to let such men get the start of him, not daring to drink to excess, yet drinking some every day."

There were plenty of hard characters for Wild Bill to worry about that summer in Abilene, including John Wesley Hardin, the notorious Texas desperado alleged to have killed more men than any other western gunfighter. Although only 18 years old in 1871, Hardin had already begun to establish a reputation of his own, and he blatantly wore his guns in town in a challenge to Marshall Hickok. In an alley where a group of Texans were playing tenpins, Hardin forced a showdown with the lawman—or so Hardin later claimed in his autobiography. All that's known for sure about the encounter is that afterwards the two famous gunmen managed to coexist without killing each other. "I have seen many fast towns," Hardin recalled, "but Abilene beat them all." As for Wild Bill, even Hardin admitted that "no braver man ever drew breath."

> "It was a very common sight in Abilene in those days to see Wild Bill sitting in a barber's chair getting shaved, with his shotgun in hand and his eyes open."
>
> JOHN CONKIE, ABILENE CITY JAILER

By most accounts, Hickok did a fine job keeping the peace during what proved to be the biggest cattle season in the history of Abilene. The city paid him $150 a month and also allowed him to keep 25 percent of the fines he collected. Mayor Joseph McCoy called Hickok "the squarest man I ever saw. He broke up all unfair gambling, made professional gamblers move their tables into the light, and when they became drunk stopped the game." Charlotte E. Northcraft, who arrived in Abilene as a young bride in May 1871, recalled that Hickok's "reputation as a dead shot was sufficient to keep the Texas cowboys from becoming too boisterous and no one was molested when he attended strictly to his own business. Women were as safe on the streets as they are now."

By the end of the 1871 season, many of the cowboys had begun to head south for the winter, while those who remained wanted to make the most of their last few nights in Abilene. "I saw this band of crazy men," recalled Thelphilus Little. "They went up and down the street with a wild swish and rush and roar, totally oblivious to anything in their path. It was a drunken mob." As the mob congregated outside the Alamo Saloon on the night of October 5, Phil Coe pulled out a pistol and fired it into the air.

Around the corner, a few doors away, Wild Bill was drinking at the bar in the Novelty Theater with a friend, Mike Williams, who had been hired to protect the chorus girls from the advances of drunken patrons. On hearing the shot, Bill rushed over to the Alamo, cutting through the saloon and pushing through the double glass doors to face the mob out on the street. When Coe admitted that he had fired the shot, Hickok ordered the Texans to surrender their guns and leave.

There are different versions of what happened next. The Abilene *Chronicle* reported that the two big men stood eight feet apart, and that Coe managed to fire two shots, one passing through Hickok's coat and another between his legs, a "truly marvelous" escape. "As quick as thought, the Marshal drew two revolvers and both men fired almost simultaneously. Several shots were fired, during which Mike Williams, a policeman, came rushing around the corner for the purpose of assisting the Marshal, and rushing between him and Coe received two of the shots intended for Coe. The whole of the affair was the work of an instant."

Some say Hickok hit Coe first, then whirled toward Williams—seeing him out of the corner of his eye and thinking he was one of the Texans. Others say the first shots meant for Coe hit Williams instead, as he ran into the line of fire, and that Hickok then blasted Coe with two more bullets. Thelphilus Little, who locked his family in their house when the trouble began, remembered that Wild Bill faced down the rest of the mob with the classic line: "If any of you want the balance of these pills, come and get them."

No one wanted the pills, and no one wanted anything to do with Hickok after he discovered that he'd killed his friend.

Wild Bill Hickock

JAMES BUTLER HICKOK (*below*) was born in 1837, youngest son of an Illinois farm family with roots in Stratford-upon-Avon, where the "Hiccox" were tenant farmers of William Shakespeare. When his father died in 1852, James helped support the family, but he and a brother moved on to Kansas in 1856, where James—a staunch antislavery man—became deeply involved in the violent conflict over slavery that earned the territory the name, "Bleeding Kansas."

After several years as a wagon driver

for the Kansas freighting firm of Russell, Majors, and Waddell, Hickok was assigned in 1861 to a Pony Express station at Rock Creek, Nebraska, where he took part in a famous gun battle in which three men were killed. Although often credited with killing all three, Hickok's role remains unclear. After Rock Creek, he joined the Union army as a civilian scout, later serving as a wagon master, sharpshooter, and spy. It was during the war, apparently after facing down a drunken mob in Missouri, that Hickok earned the nickname, "Wild Bill."

In July 1865, Hickok shot and killed a man in the public square of Springfield, Missouri, one of the few classic gunfights in the Wild West. As was often the case in Hickok's life, the conflict arose from a combination of gambling, women, and North-South antipathy. Two months later, Hickok met Colonel George Ward Nichols, who wrote an article for *Harper's New Monthly Magazine* that spread the name "Wild Bill" across the nation. "Yes, Wild Bill with his own hands has killed hundreds of men," Nichols wrote with wild exaggeration. "...'He shoots to kill,' as they say on the border." ■

"For once the *real* Wild Bill Hickok emulated his legend," wrote biographer Joseph G. Rosa. "Like a man possessed, he swept into the few saloons and gambling houses still in business and in no uncertain manner kicked everybody out. Those who resisted he knocked aside. Others took one look at the death in his eyes and fled." Williams had died instantly; Coe died in agony a few days later from wounds to the abdomen.

Hickok paid for Mike Williams' funeral, and it's said that Phil Coe's mother offered a reward of $10,000 to anyone who would kill Wild Bill and bring him her head. Fending off at least one assassination attempt on a railroad trip to Topeka, Hickok continued as marshal of Abilene until December 1871, when he was dismissed. Most citizens remembered Hickok with great respect, but times were changing in Abilene. There were children in town now, and their parents shuddered at what they might see on the other side of the tracks. Beyond the city limits, farmers filled the Kansas prairie, some staking claims along the Chisholm Trail. Although Joseph McCoy fought to keep the cattle trade he had created, a faction led by Theodore C. Henry, later known as the "Wheat King of Kansas," looked to a more peaceful future of farming that wouldn't require the services of a high-dollar, high-profile gunman like Wild Bill Hickok. In February 1872, the citizens sent the following notice to Texas:

We the undersigned, members of the Farmers' Protective Association, and officers and citizens of Dickinson County, Kansas, most respectfully request all who had contemplated driving Texas cattle to Abilene the coming season, to seek some other point for shipment, as the inhabitants of Dickinson County will no longer submit to the evils of the trade.

The Texas drovers offered no resistance; new towns further south and west were already competing for their business, and the land around Abilene was getting too settled for their liking. Without the drovers, Abilene shriveled. "Four-fifths of her business houses became vacant," McCoy wrote bitterly, "rents fell to a trifle, many of the leading hotels and business houses were either closed, or taken down and moved to other points.…The luxuriant sunflower sprang up thick and flourished in the main streets, while the inhabitants, such as could not get away, passed their time sadly contemplating their ruin."

Joseph McCoy clearly had reasons for feeling discouraged; he had cattle in his blood and soon left to pursue the trade in other markets, though he would never repeat the initial success he had in Abilene. Others felt differently about the cattle trade moving on, contemplating peace and potential rather than ruin. "Abilene is as quiet as any village in the land," wrote the editor of the *Chronicle*. "Business is not as brisk as it used to be during the cattle season, but the citizens have the satisfaction of knowing that hell is more than sixty miles away."

The new "hell" was Ellsworth, about sixty miles southwest on the Kansas Pacific Railroad. Already competing with Abilene in 1871, it attracted a good share of the cattle market in 1872 and became the dominant cattle town in 1873, when one observer noted that "great droves cover the hills and knolls and the valleys are dark with them for miles around." Over 150,000 longhorns arrived in Ellsworth that year, while the Texas cowboys who drove them filled the saloons, dance halls, and bordellos. Ellsworth had learned from the Abilene experience, opting to make money from the gamblers and soiled doves rather than fight them. "The city realizes $300 per month from prostitution fines alone," a Topeka newspaper reported of Ellsworth that July. "The authorities consider that as long as mankind is depraved and Texas cattle herders exist, there will be a demand and necessity for prostitutes."

Unfortunately, there was apparently a demand and necessity for violence as well. Five men died on the wrong end of the gun in Ellsworth that summer, one of the bloodiest seasons of any cattle town. County sheriff Chauncy B. Whitney was shot and killed as he tried to settle a dispute involving several gamblers, including Ben and Billy Thompson, two Texans with whom he'd been on good terms. Ben had been a partner of Phil Coe in Abilene, but it was Billy—drunk and belligerent—who hit Sheriff Whitney with the shotgun blast that tore through his

Ranch hands stop at an Oklahoma Territory stream to cool off and clean up in this 1890s photograph. Though the lower halves of their faces are deeply tanned, the wranglers' wide-brimmed hats spared their foreheads from the blazing sun. From April "till the wagon made tracks through four-inch Christmas snow," in the words of one woman, cowboys like the ones above were on the trail. Ranging from Texas to Montana, they braved scorching heat, freezing snows, and terrifying stampedes to bring their cattle to market. Once they reached their destination the cowboys would blow off steam at bars and bordellos—often spending all the money they would make for the entire cattle drive—before heading back home.

right arm, shoulder, and chest. When Ben tried to bring his wild younger brother to his senses, shouting, "For God's sake leave town; you have shot Whitney, our best friend!" Billy supposedly replied, "I don't give a damn! I would have shot if it had been Jesus Christ!" Billy left town as Ben advised, but he returned several years later to stand trial for murder, only to be acquitted by a jury that accepted his simple explanation that the shooting was a drunken accident.

The other big, new cattle market was Wichita, about 85 miles south of Abilene, where the Chisholm Trail crossed the broad, cottonwood-lined Arkansas River. The tracks of the Atchison, Topeka, and Santa Fe arrived just in time for the 1872 season, and Wichita competed aggressively with Ellsworth, hiring a couple of well-known cattlemen to work in public relations, including Joseph G. McCoy, who traveled by rail to the north and east, trumpeting the wonders of Wichita to cattle buyers just as he had once promoted Abilene.

Like every cow town, Wichita struggled with the basic conflict of the Texas-Kansas trade—how to lure the Texans and their money into town without getting anyone killed. "Everything goes in Wichita," read signs at the edge of the city, an invitation to fun that belied the rest of the message: "Leave your revolvers at police headquarters and get a check. Carrying concealed weapons strictly forbidden." Naturally, some cowboys didn't read the signs, and in the summer of 1874, a Texas desperado named Hurricane Bill terrorized the town until he found himself staring into the double-barreled shotgun of a local lawyer, and decided he'd give up his guns after all.

A Wicked Little Town

By 1875, Wichita had won the battle for the Texas trade, but it wouldn't last for long. As settlers crowded around Wichita and Ellsworth just as they had around Abilene, the Kansas legislature passed a new quarantine law for the 1877 season that moved the "dead line" further west, effectively cutting off the old Chisholm Trail through Kansas. By this time, the Texans had their own railroads and their own wild cow towns; in fact, they had enjoyed

direct rail access to the north for several years. Yet the experienced drovers still found it cheaper to walk their cattle north rather than pay the extra shipping charges. At the same time, more and more herds were driven beyond the Kansas railroads, on to the north and west where they were fattened on the lush grasses of Montana or Wyoming, or butchered on arrival to feed reservation Indians, soldiers, and miners. These herds—and the men who drove them—needed a stopping place on the trail, a place where the herds could graze on good prairie grass.

And so the Kansas drives continued, heading up the Chisholm Trail and cutting northwest along the Cimarron River through the Indian Territory, or taking a new path, the Western Trail, that curved north from the heart of Texas, both converging on an isolated little town on the dry and desolate plains of southwest Kansas: a town called Dodge City.

Originally a center for the buffalo trade, hunters shipped over 850,000 buffalo hides out of Dodge between 1872 and 1874, almost a third of three million animals killed as the native people fought desperately to hold onto the vanishing herds. By 1875, the big buffalo herds were gone from the southern plains, only rotting carcasses and bleaching bones remaining where sky and earth had once "merged in a purplish haze covered with one mass of buffaloes." A new industry was created as the bones were collected and hauled into Dodge by the ton, to be carved into buttons and combs, ground into powder for sugar refinement, or pulverized into meal for fertilizer. "Bones Wanted," read an advertisement of the time. "We are undertaking to buy a car load of Bones and will pay $8.00 a ton cash...."

Founded on dead buffalo, it was appropriate that Dodge became the last wild town devoted to Texas cattle, the animals that replaced the buffalo on the plains from Mexico to Canada. "Dodge City is a wicked little town," reported the *Washington Evening Star*. "The Texas cattle drovers...loiter and dissipate sometime for months, and share the boughten dalliances of fallen women."

A paper from the "civilized" Kansas city of Hays echoed

the eastern sentiments: "Dodge is a fast town....The employment of many citizens is gambling, her virtue is prostitution and her beverage is whiskey. She is a merry town, and the only visible means of supports of a great number of her citizens is jocularity. Here rowdyism has taken its most aggravated form....Seventeen saloons furnish inspiration, and many people become inspired...."

"Standing out on the extreme border of civilization, like an oasis in the desert, or like a light house off a rocky coast, is 'the beautiful, bibulous Babylon of the frontier' Dodge City."

KINSLEY GRAPHIC, 1878

To manage this "rowdyism," Dodge and surrounding Ford County hired the most storied parade of law officers in the history of the Wild West, including Wyatt Earp and Bat Masterson. Earp had served as a policeman in Wichita before coming to Dodge in the spring of 1876, the first year that significant herds of Texas cattle arrived in the dusty town. He was appointed assistant city marshal, a position generally awarded to a man who was good with a gun. Earp also served as deputy sheriff of Ford County, along with his younger brother Morgan and Bat Masterson, a former buffalo hunter who became Earp's lifelong friend.

Dark, handsome and intense, Wyatt Earp presented a very different appearance from the equally handsome, yet foppish Hickok. Eleven years younger than Hickok, Earp had also been born on an Illinois farm. He had driven one of the family wagons all the way to San Bernardino, California at the age of 16, while his older brothers fought in the Civil War. Earp later learned to gamble in the tough tent towns of the Union Pacific Railroad, and like Hickok, gambling and occasional law enforcement became his stock in trade. Both men gained reputations as the "fastest gun in the West," but most historians agree that Hickok's was more richly deserved. Still, Earp knew how to handle a gun. His favorite technique, called "buffaloing," was to smash an offender on the side of the head with the butt of a good-sized pistol, before dragging the dizzy troublemaker off to the "dog house" or "calaboose."

Whatever his methods, the citizens of Dodge appreciated Earp's efforts on their behalf. When Earp returned in July 1877—the height of the first big cattle season—the Dodge City *Times* noted his reappearance with the most complimentary words ever written in Dodge of a local officer:

Wyatt Earp, who was on our police force last summer, is in town again. We hope he will accept a position on the force once more. He had a quiet way of taking the most desperate characters into custody which invariably gave one the impression that the city was able to enforce her mandates and preserve her dignity. It wasn't considered policy to draw a gun on Wyatt unless you got the drop and meant to burn powder without any preliminary talk.

It's unclear whether Wyatt joined the force that summer. The only other mention of him in the local press came that same month when it was reported that he was involved in an altercation with a brawling prostitute who proved to be as tough as any Texas cowboy: "Miss Frankie Bell, who wears the belt for superiority in point of muscular ability, heaped epithets upon the unoffending head of Mr. Earp to such an extent as to provoke a slap from the ex-officer, besides creating a disturbance to the quiet and dignity of the city, for which she received a night's lodging in the dog house." While Miss Bell was fined "about twenty dollars," Earp was fined a dollar, "the lowest limit of the law." A week later, she attacked the editor of the Dodge City *Times* and ended up in the dog house again, finally making an oath before a local judge, "not to indulge in spirits fermenti before next Christmas. Then won't she make Rome howl."

The next year, 1878, proved the most violent cattle season in the history of the town. In January, long before the herds arrived, the newly-elected county sheriff Bat Masterson captured four train robbers who had tried to hold up the station at Kinsley, about 35 miles northeast of Dodge on the Atchison, Topeka and Santa Fe. A local newspaper called it "a brilliant achievement…accomplished so adroitly and maneuvered with the skill of a warrior."

Unfortunately, Masterson's skill couldn't help his older brother Ed, who served as city marshal that year until he was gunned down in April by two Texas cowboys who shot him at such close range that his clothes caught fire. One of the cowboys who killed him died as well, while the other was severely wounded; some say Ed shot them while dying himself, but others point to Bat, who also rounded up four accomplices. All but the dead man went free, because no one in the crowd of onlookers could clearly describe what happened.

The violence continued throughout the summer. Deputy U.S. Marshal H.T. McCarty was killed in mid-July by a drunken, half-witted camp cook at the famous Long Branch Saloon. A week later, at three o'clock in the morning, drunken cowboys decided to shoot off a few rounds into a dance hall called the Lady Gay, where famed comedian Eddie Foy was performing. No one was hurt—Foy claimed the bullets passed through the coat of his brand-new "eleven-dollar suit" hanging in a dressing room—but one of the cowboys was mortally wounded by Wyatt Earp, who was again serving as assistant marshal, and policeman Jim Masterson, younger brother of Ed and Bat. Despite Earp's reputation, the Texan was probably the first man he killed and the only man he killed while serving in Dodge.

In September, Cheyenne chiefs Dull Knife and Little Wolf fled from a reservation in Indian Territory and led their starving people across western Kansas on an epic journey to the north, throwing Dodge City into a panic and stirring already short tempers to fever pitch. "No less than half a dozen shooting scrapes occurred in our city the last week," reported one local paper. "There seems to be more danger of being shot in the city than there is danger of being scalped by the Red Man out on the plains." Although no one was killed in the September shootings, the following month a popular dance hall actress and singer named Dora Hand was murdered in her sleep, the innocent victim of a bullet that was actually intended for the mayor. As Fredric R. Young wrote in his history of Dodge, "It was a year that provided material for many exciting episodes of shoot-'em-up folklore. It was all there—plenty of cowboys, Indians, train robbers, killers, dance hall girls, sheriffs and marshals."

Dodge continued to be the "Cowboy Capital" into the 1880s, but it was never again as wild as 1878. By the end of the following season, the *Ford County Globe* noted the changing times with civic pride, tinged with sarcasm: "There have been only two men killed in Dodge this summer, for which we deserve due credit. The police, under Marshal Bassett, are compelled to practice on cold oyster cans in order to keep their hands in. The morals of our city are rapidly improving. There are only 14 saloons, 2 dance halls, and 47 cyprians [prostitutes] in our metropolis of 700 inhabitants."

The last great cattle season in Dodge was 1885, but a few Texas cattlemen continued to point their herds north for another decade, usually trailing through Colorado and up to Wyoming, Montana, or the Dakotas, where the buffalo had been exterminated just as they had been in the south. Ironically, the Texas longhorns were passing as well. As early as 1872, Joseph G. McCoy had noticed that the cattle coming into Kansas looked different—with shorter horns and fuller, squarer bodies—as Texas cattlemen upgraded the quality of their beef by introducing shorthorned Durham bulls into the herds. On the northern ranges, the process accelerated, as the longhorns mixed with high-grade shorthorned cattle driven east from

Oregon and Washington along the old Oregon Trail.

By the last long drive in 1896, the half-wild longhorn was more a curiosity than a staple, and the half-wild men who drove them had entered the realm of American myth—giving way to the stolid, hardworking cowboy who rode the ranges in the pay of wealthy cattle barons, much as the early prospectors in California gave way to wage-earning miners who worked for big mining companies. Cattle, like mining, was big business, and the big cattlemen were kings, with fancy homes and luxuries on a par with other industrialists who had made their money in railroads, steel, or oil.

Many cattle barons had sown the seeds of fortune in the desolate days after the Civil War, and though the lingering animosity of the war played out again and again in cow towns from Abilene to Dodge City and beyond, it was northerners like Joseph G. McCoy, Wild Bill Hickok, and Wyatt Earp who helped the Texans build their longhorns into a business that brought prosperity, not only to the Lone Star State, but to towns across the plains from Mexico to Canada. The cattle trade brought North and South together in the West, and ultimately did much to heal the wounds of war. "The Western Cattle Trade has been no feeble means of bringing about an era of better feeling between Northern and Texas men," wrote McCoy in 1874, "by bringing them in contact with each other in commercial transactions. The feeling today existing in the breasts of all men from both sections are far different and better than they were six years ago."

The cattle trade also brought affordable meat to the tables of eastern cities while supplying cargo for the booming western railroads. Though the trade cannot be blamed for the destruction of the buffalo or the Indian way of life, cattle quickly filled the plains they vacated. The trade brought development to the plains, and forced issues of land use that extended well into the 20th century. And ultimately, it was the cattle trade, more than any other western movement, that was responsible for the myth of the Wild West—the cow towns, the lawmen, the shoot-outs, the gamblers and dance hall girls, and the most enduring icon of all, the American cowboy.

In 1876, a young Illinois entrepreneur named John Gates tried to sell Texas cattlemen barbed wire fencing (above), developed just a few years before. They didn't believe the flimsy strands would stop the wild longhorns until Gates built a corral in downtown San Antonio and bet the cattlemen that his fence could stop their steers. It did—earning Gates the nickname "Bet-a-Million" and offering cattlemen and farmers a cheap, easy way to fence their land. In the end, "bob war," as the Texans pronounced it, spelled the end of the open range.

MEN FROM MISSOURI

"*I consider Jesse James the worst man, without exception, in America. He is utterly devoid of fear...*"

ROBERT PINKERTON, NOVEMBER 1879

MEN FROM MISSOURI

--- 1866-1882 ---

At about two o'clock on a mild February afternoon in 1866, two men in long blue overcoats once worn by Union soldiers entered the Clay County Savings Association, a redbrick building on the picturesque town square of Liberty, Missouri. Inside the bank, cashier Greenup Bird and his son William sat writing at their desks. The heavy metal door of the vault was open. • After the men in overcoats warmed their hands at the stove, one of them approached the counter and asked for change for a ten-dollar bill. When William Bird rose from his desk and began to make change, the man drew a revolver and demanded all the money in the bank. Bird backed away as the man with the gun jumped over the counter, followed by his accomplice, who had drawn his revolver as well. The second man covered the cashier, while the first forced William into the vault, smashing him on the back with his pistol and barking, "Damn you, be quick!" • Inside the vault, the robber presented a heavy cotton seed sack and forced William to place the deposits of gold and silver into the sack. At the same time, the other

---

During the Civil War, Jesse and Frank James participated in bloody guerrilla raids in Kansas (previous page) and their home state of Missouri (opposite). After Jesse's death, Frank gave 50-cent guided tours of the family homestead (above) and sold souvenir pebbles from his brother's grave.

robber took the government bonds, which were kept in a tin box outside the vault. Ordering the elder Bird into the vault with his son, the two men closed the heavy door and made their escape.

"After they left the vault door," Greenup Bird reported, "I found it was not locked….We then opened the door, rushed to the front window, hoisted it and gave the alarm. As we were going from the vault door to the window, I saw several men on horseback pass the window, going east, shooting off pistols." Other witnesses estimated the number of outlaws at between ten and twelve, riding two abreast, in good military order.

One of the pistol shots killed a teenage college student named George C. Wymore, "one of the most peaceable and promising young men in the county," who just happened to be standing on the opposite corner with a friend at the time of the robbery. "The killing was a deliberate murder," claimed the Liberty *Tribune*, "without any provocation whatever, for young Mr. Wymore, nor none of the citizens of the town previous to the shooting, knew anything of what had taken place." Although the people of Liberty quickly gathered a posse and skirmished briefly with the outlaws, they were forced to turn back when a sudden snowstorm swept down on the rolling, western Missouri countryside, obliterating the tracks of the criminals.

The robbery of the Clay County Savings Association was apparently the first daylight robbery of an American bank during peacetime. Escaped Confederate prisoners in civilian clothes had staged a daylight raid on a bank in Vermont during the Civil War, but that crime was prompted by military necessity. The Liberty robbery, which netted over $60,000 in coins, currency, and bonds was a first: a bank robbery by criminals who had simply walked into a bank during business hours and demanded money for no other reason than because they wanted it.

Bushwhacking Desperadoes

"The murders and robbers are believed by many citizens, and the officers of the Bank, to be a gang of old bushwhacking desperadoes who stay mostly in Jackson county," the Liberty *Tribune* reported three days after the robbery. The bank itself offered a $5,000 reward for return of the money and blamed the robbery on "a band of Bushwhackers, who reside chiefly in Clay county, and have their rendezvous on or near the Missouri River, above Sibley, in Jackson county."

Although the exact identity of the outlaws remains unknown, the newspaper and the bank were both close to the mark. The men who robbed the Clay County Savings Association were former Confederate guerrillas, or "bushwhackers" in local parlance. They came from both Clay and Jackson counties, a region of rolling hills and dense hardwood forests on either side of the Missouri River, near Kansas City, where the Big Muddy makes its great bend toward the north forming the Missouri-Kansas border.

As much as any single area of the nation, the border region was ripped apart by the conflicts of the war, with neighbor fighting neighbor and atrocities committed by both sides. Although never seceding from the Union, Missouri governor Claiborne F. Jackson refused to supply troops for the Union army, while Missouri men with Southern sympathies joined quasi-official guerrilla outfits under ruthless, yet charismatic leaders like William C. Quantrill and "Bloody Bill" Anderson. When the war ended, the Missouri legislature, dominated by Radical Republicans, offered amnesty for war crimes committed by Union men, while disenfranchising those who had fought for the South and denying them the right to work in professional jobs. Many former bushwhackers settled down to peaceful lives nonetheless; yet others—driven by a combination of rage, necessity, and hunger for the old excitement—turned to the outlaw trail.

Frank and Jesse James were not mentioned in contemporary accounts of the Liberty robbery, nor were they charged with the crime, yet the bank robbery is the first in a long list of crimes later attributed to a mysterious and elusive group of men who became known as the James gang. The sons of an educated Baptist minister who died in the California gold fields and a strapping, tough-minded southern woman named Zerelda, Frank and Jesse had both fought as Confederate guerrillas. Like others of their time and place, they had seen more death and violence in a few short years than most men experience in a lifetime. At the time of the Liberty raid, Frank had just turned twenty-three while Jesse was only eighteen.

In modern Clay County, the study of the James boys remains a local passion. Jack Wymore, a cousin of the college student killed during the Liberty robbery, now owns the old brick bank building and has spent a lifetime investigating the events of that day. He believes that Frank James was one of the men inside the bank, and that it was probably Frank who shot George Wymore in cold blood on his way out, an act consistent with reports of Frank's character. He also believes that Jesse was one of the riders waiting outside, pointing to a long-lost Wymore family letter allegedly signed by Jesse, in which the more sentimental James brother offered sincere apologies for the killing. On the other hand, another local historian, Bill Breckenridge, who works as a guide at the James Farm in nearby Kearney, remembers listening to family stories told by Jesse's grandson, and believes that Jesse was still too weak from a wound he suffered toward the end of the war to participate in the Liberty affair.

The truth will never be known for sure, and it is this uncertainty, a still-powerful aura of mystery surrounding their activities, that makes Frank and Jesse James the paramount figures among Wild West outlaws. Operating in the shadows, they forged an extraordinary career of crime which served as the model for countless desperate men who followed in their footsteps.

THE LIFE OF AN INNOCENT MAN

In the two years following the Liberty robbery, at least four other banks were robbed under similar circumstances, three in Missouri and one in Kentucky. Although one of the robberies failed completely, the bandits got away with around $18,000 in the others. As in Liberty, the money came at the price of human life. In Richmond, Missouri, where a dozen men rode up to a bank in May 1867, townspeople resisted the gang while the robbery was still in progress; by the time the desperadoes

MEN FROM MISSOURI 1866-1882

State and territory borders as of 1876
Present-day state borders and names in gray

Though Union forces occupied Missouri early in the Civil War, it remained a hotbed of Confederate guerrilla activity. Frank James served under the infamous William C. Quantrill while both

Frank and Jesse later rode with "Bloody Bill" Anderson. Four days after Quantrill's raiders sacked the pro-Union town of Lawrence, Kansas, in August 1863, Union General Thomas Ewing issued Order

Number 11, which evicted the citizens of four northern Missouri counties unless they could prove their loyalty to the Union.

Under the Black Flag

As SLAVE OWNERS with roots in the South, the James family naturally supported the Confederacy. Frank James enlisted in the Confederate army in 1861 but was apparently captured the following year and released after swearing allegiance to the Union—only to join a band of Confederate guerrillas led by William C. Quantrill. According to family tradition, in the spring or summer of 1863, pro-Union militiamen looking for information on Quantrill's movements bullwhipped Jesse in the fields and repeatedly hung his stepfather, Dr. Reuben Samuel, who survived with serious brain damage. That August, Quantrill's raiders attacked Lawrence, Kansas, killing over 150 unarmed men and boys before burning the town to the ground.

By 1864, both Frank and 16-year-old Jesse (below) had joined Quantrill lieutenant, William "Bloody Bill" Anderson. In September 1864, Anderson's men stopped a train in Centralia, Missouri, by piling railroad ties on the track, a technique later used by the James gang. After stealing $3,000 from the express car and shooting 24 unarmed soldiers, the guerrillas fought a lopsided battle with Union troops, killing over 100 men while only losing three of their own. Young Jesse James was credited with killing the Union commander. ■

Opposite: In this 1865 photo, taken in Nashville, Tennessee, Jesse *(right)* looks emaciated from a severe chest wound he suffered toward the end of the war, some say while surrendering under a flag of truce. Frank *(center)* wears a Civil War studio costume, while fellow guerrilla, Charles F. "Fletch" Taylor stands on the left.

escaped, the mayor and two other citizens—a father and his son—were dead in the streets.

Various bushwhackers were charged with these crimes, and three were lynched by angry mobs in response to the bloodshed at Richmond. Yet the James brothers were not mentioned in any reports or warrants of the period. That changed in December 1869, when two men entered the Daviess County Savings Bank in Gallatin, less than fifty miles north of the James' family farm in Kearney.

When the first man asked for change for a $100 bill, Captain John W. Sheets, cashier and principal owner of the bank, went to the safe for the money. The second man then entered and said, "If you will write out a receipt, I will pay you that bill." As the banker sat down at his desk, the man pulled out a gun and accused Sheets of helping to kill his "brother Bill Anderson," the Confederate guerrilla leader with whom both Frank and Jesse James had served during the war. The outlaw shot the banker twice—through the head and the heart—before turning on the bank clerk, who took a bullet in his arm as he escaped into the street, shouting that Captain Sheets had been murdered. Grabbing a few hundred dollars, the bandits tried to make their escape, and almost immediately drew fire from the aroused townspeople. One outlaw was unable to mount his mare, who had been frightened by the shooting. With his foot caught in the stirrup, the horse dragged the outlaw down the street before he freed himself and leaped up behind his partner, riding double as they galloped away.

The fine mare left behind was soon identified as belonging to a young man from Kearney named Jesse James. Two men from Gallatin rode south to Liberty, where they enlisted the deputy sheriff and his son for a raid on the James' farm. Located about ten miles north of Liberty, the simple wooden house and stable lay hidden from the road by a rolling ridge. The Gallatin men waited in the thick woods behind the farmhouse, while the sheriff and his son approached the house. Suddenly a small black boy emerged, scurrying quickly out to the stable—where the door flew open to reveal Frank and Jesse James on horseback, jumping the barnyard fence and shooting their pistols as they escaped over the ridge and down the road.

From that moment on, Frank and Jesse James lived a life on the run. That they were able to elude capture for another dozen years is perhaps the most remarkable aspect of their story, for their faces and family were known, and they often visited the farm at Kearney even while being hunted by a long parade of law officers and private investigators. Their success as outlaws owed much to the fact that they were intelligent young men from a good family, a family that had suffered much at the hands of Union forces during the war, as had many other families in Clay County, where the majority of citizens could trace their roots to the South. It wasn't considered right to turn your neighbors over to the law, especially when the law was dominated by Radical Republicans; and in the shattered post-war Missouri economy, many folks in Clay County figured that the money in the banks was Northern money anyway.

In June 1870, about six months after the Gallatin robbery, a letter signed by Jesse James appeared in the Kansas City *Times*. In it Jesse denied having ever been at Gallatin while pointing out that he could not surrender for fear of the mob justice that had greeted other former bushwhackers. "…I never will surrender to be mobbed by a set of bloodthirsty poltroons," he wrote. "It is true that during the war I was a Confederate soldier, and fought under the black flag, but since then I have lived as a peaceable citizen, and obeyed the laws of the United States to the best of my knowledge." A few weeks later, a second letter appeared addressed to the Governor of Missouri, promising to supply an alibi "to let those men know who accuse me of the Gallatin murder and robbery that they have tried to swear away the life of an innocent man." Affidavits from Clay County citizens vouching for Jesse's character soon followed, as did statements from his family, swearing that the missing mare had been sold two days before the robbery.

These letters were the first of many to appear in the *Times* and other papers that would protest the innocence of Frank and Jesse James. It is unknown whether Jesse actually wrote any of the letters; it is clear that the letters invariably appeared in newspapers associated with John Newman Edwards, a former

Confederate officer, and cofounder and editor of the *Times*. Edwards now became a literary and political advisor to the James brothers. He certainly polished the letters, and may have written them. As the brother who signed the missives, Jesse became the front man for the gang, possibly for no other reason than his was the horse left behind. Or perhaps Edwards—who loved a felicitous turn of phrase—recognized the alliterative properties of the young man's name. Though he disavowed involvement in criminal enterprise, Jesse James was now a force to be reckoned with on the American frontier.

THE CHIVALRY OF CRIME

In June 1871, a year after Jesse's public denial of guilt, four men robbed a bank in Corydon, Iowa, escaping with $6,000. The heist went smoothly; except for a lone cashier, the bank and surrounding streets were all but deserted, as most of the citizens had gathered in a local church to listen to a speech about the coming of the railroad. On their way out of town, one of the outlaws—probably Jesse—stopped at the church and interrupted the speech to announce, "We've just been down to the bank and taken every dollar in the till." By the time the startled townspeople realized he wasn't joking, the four robbers had left town and were riding south toward Missouri. The robbers were later identified as the James brothers, Cole Younger, and a young man from Kearney named Clell Miller. Miller was arrested for the crime, but went free when witnesses from Missouri swore he had been somewhere else on the day of the robbery.

The Corydon robbery revealed a puckish side of Jesse James that would appear on and off over the years, even as he and the gang left a trail of bodies. It also may have represented Jesse's gradual emergence as a leader. Although Frank was almost five years older, he was an intense, violent, and brooding intellectual who liked to quote Shakespeare, yet would shoot a man down without a second thought. Men feared Frank, but it's unlikely they followed him. Jesse was more charismatic, equally intelligent and far more engaging. John Newman Edwards referred to Frank as "sober, sedate, a dangerous man always in ambush in the midst of society," while Jesse was "light-hearted, reckless, devil-may-care."

In April 1872, five men robbed a bank in Columbia, Kentucky, killing a cashier when he resisted. A local detective believed Cole Younger had led the operation, and that Frank and Jesse had participated. A big, fleshy man who had distinguished himself for both bravery and cruelty during the war, Cole was the eldest of four brothers from a well-respected family in Jackson County. At various times, all the Younger brothers—Cole, Jim, John, and Bob—rode with the James brothers, but it was apparently Bob, the youngest, who joined them in their next big heist.

On September 26, 1872, three men rode up to the ticket booth of the Kansas City Fair. In broad daylight, and surrounded by thousands of people, one of the bandits grabbed the tin cash box and pocketed the money. When a cashier ran out of the booth to resist, another bandit fired a shot that wounded a young girl. The man with the money leaped onto his horse and the three men escaped through the milling crowd. The daring, dangerous robbery netted a grand total of $978.

Following the robbery, John Newman Edwards wrote an editorial entitled "The Chivalry of Crime," an essay that reveals much about how the James gang was perceived in their time and place—at least by some who had fought for the South:

> There are men in Jackson, Cass, and Clay—a few there are left—who learned to dare when there was no such word as quarter in the dictionary of the Border. Men who have carried their lives in their hands so long that they do not know how to commit them over into the keeping of the laws and regulations that exist now, and these men sometimes rob. But it is always in the glare of day and in the teeth of the multitude. With them booty is but the second thought; the wild drama of the adventure is first….These men are bad citizens but they are bad because they live out of their time. The nineteenth century with its Sybaric civilization is not the social soil for men who might have sat with *Arthur* at the Round

Table, ridden at tourney with Sir Launcelot or won the colors of *Guinevere....*

...What they did we condemn. But the way they did it we cannot help admiring....It was as though three bandits had come to us from the storied Odenwald, with the halo of medieval chivalry upon their garments and shown us how the things were done that poets sing of.

Edwards neglected to reconcile chivalry and a bullet in a little girl's leg, an oversight the Times soon remedied when a letter appeared in which the bandits offered to pay the girl's medical expenses. "We kill only in self-defense," they claimed. "We rob the rich and give to the poor." It was signed "Jack Shepherd, Dick Turpin, Claude Duval," the names of three storied European highwaymen. The myth of Jesse James as the American Robin Hood was now established in the popular mind, and it would be told and retold in folktales for decades—though there is no evidence that the robberies ever benefited anyone but the robbers and their immediate families.

"These bold fellows only laugh at the authorities, and seemingly invite their sleepy enterprise, by bearding the legal lion in his lair."

Lexington (MO), *Caucasian*, August 30, 1873

Unable to survive for long on $978, the James gang helped themselves to $4,000 from a bank in Sainte Genevieve, Missouri, the following spring, a heist that led a competing Kansas City newspaper to suggest that the crime offered "a splendid chance" for the *Times* "to talk about IVANHOE, Sir LANCELOT and other knights of the middle ages." The robbery was well-organized, but again a horse gave the outlaws trouble, bolting in the midst of their escape. This time the robbers forced a local farmer to retrieve it, and rode off shouting "Hurrah for Hildebrand," invoking the name of a famous local bushwhacker, Sam Hildebrand.

While the Sainte Genevieve robbery produced more than four times as much money as the Kansas City Fair heist, the crimes were not lucrative enough for the increasingly daring gang. The original heist at Liberty yielded well over $60,000—probably closer to $72,000—which amounted to an average of at least $5,000 per man. Ste. Genevieve yielded $4,000 for four men, still more than annual wages for most working people at the time, but it cost more to live on the outlaw trail, and it was said that the James boys, especially Jesse, had a passion for gambling. So they set their sights on richer prey: the railroads.

No Damn Common Robbers

Just before sunset, on July 21, 1873, a group of five to seven men waited beside the tracks of the Chicago, Rock Island & Pacific Railroad on a desolate, broken prairie near Adair, Iowa. The men had already loosened one of the rails, tying a rope and a strap through the bolt-holes on one end, and stretching the rope across the tracks and down an embankment on the other side. When the train approached from the west, they pulled on the rope, derailing the huge engine, which toppled over and plunged down the opposite embankment, crushing the engineer to death.

"As soon as the rail was replaced," an Iowa paper reported, "the robbers on the bank, seven in number and all masked like the Ku Klux Klan of the south, commenced firing guns and revolvers and shouting with frightful oaths to the passengers. A moment later and two of them had entered the express car, compelled the messenger with the potent argument of revolvers held at his head, to unlock the safe, and robbed it of about $1,700—all its contents....All the time the passenger cars were the scene of the

She was the Bandit Queen, the Female Jesse James, a high-spirited beauty who rode with Confederate guerrillas and killed four men by the age of eighteen. She married Cole Younger and led a notorious band of outlaws, twisting men around her fingers and dazzling high society even as she plundered it. That's the Belle Starr legend, but not a word is true.

Born Myra Maybelle Shirley, the well-educated daughter of a businessman in Carthage, Missouri, Belle Starr was a product of the same fierce border warfare that forged Frank and Jesse James. She never rode with Confederate guerrillas, but her older brother did, and his death at the hands of Union troops marked a turning point in her life. After the war, Myra married Jim Reid, an ex-guerrilla friend of the James and Younger boys, who became one of the most wanted men in Texas before he was killed in 1874, leaving Myra with two small children. Drifting in the border country, she later lived with Bruce Younger, a horse-thief cousin of the more-famous Youngers, giving rise to the rumor that she married Cole.

In 1880, Myra did marry Sam Starr, the handsome 23-year-old son of a Cherokee outlaw named Tom Starr.

Belle Starr

I Regard Myself as a Woman

By this time, she had taken to calling herself "Belle Reed," so Myra Maybelle Shirley—nine years older than her new husband—became "Belle Starr," settling on a ranch in the Cherokee Nation, along a big bend of the Canadian River that Sam's father had named in honor of the Younger brothers. Jesse James apparently visited Belle in 1881, inspiring the notion that she ran a sort of outlaw hotel at Younger's Bend; actually she wasn't too happy about Jesse's visit and introduced

him to her husband as "Mr. Williams."

In April 1882, Belle and Sam stole two horses from their neighbors, her first and only substantiated crime. They were tried in Fort Smith, Arkansas, before "Hanging Judge" Isaac Parker. "The very idea of a woman being charged with an offense of this kind," reported a local paper, "and that she was the leader of a band of horse thieves and wielding a power over them as their queen and guiding spirit, was sufficient to fill the courtroom

with spectators." The "band of horse thieves" was questionable, but Belle Starr the Bandit Queen was born.

After she and Sam served nine months in federal prison, Belle began to act the part, riding into Fort Smith dressed in a black velvet outfit, carrying a Colt .45 revolver she called "my baby." Although she got into some unearned trouble over a one-eyed horse, she lived on the periphery of Sam's scrapes with the law until he died in a shoot-out in December 1886. Belle publicly proclaimed she was going straight, only to take up with another handsome young Indian who was arrested for horse theft as well. In February 1889, Belle was ambushed and killed with two shotgun blasts, just across the river from Younger's Bend—apparently by a neighbor in a quarrel over some land.

Belle Starr was no Bandit Queen, but she had bad luck with bandit men. A cultured woman who loved books and brought a piano into her rough cabin, "she was more sinned against than sinning," according to an early chronicler, "…the victim of surroundings from which she could not escape." A few months before she died, Belle described herself with simple eloquence: "I regard myself as a woman who has seen much of life." ■

Myra Maybelle Shirley left her native Missouri (opposite) to become the "Bandit Queen" of the Indian Territory. The role was more imagined than real, but Belle willingly played the part, posing in the photo above on her beloved black mare, Venus, in Fort Smith, Arkansas.

American Robin Hood

IN THE AMERICAN SONGBAG, Carl Sandburg wrote, "Jesse James is the only American bandit who is classical, who is to this country what Robin Hood or Dick Turpin is to England, whose exploits are so close to the mythical and apocryphal."

The myth of Jesse James as an American Robin Hood began during his lifetime, created in large part by newspaperman John Newman Edwards, who portrayed the James boys and other former Confederate guerrillas as good, heroic men driven to outlawry by the persecution of Northern authorities. The idea struck a popular chord, growing and developing in both oral and written traditions well into the 20th century. The classic story of Jesse as Robin Hood, told in many forms and many towns throughout the border region, goes something like this:

Jesse and his gang have just robbed a bank or a railroad when they stop at a farm house and ask for a meal. A poor widow, often said to be the wife of a Confederate soldier, offers the gang the best she has and begins to cry as Jesse pays for the meal. She will lose her house and farm that very day, she explains, if she cannot pay her mortgage. Jesse gives her the money she needs, warning her to recover the official papers when she makes payment. After Jesse and his gang ride off, the banker comes to foreclose the mortgage, only to gasp in amazement when the widow produces the required funds. On the way back to town, the befuddled banker is surprised at gunpoint by Jesse James, who takes back the money, along with the banker's watch and chain.

Although it's possible that something like this happened, there is no evidence that it did—no evidence, in fact, that the James gang ever gave away any of their ill-gotten wealth. And the story could certainly not have happened in all the places it was said to happen. It is folklore, a creation of the popular imagination, as is the classic ballad that offers much the same sentiment: "Jesse James was a lad who killed many a man./He robbed the Glendale train./He stole from the rich and he gave to the poor,/He'd a hand and a heart and a brain." ∎

wildest agitation. Women and children were screaming."

While the men in the express car robbed the safe, their cohorts marched back and forth on either side of the train, firing at any passenger who dared poke his head out the window. When a Chicago man asked them not to shoot the women and children, "they swore with frightful oaths that they were 'no damn common robbers' and only took from the rich to give to the poor." In a matter of fifteen minutes, they were on their way, riding off to the south with a total take of around $2,500— a disappointing haul, especially since a train carrying a large shipment of western gold passed through Adair a few hours later.

The Adair incident was not the first American train robbery, but the James gang brought a new dimension to this type of crime with their bold, military precision. A farmer with whom five men had stopped for dinner on the day after the robbery provided descriptions that seemed to match Frank and Jesse James, and for the first time Jesse was publicly proclaimed as the leader. "This Jesse James is known to be the chief of a gang of robbers, which is a terror from their headquarters in Clay County to Sherman, Tex." wrote an Iowa reporter. "Indeed, when it is known that they have committed any depredations, everyone gives up further efforts to capture them."

Actually, Iowa officials made extensive efforts to capture the outlaws, but Frank and Jesse laid low. Six months after the robbery, in early January 1874, the usual denial appeared, but this time it was published in the St. Louis *Dispatch,* where John Newman Edwards had recently joined the staff. The letter asked the governor of Missouri to guarantee the boys a fair trial, and promised that they would "come to Jefferson City, or any other place in Missouri, except GALLATIN, surrender ourselves and take our trial for everything we have been charged with."

In mid-January, five men robbed a stagecoach on the road to Hot Springs, Arkansas. The leader seems to have been Cole Younger who returned one passenger's watch and money when he discovered that the man had served in the Confederate army. This was the only time the gang differentiated between Northerners and Southerners, but it contributed to the growing legend—as did a train robbery two weeks later at Gads Hill, Missouri, a tiny whistle stop about a hundred miles south of St. Louis.

There, five men took over the station and signaled the train to halt. As the outlaws walked up and down the passenger car, robbing the occupants, they examined the hands of each male passenger. "Hard-handed men have to work for their money," explained the leader, apparently Jesse James. "The soft-handed ones are capitalists, professors, and others that get money easy." The robbers only stole from the "soft-handed" men, as well as the express car, and escaped with between $2,000 and $22,000. Ironically, the farmer who had identified them in Iowa commented that one of the gang members had "long slender hands, and did not look as though he had ever done any work in his life."

After Gads Hill, Missouri Governor Silas Woodson offered a reward of $2,000 for the "bodies of each one of the robbers." Others wanted the James gang dead as well. The Pinkerton Detective Agency of Chicago had been pursuing the gang off and on since the Corydon bank robbery of 1871; in 1874 they entered the case full-time, with disastrous results. A Pinkerton detective named John W. Whicher arrived in Liberty on March 10, 1874, planning to obtain work as a hired hand on the James farm and get the drop on Frank and Jesse. Two local citizens tried to discourage the simpleminded plan. "The old woman would kill you if the boys don't," said one of them, a reference to the boys' mother, Zerelda, who was just as tough as her sons. The Pinkerton man went out to the James farm anyway. His body was found the next morning in Jackson County on the other side of the Missouri River with bullets through the head and the heart.

A few days later, two other Pinkerton detectives and a local man who was helping them got into a bloody shoot-out with John and Jim Younger, who discovered them snooping around the countryside. When the smoke had cleared, the local man and John Younger were both dead, while one of the Pinkertons died of his wounds six weeks later. "Poor John," wrote Cole Younger of his brother, who was wanted for murdering a sheriff in Texas. "He has been hunted down and shot like a wild beast, and never was a boy more innocent."

Bob, Jim, and Cole Younger (left to right) pose with their sister Henrietta Younger Hall in this photograph, taken while the men were still in prison. The Younger brothers, much like Frank and Jesse James, were peculiar mixtures of civility and savagery. Although Southerners considered them honorable men, Northern assessments were less favorable. During the Civil War Cole Younger was said to have tested a new rifle by shooting into a line of Union prisoners to see how many of them the bullet would pass through.

After the deaths of the Pinkertons, the gang became a volatile political issue, not only in Missouri but throughout the nation. The Radical Republicans had been out of power for several years now, and the state was once again controlled by southern Democrats, whose apparent protection of the James gang offered an easy target for northern Republicans. "The murderous operations of the Missouri highwaymen," the Chicago *Tribune* proclaimed, "...are a disgrace to that state, and argue a degree of inefficiency or cowardice upon the part of the state authorities." A Pittsburgh paper pilloried "the bandit State of Missouri," where "officers of other Commonwealths...are promptly murdered on sight." Stung by such criticism, Governor Woodson obtained a special appropriation of $10,000 to hire secret agents to capture the outlaws.

A Hunted Honeymoon

In the midst of mounting pressure, Frank and Jesse James decided to get married. The two notorious outlaws wed attractive and respectable women and managed to carve out strangely domestic lives. On April 24, 1874, Jesse married his cousin, Zerelda "Zee" Mimms, who had nursed him back to health at the end of the war, and to whom he had been betrothed for almost nine years. The wedding took place in Kearney at the home of Zee's sister, Lucy, and, according to a story passed down from Zee to her daughter-in-law, it had all the excitement one might expect from the wedding of Jesse James:

The wedding ceremony was just about to begin when they received word that two detectives were riding toward Kearney from Liberty, Missouri, a few miles away.

Everybody looked for a place to hide Zee. There just did not seem to be a hiding place in the small three-room house, until Jesse thought of the big fat feather bed.

Zee was small, and she was placed between the feather bed and the mattress with just enough space at the top for air. The bed was then made smooth again.

Jesse left by the back door to go to the barn at the home of a friend, where two horses had been left saddled and ready. He watched until the detectives were inside Lucy's house, and then rode by, making all the noise that a fast traveling horse could make. Headed in the direction of Liberty, he quickly disappeared into the darkness.

As soon as the detectives set out in pursuit, as they supposed, Jesse returned for a quick wedding. Then he and Zee left immediately on a hunted honeymoon.

In June, Frank married Annie Ralston, a beautiful young school teacher with a B.A. in Science and Literature. Although Annie's father had been a staunch Confederate supporter during the war, he disowned his daughter when he discovered she had run away to marry an outlaw.

The brothers and their wives honeymooned in Texas, but were back home by late August when two large stagecoaches were robbed in western Missouri on the same day. The three men who robbed the coach near Lexington, Missouri, were identified as the James brothers and one of the Youngers. The whole affair took place in good humor, the bandits admitting that robbing stagecoaches was a little small for them, while one of the victims announced that he was "exceedingly glad, as he had to be robbed, that it was done by first class artists, by men of national reputation."

That reputation was so substantial that the James gang was now blamed for every major crime committed within hundreds of miles. In early December, a bank robbery in Mississippi was followed a day later by a train robbery in Kansas, and the gang was blamed for both—a physical unlikelihood. Six weeks later, in the cold midnight darkness of January 26, 1875, the Pinkertons again tried to close in on the James brothers' Missouri stronghold, surrounding the Kearney farmhouse where the boys' mother, Zeralda, lived with her husband, Dr. Reuben Samuel. In a recently discovered letter, Allan Pinkerton described the disastrous attack:

About half-past twelve...We commenced firing the building. Our men battered in the window, then flung the fireballs into the house. Wild cries of dismay were heard from the inside and soon the residents ran from the house which was lit up as bright as day. Mrs. Samuel was bitter…and used anything but polite language.

Mrs. Samuel had good reason to be bitter. One of the "fireballs" was a bomb that exploded with awesome force when Dr. Samuel kicked it into the fireplace—spewing metal fragments that ripped into Zerelda's 8-year-old son Archie, stepbrother of Frank and Jesse, tearing a gaping wound in his side that killed him within an hour. The blast mangled Zerelda's arm so badly it had to be amputated, and caused lesser injuries to a family servant. It's unknown whether Jesse or Frank were home at the time, but the bungled and bloody attack produced outrage even among those who regarded the James boys as nothing but common criminals.

Surprisingly, despite the countless accusations and pervasive innuendo, neither the James brothers nor the Youngers had yet been positively identified in any of their alleged crimes. There was plenty of circumstantial evidence, but nothing definitive, and the tireless public relations campaign of John Newman Edwards—who continued to deny their guilt even as he praised their daring—further obfuscated their criminal careers. That changed in the summer of 1876 when eight men robbed a train at Rocky Cut, Missouri, and escaped with a reported $15,000, though one insider later estimated it was ten times that much. Agents dispatched by the police chief of St. Louis arrested a newcomer to the gang named Hobbs Kerry, who not only confessed to the crime, but named his accomplices in clear and certain terms: Jesse James, Frank James, Cole Younger, Bob Younger, Clell Miller, Charlie Pitts, and Bill Chadwell.

GET YOUR GUNS, BOYS!

Unmasked in their home territory, the gang set their sights on small and prosperous Northfield, Minnesota. Many explanations have been offered for the Northfield raid, but the most likely is that native Minnesotan Bill Chadwell, whose real name was

The career of the James and Younger brothers grew out of the bitter conflict over slavery between pro-Southern citizens of Missouri and abolitionists of neighboring Kansas (above). In fact, only 9 percent of the Missouri population owned slaves, but three-fourths of the people had roots in the South. When abolitionist organizations sent antislavery settlers into Kansas during the mid-1850s, the border exploded with violence that continued throughout the Civil War.

William Stiles, convinced his partners that Northfield would be easy pickings.

On September 7, 1876, eight men—Jim Younger, and the seven named by Hobbs Kerry—gathered just outside of town. According to a newspaperman who witnessed the events, Bob Younger, Charlie Pitts, and one of the James boys rode into town at about two o'clock in the afternoon, and hitched their horses outside the First National Bank. Cole Younger and Clell Miller soon followed, taking positions as lookouts outside the front door while the first three entered the bank. The others waited on the outskirts, ready to aid in their escape.

The carefully considered plan began to unravel when two local men noticed the suspicious activities and went to the bank to investigate. Clell Miller grabbed one of them, a medical student named Henry Wheeler, and threatened him with his revolver, but the young man twisted out of his grasp and ran down the street shouting, "Get your guns, boys! They're robbing the bank!" Within minutes, the town turned into a battlefield, with the three outlaws on the outskirts thundering in to help their companions, while the citizens of Northfield peppered the gang with bullets, buckshot, and rocks. In the early stages, one outlaw killed a Swedish college student who didn't understand his command to get out of the way, but it was soon the outlaws who were fighting for their lives. A sharpshooting hardware store owner named Anselm Manning shot a horse out from under one man and wounded Cole Younger before killing Bill Chadwell with a bullet through the heart. Henry Wheeler killed Clell Miller with a carbine slug in the neck and shattered Bob Younger's elbow as he tried to leave the bank.

Even before the shooting started, the men inside the bank met with resistance from three employees, including acting cashier Joseph Heywood, who refused to unlock the safe, saying it was on a timing mechanism. After one robber smashed Heywood on the head with a revolver, Clell Miller slashed his throat lightly with a knife. The other employees still refused to open the safe—which was unlocked throughout the entire affair, though the bandits never had a chance to find out. "The game is up!" shouted one of their partners out on the street.

"Better get out, boys. They're killing all our men." The three men inside jumped over the counter and rushed into the street; the last one out decided to turn around and shoot Joseph Heywood through the head.

Unlike the people of Missouri, the citizens of Minnesota had no compunctions about going in pursuit of the outlaws, organizing the biggest manhunt in the history of the state. The James boys—who had also been wounded, though not as severely as the Youngers—split with the others soon after the robbery, because Jesse reportedly wanted to kill or abandon one of the badly wounded Younger brothers who was slowing them down. Two weeks after the robbery, a posse tracked down the stragglers, killing Charlie Pitts in a shoot-out while capturing the Youngers—bloody, cold, and beaten. Expecting to be strung up by an angry mob, they were surprised when their captors treated them kindly and offered them medical attention. Although they refused to name their missing accomplices, the Youngers pleaded guilty and accepted life imprisonment in the state penitentiary.

For the next few years, the James brothers kept a low profile. Although there are many reports and rumors of Frank and Jesse appearing throughout the West, most of their activitites during this time seem to have centered around Nashville, Tennessee. Jesse had moved Zee to the Nashville area prior to the Northfield raid, and Jesse Edwards James, named after John Newman Edwards, was born there in late 1875. Frank and Annie arrived in the Nashville vicinity around 1877, and their only child, Robert, was born there in 1878, while Jesse and Zee's second child, Mary, was born in 1879. Working and living under assumed names, the brothers conducted themselves like respectable husbands and fathers, though their neighbors later remembered they were often gone for weeks at time. One photograph taken in 1880 shows Jesse and Frank posing with a group of workers at a cedar-bucket factory in Nashville.

In October 1879, while his family was still living in Tennessee, Jesse—apparently without Frank—led a successful train robbery at Glendale in Jackson County, Missouri. The cool efficiency of the bandits convinced many observers that the James gang was back in business, but speculation turned to confusion that November when a former bushwhacker claimed he had killed Jesse James in a bizarre plot to capture him. He hadn't.

"We tried a desperate game and lost. But we are rough men used to rough ways and we will abide by the consequences."

BOB YOUNGER, AFTER THE NORTHFIELD RAID

The final episode of the gang's career began to play out in July 1881, when between five and seven men robbed a train in Daviess County, Missouri, not far from the old bank robbery at Gallatin. The men boarded the train at two different stops, and a few miles beyond the town of Winston, a tall bearded man wearing a linen duster surprised the conductor and shot him twice from behind before he tumbled dead out of the still-moving train. The bearded man and his partners then killed a passenger in a wild display of gunfire, before two of the outlaws headed to the express car—where they beat the messenger with their pistols, stole his keys, and opened the safe. In the meantime others forced the engineer to stop the train on a siding, where the train robbers jumped off, escaping into the night.

The savagery of the Winston robbery elicited a tide of public condemnation beyond anything Missouri had seen before. The Civil War had now been over for sixteen years, and it was difficult to blame the crime on anything but lawless greed, though many extended the blame to those they believed were protecting the outlaws. A Republican newspaper, the Kansas City *Journal,* expressed the prevailing feeling: "If it shall turn out that the James boys or any of their old gang had a hand in it, then the Democratic party of this state is responsible, for had it not been for sympathizing friends, all of whom are Democrats, the whole gang would long since have been caught and made to pay the penalty of their crimes."

Recently-elected Democratic Governor Thomas T. Crittenden decided to prove his critics wrong; although a law prohibited the state from offering more than $300 in rewards, the governor enlisted the help of railroad and express companies to offer huge rewards by the standards of the time: $5,000 each for the delivery of Frank and Jesse James, $5,000 each for their conviction in certain murders and train robberies, and $5,000 more for the arrest and conviction of other participants in the crimes. Crittenden expected the rewards to induce one of the gang to turn traitor, and he was right—though they robbed one more train before the wheels of justice began to turn.

On September 7, 1881, the bandits stopped a train at Blue Cut, Missouri, by blocking the tracks with rocks and logs. After robbing the express car and more than a hundred passengers, the tall, black-bearded leader handed the engineer two silver dollars and said, "You are a brave man and I am stuck on you; here is two dollars for you to drink the health of Jesse James tomorrow morning."

A few weeks after Blue Cut, an outlaw named William Ryan was sentenced to 25 years in the Missouri penitentiary for his part in the Glendale train robbery. The star witness for the prosecution was Tucker Bassham, another gang member, who had been pardoned by Governor Crittenden in return for his testimony. Bassham offered details and named names—including Jesse James as the leader of the gang. Friends of the James family burned down Bassham's house in retribution, but he managed to get out of Missouri alive.

The leaks got worse when yet another gang member, Dick Liddil, surrendered in January, also offering testimony in return for clemency. Liddil had deserted Jesse after the Ryan trial, fearing that the outlaw planned to kill him, but he found himself in deeper trouble when he killed one of Jesse's cousins, Robert Woodson "Wood" Hite, in a fight over a woman—who happened to be the sister of Charles and Robert Ford, two young men who would soon be famous across America. Tipped off by the informer, the authorities arrested one of Hite's brothers, who pled guilty to robbing the Winston train, knowing Liddil would testify against him. The gang was falling apart, and these new men were willing to talk to save their skin.

I Drew My Pistol and Shot Him

Liddil's surrender was kept a secret until March 31, but Jesse James apparently didn't learn of it until he read the newspaper on the morning of April 3, 1882. By this time, Jesse was living with Zee and the children in St. Joseph, Missouri, under the alias Thomas Howard. Two "cousins"—actually Charles and Robert Ford—had recently moved in with the "Howard family" in their small rented house on an arching hill above the city. Jesse was planning a bank robbery with the Ford boys, hoping for one last haul so he could buy a farm in Nebraska and retire. The Fords were planning murder; Robert had met with Governor Crittenden sometime earlier, agreeing to deliver Jesse James dead or alive for a reward of $10,000.

When Jesse read about Dick Liddil, he questioned the Ford brothers closely; they were Liddil's friends, and it was said that Robert had helped Liddil kill Wood Hite, but they denied any knowledge of his treachery. The tension passed, and Jesse stepped into the tiny living room, where he opened the door to air the stuffy house and raised the window blinds to let in the sun. He then removed his coat, his vest, and his gunbelt—explaining that he didn't want the neighbors to see them—a strange, uncharacteristic action, for Jesse never went unarmed except with his family. Maybe he trusted the Fords after all; maybe he was testing them. Or maybe he didn't fear them because they were inexperienced boys, and he was Jesse James.

A few moments later, Jesse got up on a chair to straighten and dust some picture frames, and the Fords drew their guns, though only Robert pulled the trigger. "I drew my pistol and shot him," he explained, a simple statement to describe the end

of a complicated life. Ford's shot traveled about four feet by his estimation, but it echoed across the nation.

"JESSE, BY JEHOVAH" trumpeted *The Daily Gazette* of St. Joseph the following day. "Jesse James, the Notorious Desperado, Instantly Killed by Robert Ford." Although there was speculation that the dead man wasn't really Jesse James— there had been many false reports of his demise in the past— the body was positively identified by his wife, his mother, and a number of men who knew him. In an interview with the authorities, Zee Mimms James provided some missing details of the family story, including their long residence in Tennessee. Perhaps the most revealing statement came when she was asked how her husband earned his living. "He had a living without getting it," she replied ingenuously, adding that the family always had plenty "and never suffered for anything." Nonetheless, whatever money they had was gone, and Zee began her widowed life in poverty.

Governor Crittenden faced substantial criticism for his role in ending Jesse's criminal career, ranging from the outright condemnation of James' partisans like John Newman Edwards, who railed that the state of Missouri had aligned itself with "self confessed robbers, highwaymen, and prostitutes," to the more considered opinions of those who approved the end result while condemning "the cowardly manner in which the deed was committed." Although the Ford brothers were sentenced to be hung, Crittenden immediately pardoned them, allowing Jesse's killers to go free. Charles committed suicide two years later; Robert was murdered in a Colorado mining camp by a drifter who wanted his five minutes of fame as the man who killed the man who killed Jesse James.

Six months after Jesse's death, Frank James surrendered to Governor Crittenden, accompanied by his good friend John Newman Edwards. On a triumphant train ride from the state capital to a jail cell in Independence, Frank was greeted with such adulation that one newspaper wondered if Frank James was surrendering to the state of Missouri or the state of Missouri was surrendering to Frank James. Although he was tried twice for specific crimes—once in Missouri, once in Alabama—no jury would convict him, and by 1885 he was a free man who lived out his life as a model citizen, working a variety of jobs including a starter at horse races, a shoe salesman, and a minor actor in traveling plays. Children in Clay County remembered him as a friendly old man who would buy them ice cream cones, but Frank kept his shooting eye sharp. In 1904, when he was over sixty, he proudly signed a small target on which the bull's-eye had been peppered with bullets at ten paces: "This was done with my old Navy cap and ball I carried during the Civil War."

While Frank began a new life, the Youngers languished in the Minnesota penitentiary. Bob Younger died of tuberculosis in prison in 1899, but Cole and Jim were paroled in 1901—25 years after the Northfield raid. Jim's jaw had been so badly shattered by a bullet that he was never again able to eat solid food, and his agony become unbearable when the terms of parole forbade him from marrying a young writer with whom he'd fallen in love; he shot himself in 1902. Following Jim's suicide, the state of Minnesota granted Cole a pardon, allowing him to return to Missouri, where he hooked up for a time with Frank James in a traveling Wild West show and gave lectures entitled "Crime Does Not Pay" and "What Life Has Taught Me."

Frank James died at the family farm in Kearney in 1915. A man of genuine, if exaggerated, literary qualities, he left a classic description of life on the outlaw trail in a newspaper interview that was published as he negotiated his surrender with Governor Crittenden. Though self-serving, it has the ring of truth more than a century after the events:

I am tired of this life of taut nerves, of night-riding and day-hiding, of constant listening for footfalls, cracking twigs and rustling leaves and creaking doors; tired of seeing Judas on the face of every friend I know—and God knows I have none to spare—tired of the saddle, the revolver and the cartridge belt; tired of the hoofs and horns with which popular belief has equipped me. I want to see if there is not some way out of it....

Though the Missouri-Kansas border area (above) was home to a number of robbers, none could match the sheer élan of the James gang. During the Gads Hill train robbery Jesse handed the conductor a press release: "THE MOST DARING ROBBERY ON RECORD: The southbound train on the Iron Mountain railroad was boarded here this evening by five heavily armed men and robbed....The robbers were all large men, none of them under six feet tall. They were all masked and started in a southerly direction after they had robbed the express. They were all mounted on fine, blooded horses. There is a hell of an excitement in this part of the country."

THE OUTLAWS

Striking Fear in the Hearts of Men

Of THE MEN WHO lived by the gun, few had a more distinguished pedigree than John Wesley Hardin. The son of a Methodist minister, Hardin's ancestors had signed the Texas Declaration of Independence and served in the Congress of the Texas Republic. But the fiery Texan, who killed his first man at the age of 15, quickly found that violence suited him better than nobler pursuits.

In one storied incident, a man snoring in an adjacent hotel room so disturbed Hardin that he fired his revolver through the wall, killing the man. Even the formidable Wild Bill Hickok, then marshal of Abilene, Kansas, reportedly treated the outlaw with kid gloves when he rode into town. Hardin was eventually apprehended and served 14 years for homicide, studying law while in prison and trying to settle down after his release. The reformation was short-lived, however, and he was shot to death while gambling in an El Paso saloon in 1895. In his heavily-embellished autobiography, Hardin boasted of killing 40 men.

Equally proud of his record was Charles Boles. Between 1875 and 1882, the industrious Boles robbed 27 stagecoaches in California—using an empty shotgun—always working alone but leaving his victims with the impression he had a gang just out of sight. On at least two occasions, he left bad poetry in the strongboxes he emptied, signed with an alias that would earn him everlasting fame as Black Bart.

One poem read:

> I've labored long and hard for bread,
> For honor and for riches,
> But on my corns too long you've tread,
> You fine-haired sons of bitches.

—Black Bart, the Po-8

The Wild Bunch: Butch Cassidy (far right), and the Sundance Kid (far left)

During his last robbery, a passenger took a shot at the highwayman, causing him to drop several items including a handkerchief—which bore a laundry mark that finally led authorities to Boles, then living in San Francisco. Upon his release after a little more than four years in prison, a reporter asked him if he intended to write more poetry. "Young man," Boles replied, "didn't you just hear me say I will commit no more crimes?"

The Wild Bunch, led by Robert LeRoy Parker—better known as Butch Cassidy—shared Black Bart's puckish sense of humor. In 1889, one of the gang entered the First National Bank

Bob Dalton and Eugenia Moore in 1889

John Wesley Hardin

of Denver, and confided to the bank president, "Excuse me, sir, but I just overheard a plot to rob this bank." When the president asked how the man heard of the plot, the outlaw replied, "I planned it. Put up your hands." Relying on "smarts" and careful planning more than violence, Cassidy's Wild Bunch became some of the West's most famous bank-and-train robbers before splitting up when things got too hot. Butch and one of his partners in crime, Harry Longbaugh—known as the Sundance Kid ever since serving a sentence in Wyoming's Sundance Prison—continued their crime spree in South America, where in 1911 they were reportedly killed in a shoot-out with Bolivian troops.

The last great outlaw gang of the Wild West was the Dalton Gang, led by Bob, Grattan, and Emmett Dalton, who were distant cousins of the Younger brothers. Aided by Bob's sweetheart, Eugenia Moore, who performed the intelligence work, the gang first achieved notoriety by robbing a series of trains. Then in 1892, they audaciously attempted to rob two banks simultaneously in their hometown of Coffeyville, Kansas. The heist turned to disaster when townsmen immediately recognized the Daltons and greeted the outlaws with a hail of gunfire as they exited the banks. Of the five who rode into Coffeyville that

Charles Boles, alias Black Bart

day only Emmett Dalton survived—with 16 bullet wounds. He was sentenced to life in prison, but was paroled after 14 years and spent his last 30 years as a model citizen.

At the age of 60, Emmett returned to Coffeyville to visit the mass grave of his brothers and partners in crime. Pointing to the grave, he told an assembled crowd, "I challenge the world to produce the history of any outlaw who ever got anything out of it but that, or else be huddled in a prison cell....The biggest fool on earth is the one who thinks he can beat the law, that crime can be made to pay. It never paid and it never will and that was the one big lesson of the Coffeyville raid."

Frank James also lived a long life as

a model citizen after his earlier years on the outlaw trail, but unlike the Daltons or his partners, the Younger brothers, James managed to avoid long imprisonment—aided by powerful friends in the Democratic party and an unwillingness of two separate juries to convict him. In 1903, a Missouri newspaper expressed the prevailing sentiment toward Frank James and Cole Younger, last survivors of the famed James-Younger gang: "Their crimes can not be excused, but they can be forgotten, now that they have been pardoned under law, and can and should be covered with that Christian charity which hides a multitude of sins." ∎

Frank James in 1898

Bob and Grattan Dalton, flanked by partners Bill Powers and Dick Broadwell

BLACK HILLS
"*My lands are where my dead lie buried.*"

CRAZY HORSE, 1877

BLACK HILLS

THE BLACK HILLS LOOM LIKE A DARK AND CRAGGY ISLAND IN A YELLOW SEA OF PRAIRIE GRASS. A HUNDRED MILES LONG AND SIXTY MILES WIDE, THEY RISE FOUR THOUSAND FEET ABOVE THE SURROUNDING PLAINS, A RICH MYSTERIOUS LAND OF THICK PINE FORESTS AND JAGGED OUTCROPPINGS, PURE SPRINGS AND LAKES, AND ASPEN-TANGLED CANYONS. IT IS THE PINES THAT GAVE THE HILLS THEIR NAME; FROM THE DISTANT PLAINS THEY APPEAR SO DARK THAT THE LAKOTA CALLED THEM *PAHA SAPA*, THE HILLS THAT ARE BLACK. • THE LAKOTA CAME TO THE BLACK HILLS AROUND THE TIME OF THE AMERICAN REVOLUTION, PART OF A GRADUAL WESTERN MIGRATION THAT BEGAN A CENTURY EARLIER WHEN THEY LEFT THE WOODLANDS OF EASTERN MINNESOTA, DRIVEN BY ENEMIES AND DRAWN BY BUFFALO. BY THE TIME THE LAKOTA REACHED THE BLACK HILLS, THEY HAD OBTAINED GUNS AND HORSES, DEVELOPING THE NOMADIC WARRIOR CULTURE THAT MADE THEM THE DOMINANT FORCE ON THE NORTHERN PLAINS. THEY PUSHED THE KIOWA OUT OF THE HILLS, JUST AS THEY LATER DROVE THE CROW OUT OF THE POWDER RIVER HUNTING GROUNDS TO THE WEST. • THE LAKOTA BELIEVE THE BLACK HILLS WERE THEIRS FROM THE

South Dakota's desolate Badlands (opposite) were inhospitable to both Indians and whites. It was the verdant Black Hills they fought over, a struggle led by Sitting Bull (above, with family) that climaxed at the Little Bighorn battlefield, where headstones mark the graves of George Armstrong Custer and his command (previous page).

beginning, that it was here that the Lakota people were created and to here that they were destined to return. "According to a tribal legend," remembered one Lakota chief, "these hills were a reclining female figure from whose breasts flowed life-giving forces and to them the Lakota went as a child to its mother's arms."

Leaving their large villages on the open plains, the Lakota went into the Hills in smaller groups—to hunt for wild game, cut lodgepoles for their tepees, or seek shelter from the winter winds. Some spoke of strange, even frightening, rumblings from deep within the earth, but these stories were later exaggerated by those who hoped to drive the Indians away. For most Lakota, the Black Hills were a sacred place, a place of visions.

It is said that when Sitting Bull was still a young warrior, he had a life-changing vision on the shore of Sylvan Lake, a crystalline oasis beneath strangely eroded outcroppings in the heart of the Black Hills. Hearing a beautiful song echo across the water, he searched for the singer and spotted a figure that looked like a man atop a towering rock. But as Sitting Bull began to climb up the rock, the singer turned around to look at him, and Sitting Bull saw that it was not a man but an eagle. As he climbed closer, the eagle flew away, but the song still lingered in the air. Already wise in the ways of *Wakan Tanka,* the Great Mystery, Sitting Bull knew that this song was a gift, a message, and so he began to sing it and make the song his own:

My Father has given me this nation;
In protecting them I have a hard time.

Sitting Bull was both a warrior and a holy man, *wichasha wakan,* and he believed that Wakan Tanka had entrusted him to lead the Lakota through their hardest time. Like many spiritual leaders, he often spoke in terms of food, for he knew that a people could exist only as long as they could eat. "I heard Sitting Bull say that the Black Hills was just like a food pack," recalled one Lakota warrior. "...Indians would rove all around, but when they were in need of something they could just go in there and get it."

The Black Hills had been promised to the Lakota in the Treaty of 1868, the agreement that ended Red Cloud's War. The hard-won treaty also ended Red Cloud's leadership of the free-ranging Lakota; he gradually moved his followers to a government agency in Nebraska, just outside the Great Sioux Reservation—a vast tract of land that had been defined in the treaty. Spotted Tail, chief of the Brulé Lakota, lived with his people near another Nebraska agency, while the northern bands, including some of Sitting Bull's Hunkpapa, lived near agencies along the upper Missouri River. The government agencies were intended to ease the Indians' transition from the "wild" hunting life to a life as farmers—providing essential food and supplies along with medical, technical, and educational services. In reality, the agencies were often corrupt or incompetent, the food and supplies inadequate, and the services inappropriate or unwanted. The agency Indians lived a strange and difficult half-life, struggling to maintain their traditional ways while becoming increasingly dependent on the federal government.

Thousands of Lakota, however, perhaps a third of the Lakota population, ignored the new reservation boundaries. Some might come in to the agencies on ration day, taking what they could from the whites before heading back to their camps; but others, including Sitting Bull—who had never signed the treaty—stayed far from the agencies, hunting the buffalo on the still unsettled expanses of the northern plains. They refused all white contact, except for traders who supplied them with guns and ammunition for hunting and warfare. "Look at me," Sitting Bull once said to a group of Indians who lingered around a trading post, seeking handouts. "See if I am poor, or my people either. The whites may get me at last, as you say, but I will have good times till then. You are fools to make yourselves slaves to a piece of fat bacon, some hard-tack, and a little sugar and coffee."

It was during this period of transition, probably around 1869, that Sitting Bull became the head chief of the free-ranging Lakota and their Cheyenne allies, an unprecedented position that was foreign to the Lakota way of thinking; for each subtribe usually had several chiefs, and each warrior followed the leader he chose to follow. Sitting Bull's uncle, Four Horns, a leading chief of the Hunkpapa subtribe, saw the need for united leadership in the face of white encroachment, a decision that was ratified in a formal election. "For your bravery on the battlefields," Four Horns proclaimed, "and as the greatest warrior of our bands, we have elected you as our war chief, leader of the entire Sioux nation. When you tell us to fight, we shall fight, when you tell us to make peace, we shall make peace." Sitting Bull, who was about 38 years old at the time, then walked through the encampments, singing his acceptance: "Ye tribes behold me/The chiefs are no more/Myself shall take courage."

Despite Four Horn's claim, Sitting Bull was never "leader of the entire Sioux nation," but he did lead the Sioux and Cheyenne who had resolved to live the old free life following the buffalo. Since the early days of treaty making, the whites had pressed the Indians to choose a single leader to speak for them; now the Lakota had done so, but Sitting Bull was not the kind of man the whites had envisioned. Unlike many 19th century Indian leaders, Sitting Bull had little interest in compromise and no great desire to understand the white man or his culture. Powerfully-built and with an intense unyielding gaze, he was Lakota—first, foremost, and forever.

Around the time that Sitting Bull assumed leadership over the hunting bands, Crazy Horse emerged as the leading Lakota warrior. Seven years younger than Sitting Bull, Crazy Horse remains a shadowy figure who seldom spoke in council and refused to pose for photographs. It is clear, however, that he forged the link from Red Cloud's War—fought mostly by southern Lakota and Cheyenne—to the war for the Black Hills, led by Sitting Bull, who drew his power from northern bands. By actions if not by words, Crazy Horse convinced battle-hardened southern warriors to join the new confederacy, and he became Sitting Bull's staunchest ally outside his own subtribe, united in a mystical vision of Lakota supremacy and survival.

This confederacy faced its first great test when the whites—*wasichus* in the Lakota language—decided to build a railroad along the Yellowstone River, through the northern hunting

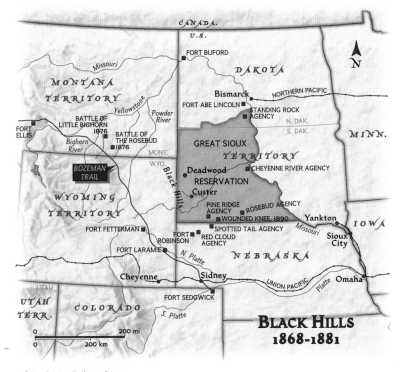

State and territory borders as of 1876
Present-day state borders and names in gray

Militarily, the Great Plains was organized into a vast jurisdiction called the Division of the Missouri, spreading from Illinois to Utah and from Texas to Montana. During most of the Indian wars its commander was Gen. Philip Sheridan, who realized that the formal strategies that made him a Civil War hero would not work against the Indians' hit-and-run tactics. It was Sheridan who conceived of the winter campaign that crushed the Cheyenne camp at the Washita, and with his three-pronged attack plan on the northern plains he hoped to crush Indian resistance once and for all.

Calamity Jane

Martha Jane Canarry (*below*) was born in Missouri around 1852. Although some say her mother was a wildly independent and beautiful woman who passed her wildness, if not her beauty, on to her daughter, almost nothing is known of Martha's early life except that she and her family moved to the gold rush town of Virginia City, Montana, in 1865. In her own fanciful autobiography, Martha Jane claimed that she worked on the Union Pacific Railroad and served as a uniformed scout for Custer. She was

actually a camp follower who wore men's clothing to sneak among the troops. She followed Dr. Walter Jenney's scientific expedition into the Black Hills in 1875, and Custer's orderly reported her following the 1874 expedition as well, dressed as a man, covered with lice and begging for whiskey. While Martha claimed that she received her famous nickname when she caught a wounded officer falling out of his saddle, the moniker probably reflected the "calamity" that befell men who shared her sexual favors.

The strangest, most persistent rumor about Calamity Jane is the story of a secret marriage or love affair with Wild Bill Hickok—a relationship that existed only in Jane's fertile imagination, born either of a genuine, unrequited love for the handsome gunslinger or a desire to connect herself with a famous man. When Hickok was gunned down in a Deadwood saloon on August 2, 1876, it's said that Jane claimed his "death chair." After Jane died of alcohol-related diseases in 1903, she was buried beside him in Deadwood's Mount Moriah Cemetery—creating a connection in death that never existed in life. ■

grounds. Accompanied by soldiers, surveyors for the Northern Pacific first entered the valley of the Yellowstone in the fall of 1871. The Lakota observed and asked questions at the agencies. The following year, however, once they understood the whites' intentions, the Lakota began to resist, skirmishing with two substantial infantry commands in August 1872.

During the first of these battles, a medicine man questioned Sitting Bull's bravery when he ordered his warriors to withdraw in the face of steady rifle fire. In response, he held a "smoking party" on the open prairie between Indians and soldiers, inviting other warriors to join him. Four accepted his dare, including his nephew, White Bull, who recalled, "We others wasted no time. Our hearts beat rapidly, and we smoked as fast as we could. All around us the bullets were kicking up the dust, and we could hear the bullets whining overhead. But Sitting Bull was not afraid. He just sat there quietly, looking as if he were at home in his tent, and smoked peacefully." After this, the Lakota began to withdraw, but Crazy Horse could not let such bravery go unanswered. He and White Bull made one last dash across the battlefield, drawing a barrage of fire that killed his horse but left the mystic warrior untouched.

Long Hair

Such individual feats of daring were the essence of Lakota warrior culture, but Sitting Bull and Crazy Horse understood that it would take a more disciplined approach to hold off the wasichus. They were tested again in 1873, when surveyors and engineers returned to the Yellowstone, this time accompanied not only by infantry, but by the Seventh Cavalry under the command of Lt. Col. George Armstrong Custer, who had been transferred north after fighting on the southern plains. The Cheyenne called him "Hard Backsides" for his relentless endurance on horseback; to the Lakota, he was *Pahuska*, "Long Hair," for his flowing, reddish-golden locks.

Custer was a man of boundless energy, a dashing and charismatic warrior who inspired absolute loyalty in those who loved and understood him, just as he elicited jealousy or condemnation in those who did not. He was a man of passion: for his county, for the plains, and for his wife, Libbie, a beautiful, intelligent woman whom he loved so much that he endured court-martial for deserting his command to visit her. She, in turn, followed him to the edge of white civilization. When her beloved "Autie" was first posted to Fort Abraham Lincoln, near Bismarck in northern Dakota Territory, Libbie opened her atlas and traced the path, later writing, "It seemed as if we were going to Lapland."

For Custer, the posting was an opportunity to forge a path through new terrain, to live, hunt and fight again on the plains he had come to love. Marching westward in the summer of 1873, he wrote Libbie long letters gushing over the unspoiled beauty of the land. "No artist could fairly represent the wonderful country we passed over, while each step of our progress was like each successive shifting of the kaleidoscope, presenting to our wondering gaze views which almost appalled us by their sublimity."

In early August, Lakota and Cheyenne warriors skirmished with Custer's troops along the Yellowstone, a game of cat and mouse that exploded when the Cheyenne recognized "Long Hair" as the officer who had wiped out Black Kettle's village on the Washita. After this first engagement, the Indians moved upriver, where they swam their horses through the rushing waters and floated their belongings in "bull boats" made of willows and buffalo hides. Though Custer tried to follow, he was unable to cross his command. On August 11, with Sitting Bull and Crazy Horse watching from a bluff, the two sides faced each other across the sparkling Yellowstone, firing steadily throughout the day, while an Indian force sneaked back across the river only to be driven off by a cavalry charge.

"The Indians were made up of different bands of Sioux," Custer reported, "...the whole under command of 'Sitting Bull,' who participated in the fight, and who for once has been taught a lesson he will not soon forget." Indeed he had, but it was not the lesson Custer imagined—what Sitting Bull had learned was that his warriors could hold their own with the soldiers, even the hard-charging Long Hair. They would fight again.

When George Custer led an expedition into South Dakota's Black Hills (above), there was every expectation that he would find gold. To ensure that any find was properly publicized, Custer took several newspaper reporters, who trumpeted the news though little gold was found. "Prepare for Lively Times," read the Yankton Press and Dakotaian. "The National Debt to be Paid When Custer Returns." In no time at all, the Sioux, to whom the government had deeded the land in perpetuity, found their sacred Hills awash in white prospectors. "All the soldiers in the United States couldn't hold back the tide then," wrote Seventh Cavalry veteran Charles Windolph.

The Panic of 1873

The Northern Pacific went bankrupt by the end of the year, victim of a national depression called the Panic of 1873. In the midst of apparent prosperity, banks closed, corporations collapsed, and the stock market crashed. Hordes of unemployed wandered the cities, while grasshoppers destroyed crops on prairies and plains, and yellow fever infected the Mississippi Valley. Many blamed the sudden financial collapse on the lack of circulating money; President Ulysses S. Grant had limited currency, creating a de facto gold standard without enough gold to support the growing post-Civil War industrial economy. Like all depressions, the dynamics were complicated, but the message that echoed from Wyoming to Wall Street was deceptively simple: The American nation needed gold, and the Lakota nation stood in the way.

Rumors of gold in the Black Hills had been circulating for years, spawned by a few small groups of prospectors, as well as Indians who traded gold for goods at Fort Laramie. By the early 1870s, settlers in the surrounding states and territories loudly pressured the government to open the land for exploration and development, not only for mining but for farming and ranching as well. The fact that the Hills had been included in the reservation "set apart for the absolute and undisturbed use and occupation of the Indians" in the Treaty of 1868 did not dim the passion of these settlers, but it wasn't until the Panic of 1873 that the government saw a compelling reason to break the promises it had made to the Lakota.

On July 2, 1874, a column of a thousand soldiers, a hundred Indian scouts, a 16-piece band and 110 supply wagons set out from Fort Abraham Lincoln under Custer's command, heading southwest for the Black Hills—an incursion of questionable legality under the terms of the Treaty of 1868. The official purpose of the expedition was to "obtain information in regard to the character of the country" and to find a location for a fort to "better control the Indians." But Custer betrayed the true purpose by taking along two "practical miners" and a geologist, as well as other scientists, a photographer, and several newspaper reporters to publicize whatever he might find.

Although soldiers and scientists alike complained about Custer's relentless pace across the plains, Custer gloried in his great Black Hill adventure, describing it, with characteristic exaggeration, as an opportunity to enter "a region of country as yet unseen by human eyes, except those of the Indians." It was the agricultural potential of the land that emerged most strongly in his official reports. "No portion of the United States," he wrote, "can boast of a richer or better pasturage, purer water,...and of greater advantages generally to the farmer or stock raiser than are to be found in the Black Hills." Those who accompanied him were equally impressed. A reporter from the Bismarck *Tribune* called the Hills, "a very paradise...no wonder the untutored savage guards it with jealous care."

> *"The American people need the country the Indians now occupy; many of our people are out of employment; the masses need some new excitement....An Indian war would do no harm, for it must come, sooner or later...."*
>
> BISMARCK *TRIBUNE*, JUNE 17, 1874

Despite this jealous care, Custer encountered only one village of five lodges. The smoke of distant fires indicated they were being watched by larger bands, but for the most part, Custer's expedition was a summer lark; the column entered the Hills by a well-worn Indian trail that the Lakota renamed the Thieves Road. They traveled "amid flowers of the most exquisite colors and perfumes," picked wild raspberries, explored caves and pure mountain streams. There were suppers of freshly bagged game, nightly serenades by the military band, and two recorded games of baseball. Although Custer didn't drink, there was plenty of whiskey as well. President Grant's son, Fred, tagged along, "drunk nearly all the time," while Custer's orderly reported that Calamity Jane followed the troops. Dressed in men's clothing, smelling badly, and covered with lice, she begged for whiskey in return for doing their laundry.

On the last day of July, Custer and five others climbed the highest peak in the Hills, named after Gen. William S. Harney, who had slaughtered the Lakota near Ash Hollow in 1855. They scribbled their names on a slip of paper and left it in a cartridge case, convinced they were the first human beings to reach the top. Professor A.B. Donaldson, who doubled as botanist and newspaper correspondent, later explained their thinking: "It is certain that no white man ever did; and it is well known that the noble, the royal, the genuine North American Indian is one of the laziest mortals on earth." Unknown to Professor Donaldson, the Lakota had been climbing Harney Peak for decades in search of visions.

Gold Among the Roots of the Grass

The day before the climbing expedition, one or both of the "practical miners" discovered about ten cents worth of gold along a stream called French Creek. They panned a little more while Custer's party climbed the peak, but it wasn't until the first days of August, after the command marched several miles down the creek to the site of present-day Custer, South Dakota, that the miners found even better prospects. "At daybreak there was a crowd around the 'diggins,'" wrote one reporter, with the men grabbing "every conceivable accoutrement," from shovels and spades to tent stakes and pot hooks. They didn't find much, but they found enough to goad them on. "Officers and privates,

mule-whackers and scientists, all met on a common level, and the great equalizer was that insignificant yellow gold dust."

On August 3, Custer sent a scout named Lonesome Charley to Fort Laramie, carrying a preliminary report of the expedition's progress which appeared in a Chicago newspaper by mid-August. Two days later, as the command prepared to leave the beautiful country they had named "Custer Park," one of the professional miners posted a notice of mining claims for "District No. 1, Custer's Gulch, Black Hills." He defined claims for himself and 20 others, stating that the men intended to work them "as soon as peaceable possession can be had of this portion of the Territory by the General Government."

Custer was carefully circumspect in his initial report of the gold discovery, cautioning that "no opinion should be formed" until there was an opportunity for further examination of the prospects. Less than two weeks later, however, on his way back to Fort Lincoln, he penned another report full of enthusiastic details about the land, the water, and the climate, including the words that spelled doom for the great Lakota nation: "The miners report that they found gold among the roots of the grass....It has not required an expert to find gold in the Black Hills, and men without former experience in mining have discovered it at an expense of but little time or labor."

By the time Custer arrived at the fort—where Libbie greeted him with a well-timed swoon into his outstretched arms— Bismarck was abuzz with the prospect of being the logical outfitting center for a new gold rush. Yankton, capital of Dakota Territory, and Sioux City, Iowa, also advertised their advantages to prospective miners and settlers, and it was Sioux City that launched the first gold mining expedition to the Black Hills, sponsored by newspaper editor Charles Collins. Although the army had started the hysteria in the first place, Gen. Philip Sheridan made it clear that civilian encroachment would not be permitted on the Sioux Reservation; Collins announced the expedition had been canceled, while sending out secret letters saying, "If you can raise $300, can handle a rifle, and mean business, be at Sioux City on or about the middle of September."

At least a hundred prospectors had answered the call by September 3, four days after Custer's return to Fort Lincoln, and the same day that Sheridan issued orders to "burn the wagon trains and destroy the outfit and arrest the leaders, confining them at the nearest military post." With troops patrolling the trails, the expedition dwindled to 26 men, one woman, and a boy by the time it set out in early October. Hiding from both Indians and soldiers along the way, they reached French Creek on December 23, and immediately built a secure stockade and six log cabins. Though the army made several attempts to find them that winter, it wasn't until the following April that troops located the settlement and forced them to leave the Hills. The frozen ground had made mining difficult, but the gold they found only fueled the growing excitement.

Even as the first party was escorted out of the Hills, another group of prospectors headed for the same diggings, only to be expelled by the army. In May, soldiers captured 176 trespassers and burned all their wagons and supplies—except one wagon load on which a resolute woman named Mrs. Brockett perched, refusing to move while the soldiers were too gallant to move her. The onslaught continued faster than the army could keep up; by July there were some 800 miners working the placer deposits along French, Rapid, Spring, and Castle creeks. One man claimed that within three months he had been run out of the Hills four times by the army and he "figured he could stand it as long as they could."

I WILL KILL THE FIRST CHIEF

Faced with a growing gold rush on Indian land, the government brought Sioux leaders, including Red Cloud and Spotted Tail, to Washington, where they were informed that the United States would like to buy the Black Hills as well as the Powder River hunting grounds. The Secretary of the Interior reminded the Indians that the government was under no obligation to continue feeding their people at the agencies. He suggested that perhaps the Sioux should consider moving to the Indian Territory in what is now Oklahoma, prompting Spotted Tail to wonder why the Great Father didn't put his red children on wheels, so he could move them wherever he wanted. Now practiced diplomats, Red Cloud and Spotted Tail informed government officials that they could not make a decision without consulting their fellow tribesmen.

Hoping to create a more conducive atmosphere for negotiation, General Sheridan ordered one of the army's most successful field commanders, Gen. George Crook, to expel the miners. Crook mingled with the men, panned a little gold himself, and assured them that he wanted to protect their claims until Indian title could be extinguished. On August 15, after giving the miners a chance to establish claims and plat out the new town of "Custer" on French Creek, Crook's command escorted several hundred miners out of the Black Hills. The following month, soldiers from Fort Laramie occupied the town.

In late September, government commissioners convened a council on the plains—halfway between the Red Cloud and Spotted Tail agencies—to discuss the idea of leasing or selling the Black Hills. Between 10,000 and 20,000 Indians attended, mostly Sioux from the agencies and the Cheyenne and Arapaho who lived with them. Sitting Bull and Crazy Horse refused to attend, but their point of view was well-represented by several hundred northern warriors under Little Big Man, who thundered into the conference stripped and painted for battle, brandishing his Winchester rifle and shouting, "I will kill the first chief who speaks for selling the Black Hills!"

Despite such threats, Red Cloud, Spotted Tail, and other agency Indians were willing to consider selling the Hills if the price were high enough. They had lived off government rations for almost seven years, and they knew that the diminishing wild game that sustained their free-ranging relatives could not sustain the whole Lakota nation. Red Cloud threw out a figure of 70 million dollars. "There have been six nations raised," he explained, "and I am the seventh, and I want seven generations to be fed....God Almighty placed these Hills here for my wealth, but now you want to take them from me and make me poor, so I ask so much that I won't be poor."

Spotted Tail expressed similar sentiments. "The amount must

George Armstrong Custer

GEORGE ARMSTRONG CUSTER (*opposite*) was the most famous field officer of the Indian Wars, yet his greatest fame came from failure, and his career was marked by an often foolhardy disregard for authority.

Born in Ohio of Hessian ancestry in 1839, Custer graduated last in his class from the U.S. Military Academy at West Point, where he was distinguished more for excessive demerits than for officer potential. The Civil War proved his salvation, as his bravery under fire and dramatic flair earned him the rank of brigadier general at the age of 23, and major general by the end of the war. Perhaps his greatest moment came at Gettysburg, a turning point in the war, where he engaged the Confederate Cavalry under Maj. Gen. J.E.B. Stuart.

Reduced to the post-war rank of captain, Custer considered leaving the army, until he received a commission as lieutenant colonel of the Seventh Cavalry. Sent to fight on the Kansas plains, the famous "boy general" was court-martialed for several offenses, including abandoning his command in the field to join his beloved wife, Libbie, who wrote of the

incident, "We are quite determined not to live apart again." Suspended for a year without pay, Custer was reinstated after ten months at the behest of his mentor, Gen. Philip Sheridan.

Custer ran into trouble again in 1876, when he testified for a Senate investigation into corruption at army trading posts. The investigation led to the impeachment of Secretary of War William Belknap, and also implicated President Ulysses Grant's brother, Orvil. This situation so displeased the president that he refused to allow Custer to leave Washington while the Seventh Cavalry prepared to take the field against the Lakota and Cheyenne, and then had Custer arrested in Chicago when he left anyway. After Gen. Alfred Terry interceded, Custer was allowed to command the Seventh, figuring he'd be able to "swing clear of Terry" and go his own way—and so he did, with tragic results. ■

On New Year's Day 1889, a Paiute Indian named Wovoka had a vision that changed the West. According to one story, reported by a fellow Paiute, the vision occurred when Wovoka heard a loud noise while cutting pine trees in the mountains, near his home in Nevada's Mason Valley:

"He laid down his ax and started to go in the direction of the noise, when he fell down dead; and God came and took him to heaven and showed him everything there; it was the most beautiful country you could imagine; he saw both Indians and white, who were all young; God told him that when the people died here on this earth, if they were good, they come to heaven, and he made then young again, and they never grow to be old afterwards.…

God came to him again that night and told him to tell all the people that they must not fight, there must be peace all over the world; that the people must not steal from one another, but be good to each other, for they were all brothers.…"

Along with his teachings of peace and harmony, Wovoka instructed the Paiute to perform their traditional Round Dance for five nights in succession so that they

Ghost Dance
"Be Good to Each Other"

might be reunited with dead friends and relatives. And so it became known as the Ghost Dance. Wovoka's blend of Indian and Christian teachings followed in a long line of spiritual renewal movements that had arisen among tribe after tribe from the Ohio River valley to the Far West, as the Indians struggled to maintain their traditional beliefs in the face of white encroachment.

News of Wovoka's "Great Revelation" soon spread beyond his own

people, and delegations from over 30 tribes visited the Paiute prophet. Many of these "apostles" came away with different ideas about the teachings and meaning of the dance. Although one delegate reported that Wovoka spoke to each Indian in his own language, he apparently spoke only Paiute and some English, and didn't know the sign language used on the plains. And like all religious teachings, each individual believed what he wanted to believe.

When a delegation of Cheyenne and Arapaho asked Wovoka to demonstrate his powers, he placed his Stetson hat on the ground, made a quick motion with his hand, and pulled something out of the hat. One Cheyenne later reported that all he saw was "something black" emerging from the hat, while an Arapaho remembered seeing "the whole world."

In November 1889, a delegation arrived including two Lakota medicine men, Short Bull and Kicking Bear. When they returned to their people the following April, the two established their own version of the Ghost Dance on the Pine Ridge and Cheyenne River reservations. Unlike the Paiute, who had fought the whites thirty years earlier and come far in adjusting to peaceful coexistence, the Lakota were struggling desperately with the harsh reality of reservation life. In the teachings of Short Bull and Kicking Bear, the Ghost Dance took on a militancy and urgency that it never had for Wovoka. And it was this militancy, fanned by white hysteria, that led to the tragedy of Wounded Knee. It's said that when Wovoka received news of the massacre, he pulled a blanket over his head and cried. ■

Founded by the Paiute prophet Wovoka in 1889, the Ghost Dance spread from Nevada to the Badlands of Dakota Territory (opposite). The Lakota fervently embraced the religion—which got its name from ritual dancing (above) and the belief that adherents would be reunited with their dead ancestors—until it failed them at Wounded Knee.

be so large that the interest will support us," he said. "…If even only two Indians remain, as long as they live they will want to be fed, as they are now." Ignoring these concerns, the commission offered $400,000 per year to lease the Hills or six million dollars to buy them. The Indians turned the offer down, and the commissioners returned to Washington in anger, suggesting that Congress set a price on the Hills and present it to the Sioux Nation "as a finality."

On November 3, 1875, President Grant held a secret meeting at the White House with the Secretary of War, the Secretary of the Interior, the Commissioner of Indian Affairs, and Generals Sheridan and Crook. Early in his administration, Grant had implemented the well-intentioned, though ultimately unsuccessful Peace Policy. Now he returned to the policy he knew best: War. Although details of the meeting remain unclear, two key decisions emerged. First, though the edict against white intrusion would remain in effect, the army would cease to enforce it. Second, all free-ranging Sioux would be required to report to government agencies by January 31, 1876, or be considered hostile and face military action.

Exactly two weeks after the meeting, the soldiers at French Creek abruptly vacated their post and headed back to Fort Laramie. Although Grant's new policy had not been publicized—for fear of alienating Easterners sympathetic to the Indian cause—its message was clear. The Black Hills were now open for anyone willing to risk the threat of Indian attack. The threat was real; in the early days of the rush, lone miners were often found dead, unscalped, with a single arrow in the ground beside their bodies. The Lakota knew that the killings were the work of Crazy Horse, who had been instructed in his vision never to take a scalp.

Though such attacks encouraged miners to travel in larger groups, they had little effect on the force of the rush; as had been proven throughout the West, the lure of gold was stronger than the fear of death. By Christmas, there were over 500 miners in the Black Hills, some earning $30 or $40 a day from easily worked placer deposits. By mid-January 1876, there were at least 4,000 with 1,000 in Custer alone. Others pushed on through the snow to work even richer deposits in the north, including Deadwood Gulch and Whitewood Creek, where the wild, wide open town of Deadwood sprang up like a sea of canvas tents.

As miners and others swarmed into the sacred hills, runners were sent out in December to inform the hunting bands of the new edict to report to the agencies. To the Lakota, the winter months were a time of quiet survival—camping in a favorable spot that offered protection from the cold winds, living off dried meat, sitting around campfires while wrapped in warm buffalo robes. Grant and his advisors surely knew this, based on years of dealing with the Plains Indians, and it seems likely that they issued the edict in full knowledge that it would not be obeyed. To men like Sitting Bull and Crazy Horse, who had never signed a treaty with the United States or asked for handouts, the idea of being "ordered" into the agencies must have seemed absurd. It was an issue to be discussed, not dictated, and if they wished to discuss it at all, they would do it in the spring.

On February 1, 1876, the day after the grace period expired, the Secretary of the Interior notified the Secretary of War that "Said Indians are hereby turned over to the War Department for such action on the part of the Army as you may deem proper under the circumstances." A month later, General Crook left Fort Fetterman in Wyoming with a force of 900 men and headed north on the Bozeman Trail. After years of fighting the Apache and Paiute on the other side of the Rockies, Crook was unprepared for the harsh winter of the northern plains. Although a detachment under Col. Joseph Reynolds managed to destroy a combined Cheyenne and Oglala village, the Indians escaped, along with their pony herd, while Crook's frozen command straggled back to Fort Fetterman.

After the attack, the homeless Indians sought refuge with Crazy Horse. Unable to provide enough food and supplies, the Oglala warrior led his own people and the newcomers down the Powder River to the larger camp of Sitting Bull, where they were greeted with pots of steaming meat and gifts of robes, tepees, and horses. "Oh what good hearts they had!"

recalled a refugee. "I can never forget the generosity of Sitting Bull's Uncpapa Sioux on that day." The attack by Crook's men had served notice that the government intended to fight, so the chiefs decided to keep their people together for protection, and fight back only if necessary. That spring, other hunting bands joined the great village of Sitting Bull until by early June there were perhaps 460 lodges—Lakota, Cheyenne, and eastern Sioux—some 3,000 people with 800 warriors. They followed the buffalo, moving every few days for fresh grass, feasting and visiting and preparing robes for trade. It was a good time, the last great time of living the old free life on the northern plains.

> *"If I were an Indian, I would greatly prefer to cast my lot among those…who adhered to the free open plains rather than submit to the confined limits of a reservation."*
>
> GEORGE ARMSTRONG CUSTER

As the hunting bands gathered in the Powder River region, thousands upon thousands of well-armed miners swarmed into the Black Hills, where tent towns like Deadwood gave way to more permanent settlements of log cabins and the false-fronted frame buildings typical of other boomtowns. With military resistance a thing of the past, the Black Hills were more accessible than any mining region yet discovered. Yankton

could be reached by river or railroad, leaving an overland trip of only a few days after the would-be prospector had bought his outfit. Sidney, Nebraska, and Cheyenne, Wyoming, both easily accessible on the Union Pacific Railroad, were even closer to the Hills. Compared to the early trek to California, the route to the Black Hills was easy and direct, though Indian attacks continued along the trails and in the eastern Hills nearest the agencies.

After the failure of Crook's first campaign, Generals Sherman and Sheridan launched a three-prong offensive, modeled on the operations that had proved successful on the southern plains. Col. John Gibbon moved out of Fort Ellis in Montana Territory on March 30, still battling winter snow as he marched east along the Yellowstone with 450 men. Six weeks later, on May 17, a column of 925 soldiers left Fort Abraham Lincoln commanded by Gen. Alfred Terry, though the bulk of the force was the Seventh Cavalry under Custer. And on May 29, General Crook set out on the Bozeman Trail with 1,000 men, later enlisting 262 Crow and Shoshone scouts. Gibbon picked up a smaller party of Crow, while Custer marched with almost 40 Arikara—all eager to fight their traditional Lakota enemies.

Although the regimental band played "The Girl I Left Behind Me" as the Seventh Cavalry rode off onto the northern plains, Libbie Custer accompanied her husband on the first day's march so that they might spend one last night together. Looking over the long column of men she noted a strange meteorological condition, an inversion layer caused by evaporating ground fog, that created an eerie reflection of the Seventh Cavalry in the sky. She called it "a scene of wonder and beauty," but found it disturbing, a portent of trouble to come. A month later, in a letter her husband never received, she wrote, "I cannot help but feel the greatest apprehension.…"

Sitting Bull was apprehensive as well, and he too had a vision of soldiers in the sky. In early June, in a camp along Rosebud Creek, he held a sun dance, offering a "scarlet blanket" of a hundred pieces of flesh to Wakan Tanka, dancing for hours around the tall cottonwood pole, fasting and feeling the powerful gaze of the hot sun. Finally he stopped, immobile in the thrall of a vision: soldiers and horses were falling upside down, as thick as grasshoppers, and dropping into an Indian village. "These soldiers do not possess ears," a voice proclaimed. "They are to die, but you are not supposed to take their spoils."

The vision caused great excitement within the camp. By this time, scouts and hunting parties had discovered Gibbon's command to the north and Crook's column marching toward them from the south.

MUCH SMOKE AND DUST

After the sun dance, the Indians moved on over a gently sloping divide toward a stream they called the Greasy Grass, known by the whites as the Little Bighorn. Before they reached their destination, scouts reported that the Rosebud Valley was "black with soldiers." Though the chiefs discouraged attack, the young warriors grew so excited at the prospect of waging war against the bluecoats that their leaders were forced to join the battle. Led by Crazy Horse and Sitting Bull—the latter so weak from the sun dance that he could only offer inspiration—some 500 warriors rode through the night.

On the early morning of June 17, 1876, the warriors approached Crook's command of about 1,250 men. It was the Crow and Shoshone scouts who saved the bluecoats, holding off the Sioux and Cheyenne long enough to allow the soldiers to mobilize. The battle raged throughout the day, up and down the long valley, a confused melee of men and horses and guns. "It was a great fight," a Cheyenne warrior recalled, "much smoke and dust." The Indians fought with a discipline and aggressiveness that amazed the American soldiers. "They were in front, rear, flanks, and on every hilltop, far and near," one later reported. "I had been in several Indian battles, but never saw so many Indians at one time before,...or so brave." Crook proclaimed victory when the Indians withdrew in the afternoon, but both sides sustained significant casualties; about 26 dead in Crook's command, and 36 among the Sioux and Cheyenne. Crook was so disturbed by the force of the Indian attack that he

retreated to his base camp on the Tongue River and spent the next weeks building fortifications, removing his substantial army from the field.

After the Battle of the Rosebud, the Indians continued on to the Greasy Grass. It was around this time that substantial numbers of Indians began to arrive from the agencies, swelling the already large encampments under Sitting Bull. "Over the span of only six days," historian Robert Utley writes, "the village more than doubled, from 450 to 1,000 lodges, from 3,000 to 7,000 people, from 800 to 1,800 fighting men." A Cheyenne woman named Kate Bighead remembered, "There were more Indians...than I ever saw together anywhere else." Now at the peak of their strength, the Indians had fought one good battle and expected another. Sitting Bull's vision had been clear— the soldiers would die coming into their village.

In mid-June, the two northern columns of the American offensive met along the Yellowstone, where they consolidated their forces and laid a plan of action, unaware that they were now the only soldiers in the field. Based on scouting reports, General Terry rightly suspected that the Indians would be gathered along the Little Bighorn, and he decided to send Custer and the Seventh Cavalry down the Rosebud valley, with orders to push beyond the Indian trail and then swing into the Little Bighorn valley from the south, while the rest of the force under Terry and Gibbon approached from the north. It was decided that the earliest the forces could meet would be June 26.

On June 22, Custer left the Yellowstone with 12 companies of the Seventh Cavalry, almost 650 men including officers, troopers, Indian and civilian scouts, and mule packers. He refused Terry's offer to take Gatling guns, fearing they would slow him down, just as he refused four additional companies of cavalry from Gibbon's command—fearing he and the Seventh might have to share the glory. On the morning of the third day, the soldiers came upon the sun-dance lodge where Sitting Bull had experienced his vision. Pictures in the sand portrayed the vision clearly enough to disturb the Indian scouts, but when they explained the vision to Custer, he simply shrugged. Late that afternoon, they reached a turn in the Indian trail which led over the divide to the Little Bighorn; though he had been ordered not to cross the divide, Custer decided to follow the trail and marched his already exhausted men and horses through the night.

On the morning of Sunday, June 25, Custer and his scouts stood on a ridge from which the scouts could see evidence of vast encampments in the hazy distance. Custer could not, but he accepted their word. His original plan had been to rest that day, and attack on the 26th, when Terry and Gibbon would arrive from the north, but he decided to attack then and there. He may have believed that his command had been detected and that the Indians would escape; or he may have rushed into battle hoping the news of his victory would reach the Democratic Convention in time to influence what he hoped would be his nomination for President. Or he may simply have been overconfident and eager to fight.

ENOUGH FOR ALL OF US

A little before noon, as the sun blazed hot in the Montana sky, Custer divided his command. One company would guard the pack train, while a detachment under Capt. Frederick Benteen scouted the edge of the valley. The main body of his command—three companies under Maj. Marcus Reno and five under Custer—would proceed toward the Indian village, spread along the tree-shaded river meandering beneath a treeless landscape of bluffs, hills, ridges, and ravines. Although the bluffs obscured the soldiers' view of the village, clouds of dust—possibly from everyday activity—suggested that the Indians were escaping, so Custer ordered Reno to attack, promising he would be "supported by the whole outfit."

As Reno's battalion thundered down toward the village, the Indian warriors quickly mobilized, while mothers gathered their children and prepared to flee. "The very earth seemed to grow Indians," Reno reported. Though his weary men established a skirmish line on the other side of the Little Bighorn, just short of the first camp circle, they were quickly driven back into the trees, and then back again across the

William F. "Buffalo Bill" Cody served as a highly-regarded scout during the Indian Wars, winning the Congressional Medal of Honor for a battle in 1872. That December, he made his stage debut, playing himself in a melodrama entitled "Scouts of the Prarie," written by Ned Buntline—who had already made Cody famous in a series of dime novels. Cody, Buntline, and another actor-scout named Texas Jack Omohundro (left to right) pose in the publicity photo above.

W ILLIAM F. "BUFFALO BILL" Cody played many roles in his long, eventful life: wagon driver, Pony Express rider, army scout, buffalo hunter, actor, writer, and fanciful hero of dime novels. But his greatest role was as director and star attraction in a series of Wild West shows that defined the frontier experience for Americans and Europeans alike.

In partnership with shooting champion Dr. W. F. Carver, Cody's show debuted on May 17, 1883, at the Omaha Fair Grounds as "The Wild West, Hon. W. F. Cody and Dr. W. F. Carver's Rocky Mountain and Prairie Exhibition." Among the attractions were an attack on the Deadwood stage by Indians in war paint, a Pony Express demonstration, fancy shooting, horse races, bucking broncos, and a buffalo hunt. Though the traveling show struggled financially, the *Hartford Courant* called it "the best open-air show ever seen."

The following year, Cody parted with Carver and formed a long-lasting partnership with fellow actor Nate Salsbury. Touring with a new show, "Buffalo Bill's Wild West—America's National Entertainment," Cody and Salsbury lost $60,000 that season, partly the result of a steamboat sinking in the Mississippi River

Buffalo Bill's Wild West

"AMERICA'S NATIONAL ENTERTAINMENT"

that cost them their equipment and livestock. Their luck changed in 1885, when the show earned $100,000 in profits during a triumphant tour of Canada and the Great Lakes region. Sitting Bull joined the cast for that one season, garnering valuable publicity, but the biggest draw of all was a pretty young woman from Ohio who could outshoot any man, including Buffalo Bill himself. Her name was Annie Oakley, and she would remain a star attraction for seventeen years.

Now a popular success, the show played to a million people during an extended run at a Staten Island resort in the summer of 1886 and a million more that winter in Madison Square Garden. "Down to its smallest details, the show is genuine," wrote Mark Twain, "cowboys, vaqueros, Indians, stage coach, costumes and all."

Having made their mark in America, Cody and Salsbury sailed for England in 1887 with over 200 performers and staff,

including 97 Indians, as well as 180 horses, 18 buffalo, and a menagerie of elk, steers, mules, and deer. The show was the rage of London, playing to 30,000 people a day for six months, with a command performance for Queen Victoria. After another run on Staten Island, Buffalo Bill's Wild West returned to Europe for a four-year tour that took them through France, Italy, Austria, Germany, and Spain.

Cody's greatest American triumph came at the 1893 Columbia Exposition in Chicago. Opened by President Grover Cleveland, "Buffalo Bill's Wild West and Congress of Rough Riders of the World," his biggest and most authentic show yet, played to capacity crowds for six months, earning profits of almost a million dollars, perhaps the most successful run in the history of outdoor entertainment.

The Wild West show toured for another 20 years, a long, downhill slide during which Salsbury died and Cody—a notoriously poor businessman—ultimately lost control of the show that bore his name. Yet to the very end, Buffalo Bill looked handsome and authentic on his big white stallion, and audiences on both sides of the Atlantic saw the American West through the eyes of a man who had lived it. ◼

Buffalo Bill Cody's Wild West show (above) featured a reenactment of Custer's Last Stand that bore little resemblance to what actually happened on the Little Bighorn battlefield (opposite). Though his show was highly embellished, the costumes, props, and performers were authentic, and Cody himself was the genuine article.

river, finally taking refuge on the high bluffs. Their casualties included 40 dead and 13 wounded, with others left behind in the trees. Captain Benteen soon arrived and showed Reno a hastily scribbled note he had received from Custer's adjutant: "Benteen. Come on. Big Village. Be quick. Bring packs....P.[S.] Bring pacs." Suddenly and mysteriously the Indians began to withdraw, heading toward the other end of the village. It was about four o'clock in the afternoon.

Custer's battalion had continued along a ridge running parallel to the vast encampment below. A sergeant recalled that when they saw the size of the village, "the boys began to cheer, [and] some of the horses became so excited that some riders were unable to hold them in ranks." "Hold your horses, boys," Custer shouted, "there are Indians enough down there for all of us."

Exactly what happened after that remains a mystery, but archaeological excavations and Indian reports indicate that Custer divided his command, leaving one wing on the bluffs while he accompanied the other down a dry gulch called Medicine Tail Coulee, drawing a charge from the Indian village. Retreating back up another gulch, Custer rode further, only to be outflanked and driven back toward a rounded hill by a massive force led by Crazy Horse.

By this time, other warriors, some with rifles, others with bows and arrows, had swarmed up Medicine Tail Coulee and surrounded the rear wing of Custer's command. "The shooting at first was at a distance," recalled a Cheyenne warrior, "but we kept creeping in closer all around the ridge." Crazy Horse and White Bull made a mad dash through the soldiers, just as they had once done on the Yellowstone, drawing a barrage of fire but emerging unscathed. Sitting Bull observed from a distance; he had participated in the first battle against Major Reno, but now his duty was to protect the women and children.

Crazy Horse's charge split the soldiers in two, with those to the rear dying in small groups, while the survivors joined Custer on the hill, a little more than 100 soldiers surrounded by 1,500 Indian warriors. A Cheyenne chief,

Two Moons, later described the scene from the Indian perspective: "The shooting was quick, quick. Pop—pop—pop very fast. Some of the soldiers were down on their knees, some standing. The smoke was like a great cloud, and everywhere the Sioux went the dust rose like smoke. We circled all around them—swirling like water round a stone. We shoot, we ride fast, we shoot again."

"...how white they looked at a distance, like little mounds of snow."

FORMER PVT. WILLIAM O. TAYLOR, DESCRIBING THE DEAD AT LITTLE BIGHORN

Evidence suggests that the men were as panicked as might be expected under the circumstances. Some were unable to fire their guns; some fired wildly into the air; some committed suicide. The last to die were not on the hill at all, but in a deep ravine, where almost half the soldiers had fled in a desperate attempt to escape. Custer himself fought well. His body was found near the top of the hill, bullet holes in the head and near the heart, stripped naked but otherwise unmutilated at least to the eyes of those who found him. Kate Bighead later reported that two Cheyenne women who recognized Custer from his campaign in the south, "pushed the point of a sewing awl into each of his ears...to improve his hearing, as it seemed he had not heard what our chiefs in the South said when he smoked the pipe with them." Many of the other bodies were mutilated beyond recognition.

The combined commands under Reno and Benteen tried to reinforce Custer, but they were slow to mobilize, and by the time they reached a high point, all they could see was "a good

TRAIL OF THE WILD WEST

many Indians galloping up and down and firing at objects on the ground." The Indians drove the Reno and Benteen commands back to their original position, where the bluecoats dug in for the rest of that day and most of the next, forming a circular skirmish line in a natural depression, firing from behind packs and dead horses, suffering from horrible thirst as Indian snipers peppered away from every undulation in the grassy landscape. "We were not very well entrenched," a private later recalled, "...I used my butcher knife to cut the earth loose and throw a mound of it in front of me upon which to rest my carbine....A bullet struck the corner of this mound, throwing so much dirt into my eyes that I could scarcely see for an hour or more....While lying face down on the ground, a bullet tore off the heel of my boot as effectively as though it had been sawed off!" The firing tapered off by the second afternoon, and that evening the Indian village began to move up the Little Bighorn. The battle was over.

The column under Terry and Gibbon arrived on the morning of the 27th. It was their approach that had caused the Indians to flee; they had fought the battle foreseen in the vision of Sitting Bull, and that was enough. "I feel sorry that too many were killed on each side," Sitting Bull said, "but when Indians must fight, they must." Including Custer's entire immediate command of 210 men, the American forces had lost 263 dead and 52 wounded, while the Indians lost between 30 and 100 dead and an unknown number of wounded. It was the greatest victory ever won by Indian warriors over the U.S. Army.

Following the Battle of the Little Bighorn, the Indian village moved east in search of buffalo, back to the Rosebud, the Tongue, and the Powder. It was difficult to find enough grass, game, and firewood to keep such a large village together, and sometime in August they split. Sitting Bull led his Hunkpapa and other northern bands toward the Missouri, and Crazy Horse led the Oglala and Cheyenne south toward the Black Hills—the next phase in the annual cycle of a Lakota lifeway that wouldn't last beyond the winter. For in their greatest victory, the Lakota had sounded the death knell of their nation.

News of Custer's defeat reached Bismarck by telegraph on the evening of July 5, the day after the gala centennial celebration of American independence. "MASSACRED" proclaimed the Bismarck *Tribune* on the 6th. "...NO OFFICER OR MAN OF 5 COMPANIES LEFT TO TELL THE TALE." Below the successive headlines typical of 19th century newspapers were two salient questions: "What Will Congress Do About It? Shall This Be the Beginning of the End?" After years of congressional vacillation on the Indian question, the answers came with astonishing speed and certainty. By the end of July, Congress had appropriated funds to build two forts on the Yellowstone, added 2,500 new cavalry troopers, and given the army control over the Sioux agencies. On August 15, the annual Indian Appropriations Act cut off all food and rations for the Sioux until they gave up their claims to the Black Hills and the Powder River hunting grounds. It was "sign or starve." The agency chiefs, including Red Cloud and Spotted Tail, signed the paper and the government considered the matter closed, despite the fact that the Treaty of 1868 required three-fourths of the adult male population to change its terms.

While their starving and desperate relatives relinquished rights to their sacred hills and hunting grounds, the bands under Sitting Bull and Crazy Horse faced starvation as more soldiers took the field, tracking them across the northern plains. In September, General Crook destroyed a village at Slim Buttes near the Black Hills, despite efforts by Sitting Bull to aid in its defense. Crook then marched into the Hills, obtaining food and supplies from the miners for his own hungry men. Once Sitting Bull had called the Hills a "food pack," and so they were. But now the food pack fed the wasichus.

That fall, Col. Nelson Miles established a winter camp on the Yellowstone, where a fort would be built the following spring. After Sitting Bull's warriors attacked a supply train they left a note on a stick in the middle of the plains, in which Sitting Bull expressed his thoughts through the words of a mixed-blood interpreter:

Dance to Wounded Knee

IN APRIL 1890, medicine men Short Bull and Kicking Bear established the Ghost Dance among the Lakota. Although the original message behind the dance was that Indians and whites should coexist in peace, the Lakota leaders recast the message in terms that reflected the desperation of their people. Short Bull prophesied that a messiah was coming to drive the whites from the earth, bringing dead Indians with him and restoring the buffalo to the land. Kicking Bear and others created ghost shirts which they believed would make the wearers invulnerable to enemy bullets.

In October, Sitting Bull invited his nephew, Kicking Bear, to introduce the Ghost Dance on the Standing Rock Reservation, where government agent James McLaughlin used growing white hysteria over the dance as an excuse for having Sitting Bull arrested. The tactic resulted in disaster when Sitting Bull and seven of his followers were killed by Indian policemen on December 15, 1890.

Refugees from Sitting Bull's camp joined another chief named Big Foot, who led his band on a 100-mile flight across the rugged Badlands *(opposite)* to the Pine Ridge Reservation. There they were intercepted by the Seventh Cavalry, who forced the Indians to camp near Wounded Knee Creek; four Hotchkiss machine guns set up on higher ground were aimed at the Indians below.

On the cold morning of December 29, the soldiers ordered the Lakota to give up their guns and began to search the camp. An old medicine man, Yellow Bird, stretched his arms westward toward the coming messiah and prayed that the ghost shirts would keep them safe from the soldiers' bullets. Suddenly, the camp exploded in violence, rifles firing, knives flashing, the Hotchkiss guns mowing the Indians down. When it was over, 146 Lakota lay dead near the creek, including 44 women and 18 children. Perhaps 30 or 40 others later died of their wounds, while 25 soldiers were killed as well. Scattered battles followed, but by mid-January the "uprising" was over—the last, tragic act of the Indian Wars. ■

I want to know what you are doing traveling on this road. You scare all the buffalo away. I want to hunt on the place. I want you to turn back from here. If you don't, I will fight you again. I want you to leave what you have got here, and turn back from here.

I am your friend,
SITTING BULL

[P.S.] I mean all the rations you have got and some powder. Wish you would write as soon as you can.

On a cold, clear October day, Sitting Bull met with Miles on the plains. The Lakota leader wore a buffalo robe, while Miles wore an overcoat trimmed with bear fur, earning the Indian name, "Bear Coat." The negotiations were strained: Miles wanted Sitting Bull to surrender unconditionally; Sitting Bull wanted Miles to leave the Yellowstone. On the second day, the talks broke off in anger, and Miles ordered his soldiers to attack. Though but a single Indian was killed, the battle created a new division among the Lakota. Many left Sitting Bull, surrendering to Colonel Miles and ultimately making their way to the agencies. Sitting Bull with thirty lodges moved on to new hunting grounds—pursued by Miles and others through the long, cold winter that followed. Finally, in the first week of May, Sitting Bull crossed the "sacred road" into Canada, seeking refuge in the land of the Grandmother, Queen Victoria.

Crazy Horse met Bear Coat as well, when Miles attacked his camp on the Powder River in early January, striking at dawn with infantry and artillery. Warriors held off the bluecoats while the women packed their belongings and fled; yet Miles pursued them through the snow, inflicting few casualties, but destroying precious food and supplies of a people who were already starving in the cold northern winter. Eating their horses and trying to warm their frostbitten children, Crazy Horse's followers held out while other bands straggled in to the agencies. Finally, on May 6, 1877, even as Sitting Bull began a new life in Canada, Crazy Horse surrendered at Fort Robinson, Nebraska, with 889 Oglalas. They sang as they approached the fort, and soon their song was taken up by the agency Indians eager to see the most famous of all Lakota warriors. "By God," exclaimed an army officer, "this is a triumphal march, not a surrender."

The triumph turned to tragedy as Crazy Horse struggled with agency life, a strange life without guns, ponies or buffalo, with little to do but wait for stringy government beef. Both Red Cloud and Spotted Tail were jealous of his stature, and it is even said that they suggested to General Crook that he be killed, though Crook preferred to send him to prison in the Dry Tortugas. In early September, after a desperate flight from the agency, the great Oglala warrior was stabbed to death while being escorted to the guardhouse. A soldier wielded the bayonet, but it was his old friend, Little Big Man—who once threatened to kill any chief who sold the Black Hills—who held Crazy Horse's arms so he could not defend himself. Thus, the final message of his great vision came true. Long ago, in the days after the Grattan Fight, he had seen himself as a mystic warrior who could only be killed by his own people.

Sitting Bull was also killed by his own people. Although the redcoats of the Grandmother treated the Lakota more honorably than had the bluecoats, Canadian officials refused to grant them a reservation and finally refused to feed them. In July 1881, Sitting Bull and 187 followers—all that remained of the great confederacy—surrendered at Fort Buford in northern Dakota Territory. After two years in prison, he made his camp on Grand River near the Standing Rock Agency, where agent James McLaughlin branded him as the primary obstacle to "progress." In 1889, despite Sitting Bull's resistance, the Sioux were forced to sign away half their remaining land in return for more food; yet rations were actually reduced once they had signed the paper. A year later, on December 15, 1890, Sitting Bull was killed by Sioux policemen, sent to arrest him by McLaughlin and his old nemesis, "Bear Coat" Miles.

"I never thought that I was against the white man," Sitting Bull had told Miles in the valley of the Yellowstone, "but I admit I am not for him....All I am looking for is to see how and where I can find more meat for my people, more game animals for my people, and to find what God has given me to eat."

THE SOLDIERS
Another War, a Different Enemy

IN THE YEARS PRIOR to the Civil War, the U.S. Army fought its initial battles with the Indians west of the Mississippi. Brig. Gen. William S. Harney struck the first big blow in 1854, destroying a Lakota village near Ash Hollow, Nebraska. The most decisive victory of the 1850s, however, was Col. George Wright's 1858 campaign against the Indians of the Pacific Northwest, which effectively ended military resistance on the Columbia Plateau.

The Civil War brought bloody fighting to the West, as the westerners' natural antipathy toward the Indians was heightened by fears of Indian-Confederate conspiracies and reports of wholesale carnage in the East. Though Harney had been nicknamed "the Butcher" by the Lakota, it was Patrick Connor and John Chivington who incited their men to massacre Indian women and children with unbridled passion at Bear River, Idaho, and Sand Creek, Colorado.

After Appomattox, the army turned its energies against the tribes. The chief architect of postwar Indian strategy was William Tecumseh Sherman, who carried the policy of "total war" that served him in the South onto the Plains, where he commanded the vast Division of the Missouri. In 1866, after 81 men were massacred by Lakota and Cheyenne warriors, Sherman wrote, "We must act with vindictive earnestness against the Sioux, even to their extermination, men, women, and children." When Grant became president in 1868, Sherman replaced him as General-in-Chief of the Army, while Gen. Phil Sheridan took

Gen. William Tecumseh Sherman

Gen. Nelson A. Miles (front) with officers at Wounded Knee

Col. George Wright

Col. Nelson A. Miles

Gen. Patrick E. Connor

Gen. George F. Crook

Col. John M. Chivington

Sherman at the 1868 Fort Laramie conference, with Harney to his right

that did not endear him to his colleagues. Worse yet, he had married a niece of General Sherman, giving even more fodder to his critics. But the steely-eyed New Yorker more than earned his stars. During the Civil War he had been wounded at Chancellorsville, and received the Medal of Honor for his bravery there. Eventually, the fiercely ambitious Miles would become General-in-Chief of the Army, taking over the position once held by Grant, Sherman, and Sheridan. ■

over on the Plains.

One of Sherman's most unusual officers was George F. Crook, who made his name fighting the Paiute and Apache. He cut a most unusual figure, with his forked beard and his habit of dressing in a canvas suit. A popular song of the day included the following verse:

"I'd like to be a packer/And pack with George F. Crook/And dressed up in my canvas suit/To be for him mistook./I'd braid my beard in two forked tails/And idle all the day/In whittling sticks and wondering/What the New York papers say."

Crook's eccentricities masked a shrewdness that made him, in Sherman's words, "the greatest Indian fighter and manager the army of the United States ever had." His straight-talking manner also earned him the trust of the Indians he battled. And despite the jokes, he was genuinely respected by his men. The general took great pains to see that they were outfitted as well as possible, and was known for letting them in on his plans.

Another man who believed a well-informed regiment fought better was Nelson Appleton Miles. The son of a dry-goods clerk, Miles was an anomaly among the army elite. He did not go to West Point and had purchased his commission during the Civil War, aspects of his career

BATTLES IN
THE SUN

"We are surrounded by the Apaches….many small children and women with us…not a soldier in hundreds of miles."

AN ARIZONA SETTLER, JUNE 15, 1885

BATTLES IN THE SUN

For over a decade Cochise waged war against the "white eyes," a war of such guile and fury that his name and the name of his people—Apache—came to symbolize all that was evil on the Arizona frontier. • Hiding behind rocks and bushes, Cochise and his warriors emerged from the land, attacking wagon trains and ranches, escaping with horses, cattle, and plunder, leaving a trail of bodies in their wake. A settler named John Spring claimed that from 1868 to 1871, "Cochise's band killed no less than thirty-four of my friends and acquaintances within a radius of 50 miles...." • Those who died quickly were lucky, for though tales of Apache torture were often exaggerated, they were based on truth. After one attack, a local paper reported that "the bodies of two men were found, tied by the feet to trees, their heads reaching within eighteen inches of the ground, their arms extended and fastened to pickets, and the evidence of a slow fire under their heads." • Cochise's war had begun in 1861 when American soldiers hung his brother, Coyuntura, from a scrub

---

Previous page: Saguaro cacti stand guard over Arizona's Cabeza Prieta National Wildlife Refuge. Opposite: The harsh southwestern terrain was the Apache's greatest ally, forcing federal troops to rely on Indian scouts like the one above, proving the adage, "It takes an Apache to catch an Apache."

oak tree, after trying to arrest Cochise for a crime he didn't commit. Within two years, the Battle at Apache Pass and the murder of Mangas Coloradas—his father-in-law and his friend—had hardened Cochise's resolve. At first, he fought a war of aggression and revenge, striking with ruthless impunity on a desolate frontier all but abandoned during the Civil War. In time, however, as soldiers and settlers filtered back into the territory, Cochise fought defensively, raiding selectively before seeking safety in Mexico or in the rugged, strangely-eroded mountains of southeastern Arizona.

As he harassed Americans, Cochise and his people continued to raid and fight in Mexico, often living there for long periods of time, even as he was blamed for raids in the north. Unbeknownst to the white eyes, he also battled other Indians south of the border, traditional enemies driven into Apache territory by encroaching Mexican settlement. By 1869, warfare on three separate fronts had begun to take its toll. Though still strong, straight, and muscular, his black hair only tinged with specks of gray, Cochise was almost 60 years old, and he worried over the future of his people. That year, he met with an army officer near the Dragoon Mountains, his first face-to-face contact with American soldiers since the war began. "I lost nearly one hundred of my people in the last year," he said sadly, "principally from sickness. The Americans killed a good many. I have not one hundred Indians now. Ten years ago I had one thousand. The Americans are everywhere, and we must live in bad places to shun them."

Although his raids continued, Cochise attended a peace conference in October 1870, at Cañada Alamosa in eastern New Mexico, near the heart of what was once the domain of Mangas Coloradas. Mangas's people, the Chihenne or Red Paint people, were now led by Loco, an elder statesman who spoke strongly for peace, and by Victorio, an inspired war leader described by contemporaries as tall and intelligent, frightening in war, yet honest in talk of peace. One Apache boy called Victorio "the most nearly perfect human being I have ever seen."

Although suspicious of the Americans, Victorio, like Loco, seemed willing to accept a reservation in the Apache homeland,

as long as it included a sacred hot springs called Ojo Caliente, a place where the Chihenne people came to be healed and sustained. Cañada Alamosa, where they were now camped, was less than 20 miles downstream from the springs. This territory was the center of their world, a land of plentiful water and wild game, with grass for livestock and sacred plants for food and medicine. Cochise, too, came to love the springs, saying later that the sacred waters "have cooled me."

In his first meeting, Cochise resisted the very idea of a reservation: "The Apaches want to run around like a coyote," he told the commissioners. "They don't want to be put in a corral." At the same time, he assured them that he wished to end hostilities, "so that the whites and everybody can travel where they please, build their fires, lay down and rest in peace." Although Cochise led only one band of southern Apache called the Chokonen, he had substantial influence among other Apache bands, much like Mangas Coloradas before him. He promised to "talk to all the tribes and learn what they want so that I can talk straight."

It was two more years before Cochise made a final peace with the Americans, after a one-armed, Bible-thumping general named Oliver Howard had the courage to visit his camp unaccompanied except for a single military aide. Howard was led by two Apache warriors and a white man named Tom Jeffords, who had won Cochise's friendship with a similar show of courage. "Now Americans and Mexicans kill an Apache on sight," Cochise told Howard, a succinct summary of anti-Apache feelings on both sides of the border. "I have retaliated with all my might. My people have killed Americans and Mexicans and taken their property. Their losses have been greater than mine. I have killed ten white men for every Indian slain, but I know that the whites are many and the Indians are few."

Although Howard tried to talk Cochise into returning to Cañada Alamosa, where he planned to reestablish a reservation, the aging chief held out for a reserve in his own homeland and Howard offered it to him, with Jeffords as agent. For almost two years Cochise kept the promised peace. Then in June 1874, the great Apache leader died, probably of stomach or colon cancer.

He was succeeded by his eldest son, Taza, who was unable to exercise the firm control that his father had.

It was around this time that Geronimo began to emerge as a leader. A member of a small band called the Bedonkohe, who once lived along the Gila River of Arizona, Geronimo had fought under both Mangas Coloradas and Cochise. He also had strong ties to the southernmost Apache band, the Nednhi, who made their homes in the Sierra Madre of Mexico. The Nednhi chief, Juh, was Geronimo's boyhood friend and brother-in-law, and with others of similar outlook, they continued to raid in Mexico while returning to the Chiricahua Reservation for refuge. The raids caused friction between the two nations and further fueled a government plan to abolish the Chiricahua reserve and concentrate all the Arizona Apache at San Carlos, on a huge low desert tract east of present-day Phoenix.

Both military and civilian officials looked for a reason to break General Howard's promise to Cochise, and they found it in March 1876, when two Chokonen warriors, brothers named Skinya and Pionsenay, got drunk on whisky sold to them by a trader. Pionsenay killed two of his sisters and then murdered the trader, because he wouldn't sell him more whiskey. Taza and his brother, Naiche, dutifully helped agent Tom Jeffords track down the offending warriors, a two-month expedition that ended when Naiche killed Skinya, and Taza wounded Pionsenay.

Despite Taza's cooperation and the alcohol-related nature of the crime, San Carlos agent John Clum was dispatched to the Chiricahua Reservation to relieve Jeffords of his duties and "if practicable, remove Chiricahua Indians to San Carlos." A young, naive Rutgers man whose proud strutting earned him the Apache nickname "Turkey Gobbler," Clum convinced Taza and Naiche to accompany him to San Carlos, but Geronimo and Juh proved less malleable. Acting as spokesman, Geronimo promised to lead their bands to San Carlos but said he needed time to gather those still living south of the border. That night, he and Juh slipped away with hundreds of followers, the first of several daring escapes that Geronimo would make over the next decade. "Every bit of superfluous camp equipment was cast aside; feeble and disabled horses were killed," Clum reported.

BATTLES IN THE SUN
1869-1886

State and territory borders as of 1880
Present-day state names in gray

In making the 1853 Gadsden Purchase, which gave Mexico ten million dollars for over 30,000 square miles of territory, America got more than it bargained for. Contained in that land—which now comprises most of Arizona south of the Gila River and the southwestern notch of New Mexico— were the ancestral territories of the southern Apache, and the infamous mining town of Tombstone. And in selling the land, Mexico was also foisting many of their problems with the Apache over to the Americans. For centuries Mexicans and Apache had battled each other ferociously; since 1837 the Mexican state of Chihuahua had placed a bounty on Apache scalps—100 pesos for a man's scalp, 50 pesos for a woman's, and 25 for a child's.

Geronimo

I**N LATER LIFE**, G**ERONIMO** *(below)* claimed he was born in 1829 on the upper Gila River, though he was more likely born several years earlier. His Apache name, "Goyahkla," means "one who yawns," an unusual description for a man of astonishing energy. By Geronimo's time, his small band, the Bedonkohe, had no chief of their own, and after the death of his father he received his warrior training among the Nednhi, who lived in the wild Sierra Madre of Mexico. It was there Geronimo formed a lifelong friendship with Juh—who would become the Nednhi

chief—and there he married a delicate Nednhi girl, Alope, who returned with him to the Gila and bore three children.

Around 1850, Geronimo and his people camped with Mangas Coloradas near Janos, Mexico. After years of bitter warfare, the Apache and Mexicans were testing a new peace, but when the men went into Janos to trade, Mexican troops attacked their women and children, killing about 25 and capturing 50 or more. Geronimo later found his mother, his wife, and three children among the dead.

Returning to Arizona, the grief-stricken warrior heard a voice telling him that no gun would ever kill him. This was his Power—a mysterious force that the Apache believed could come to anyone, but which they did not seek in vision quests like the Indians of the Plains. Geronimo's Power came to him in his darkest hour, and it was this Power that gave him the strength to fight long after others had surrendered or died for the dream of Apache freedom. ■

"Dogs were strangled, lest their bark betray the route taken by the fleeing renegades."

Of some 1,000 Indians who were living on the Chiricahua Reservation, Clum was only able to find 42 men and 280 women and children to accompany him to San Carlos. There they were thrown in with thousands of other Indians of various Apache and non-Apache tribes, some their natural enemies. All were subjected to regulations that contrasted sharply with the freedom that Cochise's people had enjoyed on the Chiricahua Reservation. But more than the degrading circumstances, it was the land itself that the southern Apache came to hate. Juh's son, Daklugie, later described it:

> San Carlos! That was the worst place in all the great territory stolen from the Apaches. If anybody ever lived there permanently, no Apache knew of it. Where there is no grass there is no game. Nearly all of the vegetation was cacti;…food was lacking. The heat was terrible. The insects were terrible. The water was terrible. What there was in the sluggish river was brackish and warm.

The sluggish river bred mosquitoes, and for the first time the southern Apache began to die of malaria, a scourge that they believed the Americans were employing to punish them. "It is because of the sickness that we must be put there—" said one San Carlos resident, "they wanted us to die." The mood on the reservation worsened when Clum escorted 22 Indians on an eastern tour, staging a Wild West show intended to raise money for his upcoming marriage. The tour lost money, and Taza, who had accompanied the tour, died of pneumonia while visiting Washington, D.C. By the time Clum returned to San Carlos with his new bride, the Chokonen were convinced that their young chief had been poisoned.

With the end of the Chiricahua Reservation, raiding once again increased in the border region. After a report that Geronimo and a hundred stolen horses had been seen in New Mexico—where Victorio's people had now resettled—Clum was ordered to go and "arrest renegade Indians.…Remove [them] to San Carlos and hold them in confinement for murder and robbery." In a daring operation that he considered the crowning glory of his career, Clum and a force of Indian policemen faced off with Geronimo at Ojo Caliente. They arrested Geronimo and his lieutenants and returned them to San Carlos in chains, along with over 100 of their followers and 343 Chihenne including Victorio. Though these Apache would hate San Carlos as much as their relatives did, and though at least eight of them died of smallpox along the way, the ever-optimistic Clum noticed "no regretful tears in this Apache exodus, just a silent hopeful migration of a weary and bewildered people to Utopia."

Geronimo remained chained in the guardhouse for at least two months, though he later claimed it was four, in either case a debilitating punishment for an Apache who feared confinement far more than he feared torture. It was a time, he said, that "might easily have been death to me." Geronimo survived due at least in part to the fact that John Clum, his bitter enemy, resigned as agent in the summer of 1877, after the Bureau of Indian Affairs refused to raise his salary. The agent who replaced Clum apparently released Geronimo, though the Apache later claimed that Juh and another leader had forced Clum to do it under threat of attack by "every Apache on this reservation."

Unchained, Geronimo investigated life at San Carlos, determining what it had to offer him. It was not until the following April that he escaped again, fleeing with Juh and their immediate families to the Sierra Madre, where they stayed off and on for a year-and-a-half. Even then, the reason for his flight was intensely personal. He had gotten drunk on *tizwin,* a mild Apache corn beer, and scolded his nephew for "no reason at all." Despondent at his elder's criticism, the young man committed suicide; Geronimo blamed himself and became a renegade again.

Victorio left San Carlos earlier, driven by a desperate longing for his beloved homeland around the sacred hot springs of Ojo Caliente. On September 2, 1877, he led 310 Chihenne off the reservation, battling troops and armed settlers on their way back to New Mexico, where they surrendered to government officials, explaining that they had no desire to make war, but only wanted to live in their own land. With temporary blessings and rations,

After surrendering in 1886, Geronimo and his band were loaded on a train and removed to prison in Florida. At virtually every stop along the way, the defeated Apache were tourist attractions; in the above photo they posed—under armed guard beside the Southern Pacific Railroad in Texas. Naiche, Cochise's son and hereditary chief of the Chokonen Apache, sits in the center; Geronimo and his son, Chappo, sit to Naiche's left wearing matching shirts. The woman third from the right in the back row has been identified as Lozen, the warrior sister of Victorio.

By THE TIME ROY BEAN became famous, he'd already led a long, adventurous life on the slippery edge of the law. Born in Kentucky around 1825, his troubles began as a teenager when he took a slave-bearing boat to New Orleans and made a quick escape for some still-hazy offense. In his early twenties, Bean killed a man in Chihuahua, Mexico, and moved on to southern California, where he fought two duels; the first led to jail, the second to the hanging tree. Though the senorita over whom he dueled cut her defender down in time, Bean bore the rope marks for the rest of his life.

When the Civil War broke out, Bean rode with Confederate guerrillas in New Mexico before settling in San Antonio, where he became a blockade runner, delivering cotton to the Mexican port of Matamoros in exchange for much needed goods brought by British ships through the Union blockade in the Gulf of Mexico. Earning plenty of money and making plenty of enemies in the process, he faced three lawsuits in 1866 and prevailed through audacious legal maneuvering. He even managed to establish his own personal neighborhood called Beanville.

Judge Roy Bean
LAW WEST OF THE PECOS

By 1881, however, Bean was reduced to hanging around the general store cadging free drinks. When the storekeeper's wife offered $900 for everything he owned—as long as he left town—Bean headed west across the Pecos River with only a wagon, a tent, a barrel of whiskey, and a supply of bottled beer. He settled for a while in the wild Southern Pacific railroad camps of Vinegaroon and Eagle's Nest, where on July 25, 1882, he advertised a new saloon with "the best wines, liquors, and cigars." That same day, the Texas Rangers brought a criminal into the saloon and Bean acted as unofficial judge; eight days later, he was appointed justice of the peace for Pecos County. In a sudden transformation typical of the Wild West, Roy Bean, saloon keeper, had become Judge Roy Bean, Law West of the Pecos.

Though he knew little of the law, Bean possessed a lifetime of common sense and an instinct for self-preservation.

Returning to Vinegaroon, he tried an Irishman accused of murdering a Chinese laborer. After gauging the strength and resolve of the 200 burly Irish workers who surrounded him, Bean thumbed through his law book and blithely announced, "There are plenty of laws against murder, but I'll be damned if I can find any law against killing a Chinaman." It wasn't justice, but it was Bean.

When the railroad was completed in early 1883, the Southern Pacific allowed Judge Bean to squat on its right-of-way in a town along the Rio Grande. He later named it Langtry in honor of English actress Lily Langtry, with whom he fell in unrequited love based on a photograph. It was here he gained national fame. Langtry became a favorite stop for railroad passengers looking for a taste of the old West, and Bean even promoted a heavyweight boxing championship—all while dispensing beer, whiskey, and his unique brand of jurisprudence. In one memorable case, Bean fined a corpse $40 dollars for carrying a concealed weapon, exactly the amount he found in the corpse's pocket. "My court is self-sustaining," he said, and so it was until Roy Bean's death in March 1903. Papers from coast-to-coast carried his obituary. ∎

Ice-cold beer and frontier justice received equal billing in the combination courthouse-saloon of Judge Roy Bean (above, with beard) in the Texas town of Langtry along the Rio Grande (opposite). A favorite practice of the judge was to sell drinks to people until they were thoroughly inebriated, then fine them for public drunkenness.

Victorio's people settled at Ojo Caliente for almost a year, "happier than they ever have been," they told one officer, "were it not that they feared removal." They were so happy, in fact, that they offered to accept half-rations if they could remain. Yet the government remained committed to its reservation policy, and in late 1878, 169 Chihenne were transported back to the San Carlos Reservation. Victorio and 90 warriors bolted for freedom, later drifting back to another reservation set aside for the Mescalero Apache. That, too, proved temporary, and in August 1879, fearing he was about to be arrested, Victorio fled to Ojo Caliente with less than 40 warriors, where they killed eight soldiers and stole a herd of horses and mules—sparking the most remarkable guerrilla campaign in the history of the American frontier.

For 14 months, Victorio left a trail of death and destruction on both sides of the border, ranging through New Mexico, Texas, and Chihuahua. Others joined him along the way, but he never had more than 110 warriors, usually closer to 75 under his command. At its height, the band including women and children numbered no more than 450. They were pursued by 4,000 American and Mexican soldiers, whom they defeated again and again with surprise attacks and sudden retreats, disappearing into the harsh dry land that proved their greatest ally. They found water where the soldiers could not, and would drink a spring dry or poison it for their pursuers—once leaving a disemboweled coyote in an otherwise pure pool.

One U.S. officer estimated that Victorio's band killed over a thousand Mexicans and Americans, a sobering if exaggerated testimony to their fury and fighting skills. Unlike many Apache leaders, even the great Cochise, Victorio had no weakness for whiskey, mescal, or tizwin. He thought clearly and led with conviction. He was aided by the ancient warrior, Nana, his equal as military strategist, and by his sister, Lozen—who rode as a warrior, "strong as a man," her brother said, "braver than most and cunning in strategy,...a shield to her people." It was said that Lozen had Power to detect the enemy—standing with arms outstretched, praying to Ussen, the creator, turning in a circle until her hands began to tingle and her palms turned purple.

In May 1880, a party of Apache scouts—traitors Victorio hated so much that he once sent a war party to kill their families on the reservation—discovered Victorio's camp and killed about 30 of his people, while wounding the chief himself. Running low on ammunition, he led the band into Chihuahua, where Mexican troops caught up with them at a desert oasis called Tres Castillos (Three Castles), named for three rocky hills that rose above seasonal pools in an otherwise barren plain. In mid-October, Victorio and 77 other Apaches were killed, while 68 women and children were taken prisoner. Nana and 16 others escaped, and were soon joined by two warriors carrying ammunition. They arrived too late to save Victorio and the rest who had died in the battle, but "not too late," Nana assured them, "so long as one Apache lives."

TOMBSTONE

In August 1877, as Victorio planned his first flight to freedom, a bedraggled prospector named Ed Schieffelin—described by one contemporary as "about the queerest specimen of humanity ever seen"—filed two mining claims in Tucson, one for himself and one for a friend. He called his own claim Tombstone and the other Graveyard, a wry comment on warnings he had received from American soldiers who told him that he wouldn't find anything but his own tombstone in the desert of southeastern Arizona, where the Apache still threatened and would threaten again. In fact, Schieffelin found the richest silver deposits ever discovered in the southwestern United States, and by early 1879, the booming town of Tombstone had begun to rise on a dry desert mesa eight miles from the Dragoon Mountains that had once provided security and sustenance to the people of Cochise.

Suddenly, "all roads led to Tombstone" said John Pleasant Gray, who arrived on a crowded stagecoach in 1880, a young man looking for adventure after graduating from the University of California. Other educated men were drawn to Tombstone as well, including John Clum, who had left San Carlos for Tucson, where he obtained a law license and published a newspaper, only to pull up stakes and start a new paper, the *Epitaph*, in the booming silver town. The *Epitaph* offered a solid Republican law-and-order point of view that competed with the more laissez-faire attitude of the Democratic *Nugget*. Both papers played a large part in the events that followed. Clum was elected mayor, but the men who made Tombstone famous were the Earps.

James, Virgil, and Wyatt Earp arrived in December 1879, just as the ramshackle mining camp was officially incorporated as a village. All three men brought their common-law wives, as well as their household possessions. Two younger brothers, Morgan and Warren, joined them in time, as did Wyatt's tubercular, trigger-happy gambling buddy, Doc Holliday. The Earps were handsome, mustachioed men who dressed alike and looked alike, especially the middle brothers—Virgil, Wyatt, and Morgan—so similar in appearance that Tombstone citizens found it difficult to tell them apart. They were a close-knit group, taught by their father to see people as either enemies or friends.

> *"Every house is a saloon and every other house is a gambling hell."*
>
> A VISITOR DESCRIBING TOMBSTONE, MARCH 1880

Wyatt Earp later said that he headed for Tombstone because "Dodge City was beginning to lose much of its snap which had given it a charm to men of restless blood." He found plenty of "snap" in Tombstone, but at first the Earps eased into the action, speculating in mining claims and town lots while trying to make a living. James dealt faro at a local gambling house, and Wyatt found a job riding shotgun for Wells Fargo, indulging his own passion for gambling on the side. Virgil held an appointment as deputy U.S. marshal, which offered no regular salary but allowed him to carry a gun and gave him jurisdiction over certain federal cases. To make ends meet, Virgil and Wyatt's wives, Allie and Mattie, took in sewing.

The Earps gradually gained influence in Tombstone, particularly Virgil and Wyatt. Wyatt's reputation as a Kansas lawman and his good work for Wells Fargo earned him an appointment as deputy county sheriff. There were two Earps wearing badges now—tough, fearless men who went about their business with an unflinching certainty that impressed those who shared their point of view and disgusted those who didn't. John Clum, the Earps' most ardent supporter, called Wyatt "quite my ideal of the strong, manly, serious and capable peace officer." Yet another Tombstone resident, who later served in the Arizona House of Representatives, said the Earps offered "absolutely nothing...for a decent man to admire in any way."

By the end of their first year in Tombstone, the Earps aggressive approach to "lawing," as they called it, had alienated an elusive and powerful faction known as the cowboys, a term that, in Tombstone at least, no longer referred to hard-working men who drove cattle up the trail, but rather "stealers of cattle" according to a correspondent who visited the town. The cowboys were generally southern Democrats, men who lived on the land instead of in town, and some of them had been in Arizona long before "boomers" like the Earps and John Clum. They were not all criminals, and the full scope of the rustling operations has never been clear; yet the problem was real, affecting both Mexican and American ranches. In February 1881, Governor John C. Fremont began his territorial address by emphasizing the need "to break up and destroy the organized bands of outlaws which now infest that region."

About the same time as Fremont's address, a new county was formed around Tombstone, named after Cochise, who had once controlled the land that now boomed with mines and ranches, saloons and gambling houses. Wyatt Earp hoped to be appointed county sheriff, a plum position that seemed a natural fit considering his experience as a lawman and his Republican politics in a territory with a Republican governor. Yet he lost the appointment to a Democrat named Johnny Behan,

Games of Chance

GAMBLING WAS A RESPECTABLE way of life in every frontier town from New Orleans to Seattle. And while a game of poker or blackjack could always be found, two of the most popular games were keno and faro. Keno was similar to bingo. Patrons would buy cards stamped with rows of numbers, and a man called the roller would then draw numbered balls from a spinning dispenser known as a "goose." Keno was a notoriously simple game to fix, by rigging the goose to dispense only those balls that would ensure victory for shills planted in the crowd. So prevalent was the game in Tombstone that an advertisement facetiously offered a $50 reward to "the man who cannot find the keno game" at the town's Alhambra saloon.

Faro had been popular in Paris since the 17th century; the name derives from the Egyptian Pharoahs that adorned the backs of French playing cards. A faro board was painted with an image of every card from deuce to ace (the suit didn't matter). Gamblers placed their bets on any one of the images, then the dealer pulled out two cards from his deck. A bet on the first card drawn lost; a bet on the second card won. If the dealer drew a pair, those who bet on the card lost half their money. Though the odds clearly favored the house, many dealers hedged by stacking the deck with consecutive pairs. Wyatt Earp worked as a faro dealer in Tombstone and was a silent partner in a number of gaming establishments. ■

Opposite: After train-robber Rube Burrow met his match—a store clerk who recognized him from a wanted poster—thousands of people thronged to view his body as a train carried it back to his Alabama home.

a self-styled ladies' man who came to law enforcement through slick talk and personal connections rather than his ability with a gun. Behan aligned himself with the cowboy faction in the battle for control of Tombstone, but Earp won a battle of the heart when he stole Behan's girl: a dark-eyed beauty named Josephine Marcus, who had come to Arizona with a traveling company of *H.M.S. Pinafore*. Earp apparently cast-off his common-law wife Mattie with little thought, and she later committed suicide. His relationship with Josephine would last for the rest of his life.

Behan's first big test as sheriff came on March 15, 1881, when a group of gunmen attacked a stagecoach a few miles outside of Tombstone, killing the driver and a passenger before they were driven off by the guard. Two posses were formed, one by Johnny Behan and one by Virgil Earp, acting as deputy U.S. marshal. Wyatt, Morgan, Doc Holliday, and Wyatt's old pal, Bat Masterson, all accompanied Virgil, and after splitting off from Behan's group, they grabbed a suspect named Luther King, who identified the killers as three men from the cowboy faction. When Earp turned King over to Johnny Behan, he sent the suspect back to town with his own deputy—who happened to be the editor of the pro-cowboy *Nugget*. King escaped from the sheriff's office the same day, prompting one citizen to comment, "Some of our officials should be hanged. They're a bad lot."

The Earps felt the same way, and their rancor toward Behan grew stronger when he arrested Doc Holliday for the crime. Though Holliday was released, rumors suggested that the Earps themselves had attacked the stage using inside information from Morgan, who had inherited Wyatt's old job as a guard. The rumors were mostly nonsense; whatever the Earps may have been, they weren't stagecoach robbers, but Holliday was not above suspicion. An undercover Wells Fargo agent named Fred Dodge—who idolized Wyatt and roomed with Morgan— believed that Doc had been in on the attack.

In the midst of the growing tensions, Wyatt apparently made a secret deal with several cowboys, including Ike Clanton and Frank McLaury, to betray the killers in return for the reward money. Earp didn't want the money himself; he wanted to be Cochise county sheriff and he figured that bringing the fugitives

TRAIL OF THE WILD WEST

in would provide him a big edge over Johnny Behan in the upcoming election. Before Ike and his cohorts could turn them over, however, two of the suspects were killed in New Mexico. Then in mid-August, the remaining suspect was killed along with Ike's father, "Old Man" Clanton, and several other cowboys by Mexican troops who caught them with a herd of stolen cattle. Ike was nervous that Wyatt might reveal their secret deal, and he became even more nervous when Virgil Earp arrested two cowboy associates for another stagecoach robbery. The Earps and the cowboys were now headed for a showdown.

THROW UP YOUR HANDS!

It came on the cool, windy afternoon of October 26, 1881. The night before, Ike Clanton had gotten into a drunken shouting match with Doc Holliday and Morgan Earp, who were just as drunk as he was. The next morning, Clanton appeared in town armed with a six-shooter and rifle. By this time, Virgil Earp was serving as Tombstone chief of police (popularly called city marshal). He arrested Clanton for carrying a gun in town, using the favorite Earp technique of "buffaloing" him across the side of the head with a revolver as he hauled him off to court. There Clanton paid a $25 fine and exchanged threats with both Morgan and Wyatt before he was released. As Wyatt left the courtroom, he ran into Tom McLaury who was coming to bail out Ike. They threatened each other as well, and Wyatt buffaloed McLaury for good measure. With sore heads and bruised feelings, Ike and Tom met their brothers, Billy Clanton and Frank McLaury. Informed that the cowboys were armed and looking for trouble, Johnny Behan made a half-hearted attempt to disarm them, later saying that only Billy and Frank had guns and they refused to give them up until the Earps gave up theirs. As Behan walked away, he passed Marshal Virgil Earp, accompanied by Wyatt, Morgan, and Doc Holliday. They brushed past the ineffective sheriff and walked steadily toward the cowboys, who stood in a vacant lot a few doors down from the back entrance of the O.K. Corral.

Virgil stopped about six feet from the cowboys, holding

Wyatt Earp
AFTER TOMBSTONE

WHEN HE LEFT TOMBSTONE in the spring of 1882, Wyatt Earp found refuge in the remote mining camp of Gunnison, Colorado. There are reports that he made a clandestine trip back to Arizona that summer to kill Johnny Ringo, last of the cowboy leaders, while others believe that Ringo committed suicide. Earp did make a quick trip to San Francisco, however, to pick up Josephine Marcus, the feisty young beauty he had stolen from Johnny Behan. Although there is no official record of marriage, Josie and Wyatt lived as man and wife for almost forty-seven years.

In 1883, Earp briefly returned to Dodge City, Kansas, where he and other gunfighters—including Doc Holliday and Bat Masterson—helped gambler Luke Short settle a business dispute known as the Saloon War, which began when three "singers" were arrested for prostitution in Short's famous Long Branch Saloon. They resolved the issue without firing a shot, though a Dodge City paper described Earp as "famous in the cheerful business of depopulating the country."

That winter, Wyatt and his brother Jim ran a saloon of their own in the booming gold town of Coeur d'Alene, Idaho, before Wyatt drifted south to the Texas gambling circuit, where Josie remembered he "struck a winning streak" in Fort Worth that left them "several thousand dollars richer"—enough to settle in San Diego. There Wyatt won a horse in a card game that propelled them into the world of thoroughbred racing, where they traveled with a higher class of sporting men and women than they had known in the rough frontier towns.

By November 1896, racing interests had brought the Earps to San Francisco, and Wyatt was asked to referee a heavyweight boxing match between Bob Fitzsimmons and Tom Sharkey. Amid rumors the fight had been fixed, the match erupted in controversy when Earp declared Sharkey the champion after he had been knocked out by a low blow that only Earp had witnessed. Although a medical investigation sustained Earp's judgment, he was pilloried in the press and fined $50 for carrying an old six-shooter into the ring.

The following summer, the Earps caught Klondike fever; they never made it to the Klondike, but Wyatt built an elegant saloon in Nome, Alaska, that netted him $85,000 when he sold his interests in 1901. Five years later, Wyatt and Josie discovered a small gold mine in the Mojave desert of southern California. They called it "Happy Days," and built a house nearby, "a roost at last" according to Josie, and so it was for over 20 years. They spent summers in Los Angeles, where Wyatt became an unpaid advisor for western films and befriended cowboy stars like William S. Hart and Tom Mix.

In 1928, at the age of 80, Earp met a talented young writer named Stuart Lake; the two began collaborating on a book, but Earp died before it was finished, passing peacefully on January 13, 1929. Lake's book *Wyatt Earp: Frontier Marshal*, was published two years later to great success, establishing the legend of Wyatt Earp as a saintly hero who preserved law and order in the Wild West. Full of fictions—some from Earp, much from Lake's imagination—the book created an anti-Earp backlash that tarnished the truth as surely as Lake polished it. In the final analysis, Wyatt Earp was neither saint nor sinner; he was simply a tough-minded, adventurous man of his time. ◼

After gambling, "lawing," and prospecting across the West, Wyatt Earp—shown above left in 1886 and right in the late 1920s—finally found a small gold mine in the Mojave Desert of southern California (opposite).

Doc's cane in his hand; the Earps and Holliday all packed pistols in their belts, and Doc held a sawed-off shotgun under his long gray coat, clearly visible as the coat flapped in the desert breeze. Someone, Virgil or Morgan or both, shouted, "You sons-of-bitches, you have been looking for a fight and now you can get it!" Then Virgil ordered, "Throw up your hands!"

What happened next is lost in the desert wind. Virgil claimed Billy Clanton and Frank McLaury reached for their guns, while others say the cowboys were about to surrender. Wyatt testified that he and Billy Clanton shot simultaneously, but the cowboys said the first shots were fired by Doc Holliday and Morgan Earp, still hotheaded and probably full of whiskey. Ike Clanton ran, shouting that he wasn't armed, and the remaining seven men faced off in a blaze of bullets that lasted less than 30 seconds. When it was over, Billy Clanton and the McLaury brothers lay dying; Virgil and Morgan Earp were seriously wounded, Holliday had a flesh wound, and Wyatt escaped without a scratch. The next day, the *Epitaph* quoted an eyewitness as saying, "Wyatt Earp stood up and fired in rapid succession, as cool as a cucumber, and was not hit....Doc Holliday was as calm as though at target practice, and fired rapidly."

The dead men were displayed in the window of the local funeral parlor—which doubled as a furniture factory and billiard-table repair shop—arrayed in fancy suits and the finest caskets money could buy, beneath a sign that read: MURDERED IN THE STREETS OF TOMBSTONE. They were given a first-class funeral, hauled to the cemetery in ornate, horse-drawn hearses accompanied by a brass band and hundreds, if not thousands of mourners. In her memoirs, Josephine Earp downplayed the significance of the turnout, saying, "A funeral in those times was like a circus; the people weren't primarily mourners but spectators." Yet sympathy for the cowboys ran high, and the coroner's verdict—that the men had died "from the effects of pistol and gunshot wounds" inflicted by the Earps and Holliday—evaded the question of guilt. "...The verdict reassures us," the *Nugget* waxed sarcastically. "We might have thought they had been struck by lightning or stung to death by hornets."

After Ike Clanton filed charges, all four men were arrested for murder, leading to a month-long inquiry that split the town and brought forth often-conflicting evidence. In the end, Judge Wells Spicer criticized Virgil Earp's judgment, but ruled that the Earps and Holliday "were officers charged with the duty of arresting and disarming armed and determined men who were experts in the use of firearms, as quick as thought and as certain as death and who had previously declared their intentions not to be arrested nor disarmed." He called the homicides "justifiable... a necessary act done in the discharge of an official duty."

"Goodbye boys; go away and let me die."

BILLY CLANTON, QUOTED IN TOMBSTONE *NUGGET*

Not surprisingly, the ruling didn't satisfy the cowboys. A month later, on the night of December 28, Virgil Earp was ambushed while crossing the street. His left arm was shattered and rendered useless for the rest of his life. Then, in March 1882, Morgan Earp was murdered while playing pool. Several Clanton friends were seen nearby, and Wyatt went after them with a vengeance. One suspect was found in Tucson, riddled with buckshot and bullets near the railroad station where Wyatt, Warren, and Doc Holliday had said good-bye to Virgil and Allie, who were taking Morgan's body to their parents' home in California. Back in Tombstone, Earp formed a posse to track down the others—claiming legal powers under a rather hazy appointment as a deputy U.S. marshal. On the way out of town, Johnny Behan tried to arrest Earp for the Tucson murder, but Earp just kept on riding, killing a cowboy associate the next morning and another two days after that. Finally, with Behan's own posse on their tail, armed with legal warrants for their arrest, the Earp party rode out of Arizona, into New Mexico and on to Colorado. The Tombstone days were over.

An Honorable Enemy

During the summer of 1881, as tensions simmered in Tombstone, a prophet rose among the White Mountain Apache, who lived north of the San Carlos agency. His name was Nakaidoklini, and he preached a religion of dance and vision that resembled the Ghost Dances of the Paiute prophets. Whites would be driven from the land, he proclaimed, not by force but by Ussen, and dead chiefs would return to life. Many southern Apache, including Geronimo, Juh, and Nana—all back at San Carlos by this time—were drawn to his teachings; Juh's son later reported that Nana "saw the bodies of three great chiefs—Mangas Coloradas, Cochise, and Victorio—rise slowly from the earth."

Such visions made white authorities nervous, and on August 30, Col. Eugene Carr, who had slaughtered the Cheyenne at Summit Springs 12 years earlier, arrived in Nakaidoklini's village with 85 soldiers and 23 Apache scouts, requested by the San Carlos agent "to arrest and send him off or have him killed without arresting." The holy man submitted peacefully, but bloody fighting broke out among his followers and the troops, with the Apache scouts defecting to fight beside their relatives. Nakaidoklini was killed along with 17 other Apache and 7 American soldiers.

The bloody battle and the death of the prophet created new fears and hysteria among whites and Apache alike. A month later, Geronimo and Juh fled in the night with 72 followers, among them Naiche, the surviving son of Cochise. They headed for Mexico, "killing everybody they encountered" according to one historian, including a lonely wood hauler in the Dragoon Mountains outside Tombstone. The citizens formed a posse, headed by Johnny Behan and Virgil Earp, accompanied by such stalwarts as Wyatt and Morgan Earp and Mayor John Clum, who was eager to track down his old nemesis. After searching for two days without seeing an Indian, the Tombstone men headed back to town for their date with destiny, while Geronimo, Juh, and the others rode toward the Sierra Madre.

The Apache decided that they would need reinforcements to battle Mexican troops, who were pursuing them as relentlessly as the Americans. In April 1882, Geronimo led a raiding party north to San Carlos, where they forced over 400 of Loco's peaceful Chihenne off the reservation, mostly women and children who followed in "gloom and despair" according to one young man. As they fled southward, American troops pursued the Apache across the border, a surprising and illegal tactic that forced the warriors to lag behind to guard against the Americans, while the defenseless women and children ran headlong into Mexican infantry—who slaughtered them as they had slaughtered Victorio's people at Tres Castillos. Of the 78 Apache killed, only 11 were warriors, while another 33 women and children were taken prisoner. The survivors straggled on to join Juh's people in the Sierra Madre.

That fall, Gen. George Crook returned to Arizona, where he had waged a brutally effective campaign against the Apache in the Tonto Basin during the early 1870s. It was Crook who had originally governed San Carlos, and the greatest regret of his first tour of duty was that he had been unable to go after Cochise. According to Nana, the Apache respected Crook as an "honorable enemy....His promise was good; his understanding of Apaches was fair." They called him "Chief Tan Wolf" for his khaki-colored civilian clothing and uncanny ability to prowl the land. It was not Crook they came to hate, but rather the Apache "traitors," mostly White Mountain people, that he used to hunt them down.

On May 1, 1883, Crook led a force that included 193 Apache scouts and fewer than 60 American soldiers across the border under a new agreement with Mexican authorities. Penetrating Juh's stronghold in the Sierra Madre, his scouts found several recently abandoned camps, killed nine Apache and captured five children. Faced with the reality of American troops in their Mexican sanctuary, 384 Apache—most Chihenne who had not wanted to leave in the first place—accompanied Crook back to San Carlos. Geronimo also agreed to surrender, but he asked for time to gather his people. He kept his promise, finally arriving in the spring of 1884 with almost a hundred followers and a herd of stolen Mexican cattle. To Geronimo, the cattle were rightfully his; he was now at peace with the Americans, not the Mexicans. But Crook confiscated them in an effort to preserve the new spirit of cooperation with the Mexican government.

Crook gave the southern Apache permission to settle on a land of their choosing, a place with good water and ample pasture called Turkey Creek, located north of San Carlos. It was the best land they had been offered since the Chiricahua reserve, but though many found a kind of happiness, living peacefully and trying to become good farmers, Geronimo and other militants chafed at the restrictions of reservation life, especially Crook's prohibition of the tizwin they liked to drink. Geronimo also claimed that he feared arrest and execution in Arizona, a reasonable explanation considering the anti-Apache hysteria of the time.

The hysteria escalated in May 1885, when Geronimo escaped with some 140 followers, including such influential men as Nana, Naiche, Chihuahua, and Mangus, son of Mangas Coloradas. By this time, Juh had died in Mexico, and Geronimo led the free Apache, though every warrior retained the right to chart his own destiny. Before they crossed the Mexican border, the band killed at least 17 American settlers and stole 150 horses. "Tan Wolf" Crook pursued them with a vengeance, fielding 2,000 men in an unsuccessful effort to seal the border, while also tracking the fugitives deep into Mexico. It wasn't until January 1886 that Apache scouts, including some of Geronimo's own people, captured his empty camp in the Sierra Madre. There was no longer any place to hide.

Two months later, in the tree-shaded Cañon de los Embudos south of the border, Geronimo met with General Crook to discuss the terms of his surrender. The Apache leader claimed he had always been committed to peace, blaming his troubles on "agents and interpreters" and "stories put in the newspaper that I am to be hanged." In his characteristically blunt manner, Crook called him a liar and told him the reservation was no longer a refuge. "You must make up your own mind whether you will stay out on the warpath or surrender unconditionally," he barked. "If you stay out, I'll keep after you and kill the last one, if it takes fifty years."

Following an Apache council, Chihuahua and Naiche pledged complete submission. "I am anxious to behave," said Chihuahua. "I surrender myself to you because I believe in you and you do not deceive us. You must be our God." Naiche echoed those sentiments in words that would never have been uttered by his father, Cochise. "I throw myself at your feet. You now order and I obey." Finally, Geronimo spoke with the eloquent simplicity of the greatest Apache leaders: "Once I moved about like the wind. Now I surrender to you and that is all."

After Crook agreed to liberal terms—all warriors to be imprisoned in the East for two years with any family members who wished to join them—the Indians got drunk on liquor supplied by an American trader who told Geronimo that he would be hung as soon as he crossed the border. Geronimo and Naiche slipped away for the final time, with a band of less than 40 followers. About half of them were women and children, including Lozen, the warrior sister of Victorio.

Even before he knew of the escape, General Sheridan rejected the terms of surrender; there would be no terms except to spare their lives. Following Sheridan's orders, Crook shipped his remaining prisoners to Fort Marion, Florida, and asked to be relieved of command—he had made a promise that his superiors said he couldn't keep. The Tan Wolf was replaced by Gen. Nelson Miles, who had once pursued Sitting Bull and Crazy Horse across the cold northern plains. Though as capable as Crook, Miles was a different breed of military officer, younger, more vain, and ambitious. Discarding his predecessor's reliance on Indian scouts, he sent 5,000 soldiers into the field, one-quarter of the United States Army. At the same time, at least 3,000 Mexican troops pursued the renegades. In five months, the soldiers failed to capture a single Indian, while Geronimo's band forged a trail of death along the troubled border. Most of the carnage was in Mexico; the governor of Sonora claimed that the band killed over 500 people in his state alone.

Unable to defeat Geronimo by military means, Miles shipped the southern Apaches remaining at San Carlos—including the peaceful Chihenne and scouts who had once aided Crook—to Fort Marion, Florida. As he planned their removal, Miles sent Lt. Charles Gatewood and two southern Apache guides to find Geronimo. Gatewood explained to the hardened warrior that his people were gone; that there was nowhere left to go and nothing left to fight for. Geronimo wanted to keep fighting anyway, but some of his warriors were tired. He agreed to meet with General Miles.

In Skeleton Canyon, about 10 miles north of the Arizona-Mexican border, Miles promised Geronimo and the renegades that they would be reunited with their families, and that "no harm will be done you." Later, he improved this offer to include a reservation with houses, horses, and wagons. The past, he said, would be "considered smooth and forgotten." These seemed good promises, and on September 4, 1886, Geronimo and Naiche formally surrendered to the United States of America.

"We stood between his troopers and my warriors," Geronimo remembered. "We placed a large stone on the blanket before us. Our treaty was made by this stone, and it was to last until the stone should crumble to dust...."

Four days after their surrender, the renegades were herded onto railroad cars and transported under armed guard to Florida. Despite Miles's promise that families would be united, Geronimo and his warriors were locked away at Fort Pickens, a damp island prison off the Gulf Coast, while the women and children joined almost 400 other southern Apaches at Fort Marion off the Atlantic coast. Suffering from malaria, tuberculosis, and hunger, all of the prisoners were moved to Alabama over the next two years but the change had minimal effect; by the end of 1889, after a little more than three years of captivity, 89 Apache died in the prison camps while 30 children died at the Carlisle Indian School—a Pennsylvania boarding school where Indian children were sent to be "civilized."

In 1893, the southern Apaches were moved to Fort Sill in what is now Oklahoma, where some began to adjust to a life as farmers, while others—including Geronimo—still pined for their desert home. A star attraction at fairs and expositions in his later years, the once-feared warrior rode in President Theodore Roosevelt's 1905 inaugural parade. "Let me die in my own country," he asked the President, "an old man who is punished enough and is free." It was not to be; Geronimo died in 1909, after 23 years as a prisoner of war. Three years later, the southern Apaches were released from captivity.

Exiled from his beloved Arizona (above), Geronimo longed to return. "I have been away from Arizona now twelve years," he told his old nemesis, General Miles, in 1898. "The acorns and piñon nuts, the quail and the wild turkey, the giant cactus and the palo verdes—they all miss me. They wonder where I've gone. They want me to come back." "A very beautiful thought, Geronimo," the general replied. "Quite poetic. But the men and women who live in Arizona, they do not miss you....The acorns and the piñon nuts, the quail and the wild turkey, the giant cactus and the palo verde trees—they will have to get along as best they can—without you."

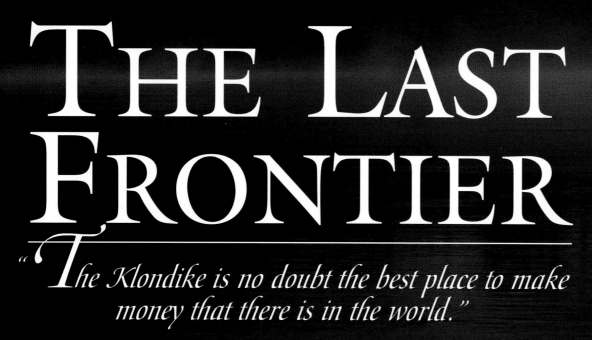

THE LAST FRONTIER

"*The Klondike is no doubt the best place to make money that there is in the world.*"

WILLIAM STANLEY, KLONDIKE MINER, JULY 1897

THE LAST FRONTIER

1873-1898

IN AUTUMN 1879, THE AMERICAN NATURALIST JOHN MUIR TRAVELED BY NATIVE CANOE THROUGH ALASKA'S INSIDE PASSAGE, A RAINY, FJORD-LIKE LABYRINTH OF MILD PACIFIC WATER FLOWING THROUGH FORESTED MOUNTAINS HUNG WITH GLACIERS AND TEEMING WITH WILDLIFE. "TO THE LOVER OF PURE WILDERNESS," HE WROTE OF THE JOURNEY, "ALASKA IS ONE OF THE MOST WONDERFUL COUNTRIES IN THE WORLD." • TRAVELING WITH A PRESBYTERIAN MINISTER, MUIR STOPPED AT NATIVE VILLAGES WHERE THE SOPHISTICATED CULTURE OF THE TLINGIT-SPEAKING PEOPLE IMPRESSED HIM DEEPLY.

"THEY MANAGE TO FEED THEMSELVES WELL, BUILD GOOD SUBSTANTIAL HOUSES, BRAVELY FIGHT THEIR ENEMIES, LOVE THEIR WIVES AND CHILDREN AND FRIENDS, AND CHERISH A QUICK SENSE OF HONOR." • TOWARD THE END OF THE JOURNEY, MUIR'S PARTY PASSED THOUGH A NARROW CHANNEL NOW CALLED THE GASTINEAU. "THE SCENERY ALL THROUGH THE CHANNEL IS MAGNIFICENT," HE WROTE, "SOMETHING LIKE YOSEMITE VALLEY IN ITS LOFTY AVALANCHE-SWEPT WALL CLIFFS." THE COMPARISON PROVED PRESCIENT, FOR JUST AS MUIR'S BELOVED YOSEMITE ABUTTED THE WEALTH OF THE

The Yukon River (previous page and opposite) was the lifeline of a vast northern wilderness that drew a gradually increasing stream of prospectors like the ones above, departing Juneau around 1895. The following year, a major gold strike on a Yukon tributary called the Klondike would turn that stream to a stampede.

Mother Lode, so did the lofty cliffs of the Gastineau Channel reveal the promise of gold riches. Prompted by Muir's observations, mining engineer George Pilz offered a hundred Hudson Bay blankets to the native people in exchange for leading his men to gold. It seemed a good offer to Kowee, chief of the Tlingit Auk clan who lived on Douglas Island—a lush, temperate rain forest just south of the Gastineau Channel. In 1880, Kowee brought ore samples to Pilz in Sitka and returned to the channel with two grizzled prospectors, Joe Juneau and Richard Harris. He led the men up a rushing creek into the mountainous mainland, but they didn't get far. A few miles inland, at a place called Last Chance Basin, Harris and Juneau traded their grubstake for native beer and returned to Pilz empty-handed.

Undaunted, Kowee followed the prospectors back to Sitka, where he offered Pilz more ore samples and explained why the whites—Boston Men in the native term—had nothing to show for their efforts. Pilz staked the prospectors again, and this time Kowee and two other Indians pushed them beyond Last Chance Basin, literally dragging the Boston Men up a rocky, precipitous incline known as Snowslide Gulch. They emerged into a broad high country that Harris named Silver Bow Basin. There Kowee showed them the source of the gold, and it's said that Juneau and Harris loaded their canoe with a thousand pounds of ore and headed south for Canada, until another Pilz prospector forced them back to Sitka at gunpoint.

So began Alaska's first great gold rush. The town that grew along the channel was originally called Harrisburg after Richard Harris, but when it came time to put the name of the town up for a final vote, it was Joe Juneau who bought the most drinks. Easily-mined placer gold gave out quickly in the Juneau area, and the tale of the Juneau Gold Belt is a saga of industrial mining, with miles of tunnels honeycombing the mountains and huge stamp mills crushing the low-grade ore. Yet even as it evolved from a rough mining camp to an industrial town, Juneau served as a springboard for restless men who pushed beyond the mountains into the vast wilderness drained by the Yukon River.

THE YUKON WILDERNESS

Rising from alpine lakes on the inland slopes of the craggy coastal mountains, the Yukon River describes a great arc of over 2,000 miles, flowing northwest through the Yukon Territory of Canada and into Alaska where it almost meets the Arctic Circle at an old fur trading post called Fort Yukon. There, as if repelled by the magnetic force of the pole, it makes a great bend toward the south, cutting across Alaska until it empties its load of silt and sand into the cold gray waters of the Bering Sea. Along the way, it drains a rugged, sparsely populated country of 327,000 square miles, larger than California and Arizona combined, a land of short, mosquito-infested summers bathed in long hours of daylight, and seemingly endless, frozen winters where temperatures drop to eighty below and the sun barely peeks above the horizon. Gold is where you find it, say the prospectors, but finding it in the Yukon offered new challenges that tested the most experienced men.

Even before the Juneau discovery, a few hardy prospectors penetrated the Yukon; among the first were Arthur Harper, Jack McQuesten, and Alfred Mayo, who reached Fort Yukon in the summer of 1873, in two separate parties that worked their way north from British Columbia, following a long, circuitous route along the Mackenzie River originally used by the Hudson Bay Company. Harper and McQuesten were "Old Californians" who had followed the call of gold into British Columbia and beyond; Mayo was a dry-witted circus acrobat driven north by his own restless nature. These three stayed in the Yukon, prospecting and establishing trading posts, where they offered generous credit to those who followed.

Sometime during the 1870s, a shadowy character named George Holt attempted a more direct route over a wind-cut notch in the towering mountains at the northern end of the Inside Passage. The Chilkoot Pass, as it was called, required a one thousand foot climb up a rocky, thirty-five degree slope covered in ice eight months out of the year. Even so it was far easier than the long route followed by Harper, McQuesten, and Mayo. The trip from the salty ocean tides of the Taiya Inlet, northern tip of the Inside Passage, to the fresh, emerald waters of Bennett Lake, head of navigation for the Yukon River system, required a hike of only 33 miles.

Although little is known of Holt's journey, it's said he was the first white man to cross the pass and return alive, somehow eluding the Chilkoot people who guarded the pass to protect their lucrative trade with the Indians of the interior. One of several coastal Tlingit groups who controlled the various passes over the mountains, the Chilkoot were closely related to the even more powerful Chilkat, "the most warlike of all the tribes" according to U.S. Naval Capt. Lester Beardslee, commander of a patrol boat in Sitka, the only American military force in the region. In 1880, Beardslee negotiated an agreement with the Chilkats and Chilkoots to allow prospectors over the Chilkoot Pass provided they did not interfere with the fur trade. The decision was driven more by economics than fear of American guns; the Tlingits saw the Boston Men as a new market for their packing services, and charged between $9 and $13 for each 100 pounds they carried over the pass.

In 1883, Ed Schieffelin, the gaunt eccentric who had discovered silver in Tombstone, attacked the Yukon from the other end, leading a party of men on a specially-built steamboat upriver from the Bering Sea. Though he found color about a thousand miles into the interior, Schieffelin turned back in the face of the Arctic winter, returning to warmer climates where he spent the rest of his life looking for another big strike. He sold the steamer to McQuesten, Harper, and Mayo, who operated it along the river, providing a key lifeline to the "Outside."

The first great breakthrough came on the Fortymile River, a small tributary of the Yukon named for its distance from Jack McQuesten's trading post. In late 1886, prospectors discovered coarse gold—nuggets that rattle the pan and excite every miner's heart. By the following summer, 250 men were working the gravel bars, and many stayed through the winter in the new settlement of Forty Mile. A town of strange, scruffy characters who had run away from towns, Forty Mile was so cold and dark in winter, so isolated in every season, that an Anglican missionary who lived there wrote, "I feel so long dead and

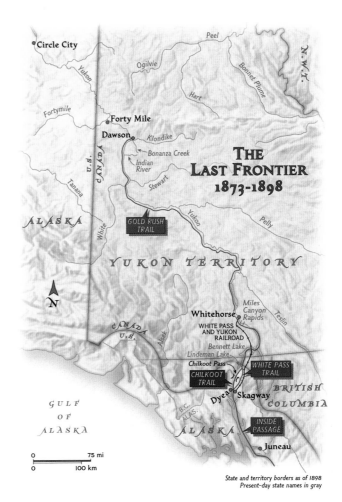

State and territory borders as of 1898
Present-day state names in gray

At the time of the Klonkike gold strike, the future site of Dawson was a moose pasture near an Indian fishing camp. Within two years, Dawson was a booming city with a population approaching 20,000. Boat fares to Skagway and Dyea jumped from $200 to $1000—scalpers sold tickets for up to $2000—and Canadian officials charged substantial fees to prospectors entering the Yukon. When the Klondike gold rush fizzled, the next target for prospectors became Nome, where gold was discovered in the fall of 1898.

Prospectors lined up to make the exhausting climb up the Chilkoot Pass. By the time this photo was taken, a rope set along the pass helped climbers maintain their balance and a series of steps cut into the snow—called the "Golden Stairs"—helped speed the procession along. Setting eyes on the long, treacherous slope, with its 35-degree incline, many people simply turned back and sold their gear at a loss. Those with money could pay to have their gear hauled up the slope; those with fewer resources and stronger backs would haul their packs up 50 pounds at a time, sliding back down the pass to pick up another load.

buried that I cannot think a short visit home, as if from the grave, would be of much use."

Though the miners were mostly Americans, they discovered that the town was in Canada when a Canadian surveyor arrived to define the border. At first the distinction was irrelevant; the men of Forty Mile governed themselves through "miners' meetings," a chaotic California-born democracy that reached its zenith in the Yukon, where the miner's natural avarice was tempered by the necessity of cooperation for mutual survival. There were two sacred rules in the Yukon: Never refuse another man food or shelter, and share news of a promising discovery. Just as sacred, though less essential to survival, was a custom that required a man who bought himself a drink to buy one for everyone in sight, "an expensive matter," according to one observer, "—if you get off with an expenditure of $100 you may consider yourself lucky."

In 1895, the growing population and questionable justice of the miners' meetings brought a contingent of 20 North-West Mounted Police to Forty Mile, an intrusion of Canadian law and order that rankled the free-spirited Americans. By that time, even richer prospects had been found on Birch Creek, just south of the Arctic Circle on the Alaska side of the border, and many left Forty Mile for the new diggings, joined by others from the Outside. In 1896, Birch Creek yielded a million dollars worth of gold, and the booming town it spawned, Circle City, the self-styled "Paris Of Alaska," boasted more than a thousand citizens, a music hall, two theaters, two churches, a 2,000 volume library (courtesy of Jack McQuesten), a hospital, a school, eight dance halls and twenty-eight saloons—all in a drab Arctic wilderness of sandbars, swamps, and muskeg. Yet even the rush that gave rise to the Paris of Alaska was but a shadow of the one that followed.

My Heart Skipped a Beat

The Klondike gold discovery is a story of dreams. Not only of dreams that drove men and women north, but of daydreams and night dreams that inspired specific actions. The gold was there

Trail Of The Wild West

waiting to be found, but it required dreams, it seems, to find it.

Joe Ladue first came to the Yukon in 1882, climbing the Chilkoot Pass and traveling downriver with a dozen men. They each dreamed of riches, but Ladue had a more compelling dream than most; he was in love with a wealthy young lady back in Plattsburgh, New York, and her parents insisted he make his own fortune before they would consent to the marriage. Twelve years later, while his aging fiancee waited patiently back in Plattsburgh, Ladue was still in the Yukon, running a trading post and sawmill in partnership with Arthur Harper, about a hundred miles south of Forty Mile. On the stretch of river between the post and the town were two major Yukon tributaries, one called the Indian, the other the Thon-diuck, a native word meaning "Hammer-Water," which whites mispronounced as Klondike.

The Klondike is a beautiful region of spruce and aspen forests, of sparkling waters under arching skies, of softly-rounded hills and distant purple mountains. Ladue had tested the Klondike himself, but he believed the Indian offered better prospects, so he staked a respected prospector named Robert Henderson to explore it. A tall, lean Nova Scotian, Henderson had spent his life looking for gold from Australia and New Zealand to Colorado and Alaska, never finding enough to satisfy his restless longing. For two years he tested the Indian River region, finding color here and there, always pushing on. Finally in the spring of 1896, he climbed a rounded dome separating the streams that flowed into the Indian from those that flowed into the Klondike. Canadian author Pierre Berton, who grew up in the Klondike region, describes the scene:

> When he reached the summit a sight of breath-taking majesty met his gaze. To the north a long line of glistening snow-capped peaks marched off like soldiers to vanish beyond the lip of the horizon. In every direction the violet hills rolled on as far as he could see, hill upon hill, valley upon valley, gulch upon gulch—and each hill of almost identical height so that the whole effect through half-closed eyes was of a great plateau

Klondike Kate

"KLONDIKE KATE" Rockwell (below), arrived in Dawson in 1900 at the age of 19. Although the great rush was over, there were still plenty of men with money, and the red-haired, violet-eyed Kate became queen of the Dawson dance halls, renowned for her beauty, talent, and personality. Kate's own favorite was a young Greek immigrant named Alexander Pantages who ran the Orpheum Theater, the beginning of the Pantages theater empire. Kate sued Pantages for $25,000 in 1905, claiming she had bought him cigars and silk shirts in Dawson and paid their traveling expenses back to the states. She settled out of court for less than $5,000 but remained an upbeat colorful personality until her death in 1957.

"We girls of the Klondike dance halls dressed in the latest fashions," she said in a 1944 interview. "My gowns and hats were from Paris, beautiful and expensive. But no short skirts nor revealing décolletage for us! My most daring costume, with its brief, rhinestone-studded tights, would seem mild today....Dawson in 1901 was the hilarious heart of the rich gold country. To its theaters and dance halls the miners came for relief from the long, lonely hours on the claims. They laughed, drank and threw their gold dust recklessly about. I was queen of that laughter and gaiety." ∎

creased and gouged and furrowed by centuries of running water.

Henderson descended the dome and dipped his pan into one of the streams on the other side. It yielded eight cents worth of gold—hardly enough to take a man's breath away, but to an experienced prospector like Henderson, enough to suggest that riches might wait beneath the ground. Returning to the Indian River, he convinced three men to join him at the place he named Gold Bottom, because, he explained, "I had a daydream that when I got my shaft down to bedrock it might be like the streets of the New Jerusalem." It wasn't, but the site yielded $750 by midsummer, when Henderson returned to Ladue's trading post for supplies. On the way back, he decided to paddle directly up the Klondike, because he feared the shallow Indian would rip the bottom of his canoe. It was this decision that brought him to the fish camp of George Carmack.

Carmack was a child of the California gold rush, a different sort of man than Robert Henderson, more sensitive and literary by nature, driven less by the yellow metal than by a desire for new experiences. In the spring of 1886, while working at a trading post in Dyea, a fishing village on the Taiya Inlet that served as the gateway to the Chilkoot Pass, Carmack befriended two native men—Keish and Kaa Goox, better known as Skookum Jim and Dawson Charlie—with whom he would change the course of Yukon history.

Jim was the tall, handsome son of a clan chief from Tagish, located on the other side of the mountains; Charlie was Jim's nephew, a smaller, leaner man with a round and pleasant face. Although originally Athapaskan-speaking people, the Tagish developed such close trading connections with the coastal Tlingit that they spoke a Tlingit dialect and adopted many aspects of Tlingit culture. Jim and Charlie had come to Dyea to work as packers, and it was on a later packing trip, arranged by his new friend George Carmack, that Jim earned the nickname Skookum—meaning "strong" in the Chinook trade jargon—by carrying 156 pounds of bacon over the Chilkoot Pass.

George Carmack spent the winter of 1886-87 at Tagish, where he enjoyed Jim's hospitality and married one of his sisters. When she died a short time later, he married another sister, whom he called by the English name, Kate. While other white prospectors looked down on the native people, Carmack tried to emulate them, learning their ways of living off the land, fishing, hunting, and trapping in the cold, dry northern interior. In the winter of 1888-89, however, George and Kate Carmack parted ways with Skookum Jim and Dawson Charlie because George wanted to prospect in a region that the Tagish men considered full of bad spirits. They didn't see each other for seven years, yet even as he lived among white prospectors, George Carmack was proud of his connections to the Tagish people. When other whites called him a "Siwash," a derogatory term for the upper Yukon Indians, George Carmack took it as a compliment.

In the spring of 1896, Carmack had a vivid dream. "I was sitting on the bank of a small stream of water," he later wrote, "watching the grayling shoot the rapids. Suddenly the grayling began to scatter, and two very large King Salmon shot up the stream in a flurry of foaming water and came to a dead stop in front of the bank where I was sitting. They were two beautiful fish, but I noticed that instead of having scales like salmon, they were covered with an armour of bright gold nuggets and gold pieces for eyes."

It says something about Carmack's interests that he interpreted this dream as a sign he should go fishing, rather than prospecting. So George, Kate, and their 3-year-old daughter, Graphie Gracie, paddled upriver to the salmon-rich mouth of the Klondike. At the end of July, they were reunited with Skookum Jim, Dawson Charlie, and Charlie's teenage brother, Patsy Henderson. The trio had decided to look for the missing couple, because so many Tagish people were dying of white diseases, and Jim was concerned for his sister. It's also said that Jim had a dream of a beautiful woman, "just like shining, gold shining," who pointed down the Yukon River and said, "You go down this way and you're going to have your luck...." George Carmack felt there was something mystical as well, explaining that "their medicine told them to hunt me up and they would have good luck as their luck had been bad ever since we parted...."

A few days after the reunion, Robert Henderson arrived at the fish camp on his way back to Gold Bottom. As was the custom in the North, he told them of his new discovery. "What are the chances to locate up there?" Carmack asked. "Everything staked?"

"I felt as if I had just dealt myself a royal flush in the game of life, and the whole world was a jackpot."

GEORGE CARMACK, DESCRIBING THE KLONDIKE GOLD DISCOVERY

Henderson scowled over at Skookum Jim and Tagish Charlie, before turning his attention back to Carmack. "There's a chance for you, George," he replied, "but I don't want any damn Siwashes staking on the creek." With that, he pushed his boat back into the water and headed upriver.

Carmack and his relatives were disgusted with Henderson's attitude, but his news of Gold Bottom inspired them to quit fishing and start prospecting. Leaving Kate, Graphie, and Patsy at the fish camp, they tested a tributary of the Klondike, Rabbit Creek, and found good prospects before moving on to Gold Bottom—where they staked claims and briefly visited Henderson's camp, only to be insulted when he refused to sell the Indians tobacco. Carmack later wrote that Henderson's "obstinacy lost him a fortune."

Crossing the divide that separated the streams, the trio worked their way up Rabbit Creek, running dangerously short of food. While George and Charlie prospected along the way,

Jim—considered the best hunter and trapper in the upper Yukon—found hunting more difficult in the Klondike region. Finally, after three days, when they were so hungry they could barely go on, Jim killed a moose and signaled to the others to come and join him, cutting off a piece of meat and eating it raw while he waited. The meat made him thirsty, so he walked down to the creek for a drink, a hunk of raw moose in his hand, and saw more gold than he had ever seen before. Jim waited until they had cooked some meat and eaten their fill before showing the gold to George and Charlie. After prospecting up and down the creek, George convinced Jim to let him stake the discovery, which allowed the discoverer an extra claim on the same creek—because the whites would never grant an Indian such an honor.

That's Jim's story, anyway, as he told it to William Ogilvie, the Canadian government surveyor who interviewed the participants shortly after the event. Ogilvie believed Jim, and the weight of evidence suggests that it was indeed Skookum Jim who found the gold that started the Klondike rush. But George Carmack told a different story, claiming that he noted a long narrow strip of bedrock along the creek, "the very thing I had been looking for."

Throwing off my pack, I walked down to the rim. As soon as I reached it, I stopped and looked down... my heart skipped a beat, I rubbed my eyes with the back of my hand to wipe away a misty film that enveloped my pupils, then I reached down and picked up a nugget about the size of a dime...and bit it like a schoolboy who had found a quarter in the garbage can.

According to Carmack, after calling to Jim and Charlie for the pan and shovel, he dug up the loose bedrock and turned over some flat pieces, where he "could see the raw gold laying thick between the flakey slabs, like cheese sandwiches." Then, walking back to the rim and settling his gold pan on the ground, George joined his Indian companions in "a war-dance around that gold-pan...a combination war-dance...Scotch hornpipe, Indian foxtrot, syncopated Irish jig, and a sort of

William Schooley
The Diary Of A Miner

HUNDREDS OF GOLD seekers kept diaries of their Klondike adventure. One of the best is that of William Schooley, a 23-year-old Missourian who was already mining in Alaska when he headed for the Klondike in late 1897. Writing from Dyea, Schooley answered the query of a younger brother who wanted to know if he should join the Klondike stampede:

"That, you see is pretty hard to answer, because a man's lifelong career may hinge on that advice. What I would like, or rather what I would endure, would cause someone else to hoist canvas and sail away....I think that if a man can and will stay with it, he will succeed in time, but it is far from a sure thing. Gold is not lying about in such quantities as the steamboat companies would have you believe. It is in spots deep down under the frozen ground."

Schooley began his diary on January 30, 1898, the day that he and partners Lafe and Frank Coleman moved "the last load of our outfit" by dogsled from Dyea to Canyon City, eight miles up the Chilkoot Trail. Four days later, he described a tragedy that occurred when a party of Indians got lost in a snow-storm, leaving a mother with an eight-year-old boy and a baby behind:

"...They found the squaw and little boy frozen to death but when the mother saw she must die, she put her own clothes on the little babe and it was found alive and warm. Just one other showing of a mother's love....About 1500 people landed at Dyea today. I think the rush is on in earnest."

Through February, Schooley moved their outfit further up the trail when the weather was good and stayed in camp reading when it wasn't, devouring novels by Dumas, Tolstoy, and Thackeray. "So many people are on the trail now that it looks like the main street of a crowded city," he wrote on February 28. By then he and the Colemans were packing gear on their backs to the summit, for the last slope was too steep for dogs. Schooley took the work in stride, noting that it was "a good day for sliding down the mountain."

All 6,000 pounds were at the top by mid-March, and they moved on to Lake Lindeman and later Lake Bennett, where patriotic Americans eagerly discussed the Spanish-American War and chafed at Canadian fees and regulations. "Here in John Bull's domain we pay dearly for the air we breathe and every move we make," he wrote on May 9. "Here an American will realize that America is still 'A land of the Free.'"

Schooley felt much the same when he reached Dawson on June 16, noting that "Many are cursing the country preparatory to leaving." Although the diary stops nine days later, he wrote to his mother in October: "The Police organization here is so corrupt that justice in anything must be bought if obtained....we decided to go to Uncle Sam's Territory, where if we made a strike all would be ours."

William Schooley and his partners found a promising claim on Wade Creek, across the Alaska border. He picked up his diary again in May 1900 and continued it until June 3, 1901, when he made a final entry: "Leave Wade Creek perhaps forever. Sold to Lafe. Leave with $525.00." ■

On April 3, 1898, approximately 70 stampeders died in avalanches along the Chilkoot Trail, some still buried in Dyea's Slide Cemetery (opposite). "It was a terrible sight and affected me deeply" wrote William Schooley, "to look on the frozen bodies twisted in all shapes." Such dangers didn't stop families like the one pictured above.

Soapy Smith

THE RUSH TO the Klondike spawned three thriving boomtowns: Dawson near the gold fields, Dyea and Skagway over 500 miles away at the head of Alaska's Inside Passage. While Dawson was downright civilized, Skagway was "the roughest place on earth," according to one Canadian Mountie. And the man behind the mayhem was Jefferson Randolph "Soapy" Smith.

Smith had earned his nickname in Leadville, Colorado, where he sold gullible miners bars of soap for $5 apiece, on the promise that there might be a $20 bill tucked beneath the wrapper. He thought bigger in Skagway, directing a band of thieves who mingled with the naive *cheechakos* to figure the size of their "pokes." A man with money was directed to various businesses controlled by Smith—where he would be expertly relieved of the poke amid a well-orchestrated disturbance.

Soapy held court at Jeff's Place, a saloon where the games were fixed and the girls would pick a man's pocket while gazing lovingly into his eyes. Perhaps his most outrageous scam was a "telegraph office" where adventurers paid $5 to send a message anywhere in the United States.

The replies always came back collect, usually asking to send more money. Few cheechakos noticed that there were no telegraph wires running out of Skagway.

Soapy had a soft streak, too, or perhaps it was just good public relations instincts. He raised money to build a church, started a fund for two widows, and another fund to save ownerless dogs. The height of his reign came on July 4, 1898, when he served as Grand Marshal in an Independence Day parade and shook hands with the governor of Alaska. Three days later, the scam came to an end when Soapy was gunned down by surveyor Frank Reid, who later died of wounds sustained in the gunfight. While Reid was given a hero's funeral and a massive stone monument inscribed, "He gave his life for the honor of Skagway," Soapy received a simple wooden marker and a lonely send-off, attended by his mistress and the minister. ■

Opposite: Gold Creek in the mountains above Juneau, site of the first Alaska gold rush in 1880.

Siwash hula-hula."

Whoever found the gold, it was George Carmack who blazed a spruce tree the following day and wrote in pencil: TO WHOM IT MAY CONCERN: I do, this day, locate and claim, by right of discovery, five hundred feet, running up stream from this notice. Located this 17th day of August, 1896. G.W. Carmack." Carmack also staked another claim for himself, and single claims for Skookum Jim and Dawson Charlie.

Leaving Jim to protect their interests, Carmack and Charlie headed for Forty Mile to officially record their claims, passing the news to other prospectors along the way. Carmack had a questionable reputation among the men—who called him "Lying George" when they weren't taunting him as "Siwash George"—so it wasn't until he produced a shotgun shell full of bright coarse gold unlike any they'd seen before that the men believed him. By August 22, six days after the original discovery, 25 miners met on a hillside above the gold-bearing stream, renaming it Bonanza Creek and appointing one of their number as mining recorder. No one told Robert Henderson, who was working just over the ridge from the golden riches he had dreamed of as long as he could remember.

Though he wasn't a drinking man, George Carmack required two shots of whiskey before announcing the news in a Forty Mile saloon. There, too, he met with skepticism until he produced the magic shotgun shell. "By the next morning, the town of Forty Mile was empty," writes historian Michael Gates, with the first exodus followed by the rest of the men on the river. "…the value of boats sky-rocketed while that of real estate plummeted. In the winter, the value of dogs surpassed that of boats….The fever spread faster than an epidemic."

Ironically, Carmack didn't have enough gold in his cartridge case—at least after buying the whiskeys—to pay the $15 filing fee, so Inspector Charles Constantine of the North-West Mounted Police agreed to hold the claims until he could return with more. Using a rudimentary sluice box, Carmack and his partners mined over $1,400 worth of gold in the first three weeks, enough to pay their fees and buy supplies for the winter. Other men also did well on Bonanza, but the richest prospects were on a little tributary, "Bonanza's pup" in the miners' term, that became known as Eldorado Creek, where the first prospectors mined six dollars worth of gold in a single pan. Though they didn't know it at the time, the creek would prove to be the richest gold-bearing stream in the world, where almost all of the first 40 claims produced a half million dollars or more at a time when gold traded for $16 an ounce.

In the fall of 1896, however, these riches lay waiting below the surface as hundreds of men scurried to stake their claims in a mad rush driven more by force of habit than genuine belief in the new gold field. Most of the old-timers didn't trust "Lying George" Carmack and didn't like the looks of the Bonanza. One sourdough, as these experienced miners were called, staked a claim upstream from Carmack's discovery and then decided not to bother recording it. "This moose pasture reserved for Swedes and Cheechakos," he wrote on the claiming stakes, a disparaging reference to Scandinavians said to work ground other men considered worthless and inexperienced greenhorns, called *cheechakos* by the Indians. Another sourdough named Louis Rhodes decided to work the same claim against his better judgment, telling his friends that for two-bits he'd forget about it. Apparently no one had the two-bits, and by the following spring that particular slice of "moose pasture" had produced over $60,000.

Such stories were even wilder on El Dorado, where men unwittingly made and lost fortunes as million-dollar claims were exchanged for hundreds of dollars in the first flurry of the rush. Some claims changed hands for nothing at all. When a group of Scotsman staked four claims only to abandon two of them to keep their options open on other creeks, a Seattle YMCA instructor named Thomas Lippy decided to leave his own claim further upstream and restake one of those abandoned by the Scotsmen. Lippy's wife, Salome, wanted to live in a cabin, and the new claim had more timber; it also had more gold: $1,530,000 worth, the richest single claim in the Klondike.

It was not until early October that the men on Bonanza and Eldorado began to understand the significance of their claims. On the third of that month, Louis Rhodes reached bedrock on

Bonanza 15 feet below the surface. There, by the light of a candle, he stared in stupefaction at the glittering seams of gold that ran through frozen clay and gravel of the old creek bed. It was the "pay streak," an apt term in more ways that one, for such rich ground allowed Rhodes to pay workmen with a few pans of gold, keeping the rest of the riches for himself.

The first to hit bedrock on Eldorado were Antone Stander, a handsome Austrian who had been among the original men on the creek, and his partner, Clarence Berry—a huge, muscular Californian who had come to the Yukon in 1894, and then returned with his new bride the following year, dragging her on a sled over the Chilkoot Pass and down the frozen river. Berry had gotten in on Stander's claim in a Forty Mile saloon, when he offered to help the impoverished immigrant arrange for a grubstake. As it turned out, there was plenty of gold for both of them; with their initial proceeds, they bought two adjoining claims and split the whole shebang. Berry cleared 140 thousand dollars that spring and ended up with 1.5 million dollars from Eldorado—all because he helped a man who needed it.

Not everyone earned their riches through such altruism. A large, slow, jowly man named Big Alex McDonald, "King of the Klondike," pioneered a canny and complicated speculative scheme known as the lay system, which began when he bought half-interest in an Eldorado claim for a sack of flour and a side of bacon. He then leased a section of the claim to two prospectors, who did the backbreaking work of mining while giving half the proceeds to McDonald. In the first 45 days, McDonald's share came to $16,500. He used the money to buy more property, which he leased as well, only to buy more and more in an ever-deepening cycle that finally had him borrowing at short-term interest rates that worked out to 1% per day. Within a year, McDonald had interests in 28 claims, investing his "whole fortune" while running up $150,000 in debt—a situation that didn't bother him in the least, for as he laconically pointed out, "I can dig out a hundred and fifty thousand any time I need it."

A Ton of Solid Gold

In the fall of 1896, as the miners dug for gold on the little creeks, a town of tents and a few lonely wooden buildings rose on the swampy flats where the Klondike itself poured into the mighty Yukon. The town was the brainchild of Joe Ladue, who arrived around the time of the great discovery, drawn not by Bonanza Creek but by Henderson's earlier find on Gold Bottom. It was a classic case of good timing, and no one deserved it more than Ladue, who had been boosting the Klondike region for years. While other men staked claims, Ladue staked out a townsite, 160 acres along the Yukon, beneath a looming hill gashed with a natural scar that looks strangely like a moose—as if Nature herself presaged the excitement that began when Skookum Jim killed a moose that led him to gold. Ladue brought his sawmill up the river and was ready for business just as the area teemed with miners who needed lumber. His cabin served as the first saloon, though there would be plenty more in Dawson, named for George M. Dawson, a tough, tiny, hunchbacked geologist who had led the first official Canadian expedition into the Yukon. After years of looking for gold, Joe Ladue made his fortune in real estate.

Dawson grew steadily that winter, fed by a local rush from Forty Mile, Circle, and Juneau. Like its predecessors, it was a strange town, locked in winter darkness, and isolated from the outside world, but in Dawson the disparity between the wealth of the mines and the "comforts" of the town was greater than in any gold rush before or since. People ate their dogs, and salt was literally worth its weight in gold; laundry was so expensive that men wore their shirts until the stench forced them to throw them away; there was no writing paper and nothing to read, except old newspapers that the miners devoured with such appreciation that they donated $400 in gold for the privilege.

In truth, there was little of anything in Dawson except gold, so much gold that on May 23, 1897, a teenage boy named Monte Snow panned out $287 worth from the sawdust on the floor of a saloon. Nine days earlier, the Yukon ice had broken with an explosive roar, and a steady stream of boats began to arrive from upriver, carrying men who wintered on the Yukon followed by others who climbed the Chilkoot Pass. These cheechakos brought welcome news of the Outside to the stir-crazy citizens of Dawson, but the real excitement came in early June when two supply boats arrived from *downriver,* carrying much-needed food and much-appreciated whiskey. Following an alcoholic binge fueled by free drinks at every saloon, the boats headed back toward the sea carrying some 80 Klondike miners and three tons of gold.

> *"It is a corker; seventy-two below and getting colder all the while. It is the coldest day of my life."*
>
> WILLIAM SCHOOLEY, WADE CREEK, JANUARY 14, 1901

At the old Russian port of St. Michael, the Klondikers boarded two oceangoing steamships, the *Portland* and the *Excelsior,* bound for Seattle and San Francisco respectively. The *Portland* departed first, carrying most of the miners, but the *Excelsior* sailed faster, arriving in San Francisco Bay on July 15, 1897. Spectators stared slackjawed as the rugged, sunburned adventurers—including Tom and Salome Lippy, Louis Rhodes, and Joe Ladue—dragged suitcases and satchels full of heavy gold down the gangplank.

By the time the *Portland* arrived in Seattle two days later, the news had spread, and the local paper sent reporters to meet the ship in Puget Sound. "GOLD! GOLD! GOLD! GOLD!" the headline screamed. "68 rich men on the Steamer *Portland;*

STACKS OF YELLOW METAL!" Within the story itself, it was reported that the ship carried "a ton of solid gold," an inspired phrase that reverberated around the world and launched the Klondike stampede. It was an understatement; the *Portland* carried over two tons of gold.

News of the Klondike find greeted America in the throes of depression, an extension of a long financial downturn that had begun with the Panic of 1873. The economy wasn't much improved in 1897, a time when the lack of circulating money made luxuries elusive for all but a few. It was in 1896, the year of the Klondike discovery, that William Jennings Bryan made his famous speech against the gold standard, thundering that "you shall not crucify mankind on a cross of gold." Now 80 men and women, all poor when they embarked for the Far North, had returned with three tons of gold—worth almost two million dollars at a time when a decent meal cost a quarter and a four-room apartment rented for $1.25 a week.

Over 100,000 hopefuls set out for the gold fields, though less than half of them made it; many departed for the Klondike without even knowing where it was. More frenzied and concentrated than the earlier rushes to California and Colorado, the Klondike "stampede" captured the imagination of millions who could dream about the great adventure even if they couldn't experience it. There were Klondike board games and Klondike songs; Klondike cough medicine, chewing gum and head rub; Klondike pulp fiction and literary Klondike novels.

Although various northwest cities competed for the Klondike trade, Seattle became the prime outfitting and transportation center. The city was infected with such acute "Klodicitis," as the papers called it, that scores of municipal employees, including the mayor, resigned to head for the gold fields. By mid-August, only six weeks after the *Portland's* arrival, some 8,000 adventurers had sailed from Seattle on 18 ships. Most were outfitted in Seattle as well, providing a cash infusion that effectively ended the depression in the Pacific Northwest. Outfits varied widely, but real sourdoughs recommended carrying enough gear for a year or more, which meant a $500 investment for some 2,000 pounds of food, 50 items of clothing

LIKE EVERY GOLD rush before it, the Klondike stampede attracted prostitutes and dazzling dance-hall girls. But coming at the end of the 19th century, it also drew tough-minded "respectable women" eager to discard the trappings of Victorian society and chart their own destiny beyond the realm of traditional feminine pursuits.

Chicago socialite Martha Purdy set her sights so firmly on the Klondike that she broke off with her husband when he decided to go to Hawaii instead. Not knowing she was two months pregnant, Purdy hiked the Chilkoot Trail with her brother. "I cursed my high buckram collar," she later wrote, "my tight heavily boned corsets, my long corduroy skirt, my full bloomers, which I had to hitch up with every step." Purdy delivered her baby in Dawson, where she managed a sawmill and obtained a lucrative mining claim. She divorced her first husband and remarried Dawson lawyer George Black, who later served in the Canadian parliament. When he retired, Martha Purdy Black won election to succeed him, becoming a Member of Parliament at the age of 69.

Belinda Mulroney was working for a Pacific coast steamship company when she first heard of Klondike gold. Already an

Gold Rush Women
"WOMAN HOLDS THE FIELD"

accomplished businesswoman, she invested her $5,000 savings in bolts of fabric and hot-water bottles, which she sold for $30,000 in Dawson. Although the Dawson folks said she was crazy, Mulroney opened a lunch counter out in the gold fields at Grand Forks, the junction of Bonanza and Eldorado creeks. The miners threw so much gold dust across her counter that she expanded it into a saloon and roadhouse, later building a more elegant hotel in Dawson—with cut-glass

chandeliers and brass bedsteads packed over the White Pass under her personal supervision. Mulroney bought mining claims as well; by 1899, she had ten good ones. "I like mining," she said that year, "and have only hired a foreman because it looks better to have it said that a man is running the mine, but the truth is that I look after the management myself."

Harriet "Ma" Pullen left her husband and four children back in Washington State when she came to Skagway in

September 1897. She started out baking pies and made so much money that she brought her family north and went into the horse-packing business, before establishing the famous Pullen House hotel—where she held court for almost fifty years, entertaining her guests with a whimsical mixture of fact and fiction about herself and the great days of the Klondike stampede.

Eighteen-year-old Mabel Long, newly and unhappily married to a much older man, fell off a boat in Lake Bennett during the great flotilla of 1898. While her ineffective husband wrung his hands in despair, a young stampeder who was traveling with them dove into the icy waters and pulled her onto a sandbar. Mabel was so disgusted with her husband that she left him right then and there and continued on with her rescuer—who turned out to be the heir to a fortune.

Flora Shaw covered the Klondike stampede as colonial editor for the *London Times,* later giving a speech in London on the question of whether "respectable women" had a place on the Yukon frontier. "…in the expansion of the Empire, as in other movements," she said, "man wins the battle, but woman holds the field." ■

Many independent women headed for the Yukon (opposite) with or without the company of men. In the photo above, a group of actresses pose on the Canadian side of the Chilkoot Pass, at a small valley called Happy Camp, "a misnomer if there ever was one," according to journalist Tappan Adney who passed through in September 1897.

Just as in all the previous gold and silver rushes, an entire industry grew up in the Klondike region to serve the miners. Photographed above at her shop in Dawson, Mrs. G. I. Lowe augmented her income from doing laundry by telling fortunes for the impressive sum of one dollar. Far removed from the rigid society in more settled areas, the Far North offered women new opportunity to chart their own destiny. Wrote one veteran of the California Gold Rush, "It is the only country that I ever was in where a woman received anything like a just compensation for work."

(include two dozen heavy wool socks), as well as tents, stoves, cooking utensils and tools. Not everyone followed their advice; many cheechakos thought they could buy what they needed along the trail, while others didn't plan at all. One man left with thirty-two pairs of moccasins, a case of pipes, a case of shoes, two Irish setters, a bull pup, and a lawn tennis set.

The first ships landed at Dyea, the old Tlingit village at the beginning of the trail to the Chilkoot Pass. The shallow, tidal waters of the Taiya Inlet, easily navigable by native canoe, proved impractical for oceangoing vessels, however, and captains were forced to anchor far offshore, where passengers and crewman feverishly unloaded cargo onto barges. Sometimes the barges didn't make it, either, as the tidal extremes turned water into land. "In an hour we were gently grating on the bottom," wrote one stampeder. "In twenty minutes we were high and dry, and wagons were coming out on the sandy bottom to get us." The chaos continued when the cargo reached the shore. "It would be difficult for one to imagine the confusion that existed," another man remembered, "when the tons and tons of boxes and sacks and barrels came ashore,…where each one of the eight hundred passengers was hurrying about looking for the goods that bore his private brand."

The solution was to build a dock, but by the time Dyea's "Long Wharf" was completed in May 1898, most of the stampeders had passed. In the meantime, ships turned toward another port on the inlet, which offered a deeper bottom, a place the Tlingits called "Skaguay," home of the north wind. The Indians seldom used the area, not only because of the wind, but because the White Pass Trail that began at Skagway (as the name was later spelled) was ten miles longer than the Chilkoot. Yet it offered a more gradual ascent over a lower pass, allowing draft animals, and later a railroad, to transport heavy loads into the interior. Observing these advantages, a visionary old sea captain named William Moore had established a 160-acre homestead in 1887, only to be swept aside in the fury of the rush, when the new "town fathers" moved his cabin because it lay in the way of a carefully surveyed thoroughfare. The resilient Captain Moore had the last laugh, however, building a dock that earned him a fortune, and ultimately receiving one-fourth of the assessed value of the booming town that grew on his homestead.

Although more stampeders followed the Chilkoot Trail than followed the White Pass, Skagway grew faster and lasted longer that Dyea, not only because of its port facilities, but because the White Pass Trail proved more difficult than anyone imagined. Stampeders passed through Dyea, but they became stuck in Skagway, just as their animals got stuck in the sloppy mud and treacherous footing of the trail. An idea that seemed so promising—to let the animals carry the load—turned to nightmares, vividly described by a young seaman from San Francisco named Jack London, whose muscular, modern prose not only evokes the time and place, but also marks a point of departure from the romantic sensibilities of the Victorian age:

> The horses died like mosquitoes in the first frost and from Skagway to Bennett they rotted in heaps. They died at the rocks, they were poisoned at the summit, and they starved at the lakes; they fell off the trail, what there was of it, and they went through it; in the river they drowned under their loads or were smashed to pieces against the boulders; they snapped their legs in the crevices and broke their backs falling backwards with their packs; in the sloughs they sank from fright or smothered in the slime; and they were disemboweled in the bogs where the corduroy logs turned end up in the mud; men shot them, worked them to death and when they were gone, went back to the beach and bought more. Some did not bother to shoot them, stripping the saddles off and the shoes and leaving them where they fell. Their hearts turned to stone—those which did not break—and they became beasts, the men on the Dead Horse Trail.

The Chilkoot Trail had no Jack London to record its vicissitudes, but it was this journey, "the meanest 32 miles in history" according to one who walked it, that came to represent the Klondike experience. The trail is gradual at first, rising less that 1,000 feet in the first 13 miles, but the next 3 miles ascend 2,650 feet—more than half a mile. "For about six hundred feet we cut every foot of the way in the ice," remembered a young woman named Esther Lyons, "and so steep is it that I had to bend forward constantly to maintain my equilibrium. It is very hard on one's lungs and legs...." Despite the pain, the climb was worth it, at least for Lyons, who crossed in the spring of 1897, before the rush began. "What pen can describe that hour on the summit of the Chilkoot?" she wrote. "Behind us civilization; before us vastness, silence, grandeur."

In February 1898, the North-West Mounted Police took possession of the Chilkoot Pass, as well as the White Pass, guarding them with small, well-armed detachments, each reenforced by a conspicuous Maxim machine gun. The maneuver was the turning point in a potentially explosive conflict between the United States and Canada over the international boundary along the Alaska Panhandle, a boundary that had little practical meaning until tens of thousands of stampeders entered with forty to one hundred million dollars worth of goods, all eligible for customs duties.

The Mounties required that every individual carry a year's supply of food along with essential clothing and equipment, a minimal outfit that weighed around 2,000 pounds. Thus a man carrying 50-pound packs would have to ascend the final slope 40 times before being allowed into Canada. For those with money, the task was easier; the Tlingit and Tagish offered packing services, though with the demand, prices rose to as high as a dollar a pound. By May 1898, motorized tramlines were operating at the pass, but these cost money, too. For many, the ascent of the Chilkoot Pass was really 40 ascents that took as many days of backbreaking labor over icy rocks and snow. To move an outfit all the way from Dyea might take three months.

Dave Curl, a ranger at the Klondike Gold Rush National Historical Park in Skagway, believes that "the Wild West ended at the summit of the Chilkoot Pass," where the Canadian Mounties enforced a brand of law and order that was seldom seen on the American frontier. But the Wild West was more than lawlessness; it was adventure as well, and there was still plenty of adventure waiting on the other side of the pass. Relatively few stampeders made it down the Yukon River before the freeze in the fall of 1897; all that winter and early spring, men and women poured over the Chilkoot and White passes until there were between 20,000 and 30,000 camped beside the alpine lakes, feverishly making boats or buying them from questionable entrepreneurs, all waiting for the ice to crack.

The great event occurred on May 29, and within two days a bizarre, ramshackle flotilla of over 7,000 boats, rafts, and canoes headed downriver into a land few had seen before, still more than 500 miles from their destination. It is one of the small miracles of the gold rush that only a score or so drowned, though thousands got wet and plenty lost their precious outfits.

The toughest test came near present-day Whitehorse, where the broad Yukon squeezed between looming rock walls at Miles Canyon, forming a treacherous whirlpool that led into even more treacherous rapids, including the dreaded Whitehorse, named for the frothing waters reminiscent of a horse's mane. When the flotilla hit this natural juggernaut, 150 boats were wrecked and at least five men drowned, forcing thousands of other craft into a giant jam as their owners decided how to proceed. Just as they had in the rocky passes, the Mounties took control, requiring women and children to walk around the rapids while only safe boats "steered by competent men" were allowed to pass. Their actions saved countless lives.

It was smoother sailing after Miles Canyon, and by July, boats were moored six-deep at Dawson for two miles along the Yukon. Some 60 steamers arrived from downriver as well, bringing supplies and well-heeled stampeders who could afford the long, all-water passage through the Bering Sea. Suddenly Dawson was a teeming city of tents and false-fronted wooden buildings, with a constantly changing population estimated at 18,000 in mid-summer. There were two newspapers, two banks, five churches, twelve sawmills, and telephone service that connected Dawson proper with Lousetown, just across the Klondike where George Carmack had once made his fish camp. There were theaters, saloons, gambling dens, bawdy houses, and moving-picture shows; hotels, restaurants, laundries, and an open-air market where you could buy almost anything, from fresh grapes and opera glasses to the complete works of Shakespeare—most at prices that were half what they cost in Seattle.

On the Fourth of July, the heavily American population exploded in the loudest, longest, and wildest Independence Day celebration ever held on Canadian soil, so loud in fact that some 400 dogs swam across the Yukon to escape the noise. It was at once a celebration and and outburst of frustration, for though the men and women in Dawson had accomplished what others only dreamed of, the simple, sad fact was that the rich claims had been staked before the rush began. "There are many men in Dawson at the present time who feel keenly disappointed," reported *The Klondike Nugget*. "They have come thousands of miles on a perilous trip, risked life, health and property, spent months of the most arduous labor a man can perform and at length with expectations raised to the highest pitch have reached the coveted goal only to discover that there is nothing here for them." While expressing "sincere sympathy," the *Nugget* pointed out that "a few moments of calm and deliberate thought" might have anticipated the situation, but such thought was lost in the madness of the rush. A young man from San Diego wrote that many stampeders "expected all they would have to do was to pick the nuggets above the ground and some even thought they grew on bushes."

The riches of the Klondike went to pioneers who earned them before the rest of the world even knew they existed. Few held onto their riches for long. Joe Ladue finally married his sweetheart only to die of tuberculosis in 1901, his body worn and weakend by too many years in the Far North. Tom Lippy, a good man and bad businessman, lost his fortune with ill-conceived investments, leaving Salome nothing but a pension of $50 a month. Big Alex McDonald lost his fortune as well, because he couldn't stop buying land, and he died of a heart attack slumped over the chopping block in front of his cabin. Louis Rhodes lost his, only to make a new one in the Fairbanks gold rush a few years later. Almost unique among the Klondike kings, Clarence Berry held onto his money and made more, living a long successful life as one of the wealthiest men in California.

George Carmack, Skookum Jim, and Dawson Charlie never made millions, but they cleared $150,000 in the spring of 1898—before the hordes arrived—and set off on a celebratory trip to Seattle and San Francisco that only emphasized the cultural gulf between Carmack and his Indian relatives. In 1900, Carmack left Kate and married a white adventuress he had met in Dawson, severing his ties with Jim and Charlie around the same time. Charlie died in 1909 when he fell off a railroad bridge after a drinking party; Jim had drinking problems as well, but he lived until 1916, leaving an estate that still provides funds for a native cultural organization called The Skookum Jim Friendship Centre. Despite their estrangement, George Carmack called his grandson Keish, Skookum Jim's Tagish name. Carmack died in 1922, leaving $150,000 which his wife and daughter fought over so intently that most of it went to lawyers. Robert Henderson left the Yukon with $1,100 which was stolen from him before he reached Seattle; he prospected until his death in 1933, living on a $200 monthly stipend from the Canadian government as the only Canadian involved in the great discovery.

And what of the hordes who came to the Klondike? By August, the *Nugget* reported that a third of them had gone home, and most had left by the end of 1899, when the cry of Gold! on the beaches of Nome drew those who still had a stomach for the chase. Of the 30 or 40,000 who reached Dawson, only half even looked for gold, and perhaps 4,000 found it—though few found enough to make it worthwhile. Yet it was worthwhile anyway, or so it seemed to many who looked back on the adventure of a lifetime. "I made exactly nothing," wrote one stampeder, "but if I could turn time back I would do it over again for less than that." Like an earlier generation who had set off for California to "see the elephant," the men and women of 1898 had seen the Klondike. They had followed their hearts and dreams instead of their heads, but they were better for it. As the twentieth century dawned with a new age of automobiles, airplanes, and skyscrapers, the Klondike stampeders could proudly say they had followed the last great trail of the Wild West.

Though he spent most of his time in California, the beauty of the Far North (above) captured John Muir's imagination. He made five more northern trips after his initial 1879 excursion , and never ceased to marvel at "the nightless days of that beautiful Northland." Well-schooled in the Bible, the great naturalist did not lack for spiritual comparisons: "I've been wandering through a thousand rooms in God's crystal temple....Solomon's marble and ivory palaces were nothing like this." When he left Alaska in 1879, he told his traveling companion "Your heart will cry every day for the North like a lost child; and in your sleep the snow-banners of your white peaks will beckon to you."

INDEX

Boldface indicates illustrations

*A group of Apache ride into a storm on the Fort Apache Reservation in this
1906 photograph by famed photographer/ethnologist Edward S. Curtis,
who took over 40,000 photographs of Indian subjects.*

Acknowledgements

I would like to thank the Bovey Restorations, Norcan Leasing Ltd., and White Pass & Yukon Route Railway • I would also like to thank the staff of the following research and historical facilities • Adams Museum • Alaska State Library • Alaska State Museum • Bannack State Park • Bighole Battlefield National Monument • Boot Hill Museum • Canadian Heritage Parks Canada • Dawson City Museum • Denver Public Library, Western History/Genealogy • Dickinson County Heritage Center • Fort Laramie National Historic Site • Fort Larned National Historic Site • Fort Phil Kearney State Historical Site • Golden Spike National Historic Site • Heritage Branch, Yukon Tourism • Jesse James Bank Museum • Jesse James Farm & Musum • Jim Gatchell Memorial Museum • Klondike Gold Rush National Historical Park • Little Bighorn Battlefield National Monuument • Marshall Gold Discovery State Historic Park • Pony Express National Memorial • Shoshone-Bannock Tribal Museum • Skagway Historical Museum • South Pass City State Historic Site • T.A. Guest Ranch • Union Pacific Historical Museum • Utah State Historical Society Library-Archives • Yukon Archives • Finally, thanks to the following individuals, who gave freely of their time and expertise • Gary C. "Andy" Anderson • Gunder C. Anderson • Norman R. Blake • Bill Breckenridge • Dave Curl • Fritz & Skyler • Michael Gates • Scott Goetz • John Gould • Kirk Hansen • Jeanine Henderson-Hodges • Earl Hudson, Jr. • Phillip Jumping Eagle • Gladi Kulp • Jacqueline Lewin • Sandra Lowry • Ruth Mather • Douglas C. McChristian • David Neufeld • Jim Richards • Jeff Sheets • Don Snoddy • Ken Spotswood • Ryan White Feather • Alex White Plume • Jack Wymore.

Bibliography

Adams, Andy. *The Log of a Cowboy.* • Adney, Tappan. *The Klondike Stampede.* • Alt, David D. and Donald W. Hyndman. *Roadside Geology of Northern California.* • Ambrose, Stephen E. *Crazy Horse and Custer.* • Ball, Eve, *Indeh.* Ibid, *In the Days of Victorio.* • Beatty, Park. *Park Beatty's Trip to Alaska 1898.* Ms., Klondike Gold Rush NHP. • Belish, Elbert D. "American Horse (Wasechun-Tashunka): The Man Who Killed Fetterman." *Annals of Wyoming,* Spring 1991. • Berton, Pierre. *Klondike.* • Bird, Greenup. "Bank Robbery Committed in Liberty, Missouri on February 13, 1866." Jesse James Bank Museum, Liberty, MO. • Brown, Dee. *Bury My Heart at Wounded Knee.* Ibid, *Hear that Lonesome Whistle Blow.* • Brown, Robert L. *the Great Pikes Peak Gold Rush.* • Browning, Peter, comp. and ed. *To the Golden Shore.* • Camp, Walter Mason. *Custer in '76.* • Carey, Charles H. *General History of Oregon.* • Carroll, John M., ed. *The Battle of the Washita* by Francis M. Gibson and *The Washita Campaign* by Edward G. Mathey. • Chaput, Don. *Virgil Earp.* • Coel, Margaret. *Chief Left Hand, Southern Arapaho.* • Conley, Robert J. "Into the Sunset." In *The West That Was.* Ed. by Thomas W. Knowles and Joe R. Lansdale. • Connell, Evan S. *Son of the Morning Star.* • Connor, Cathy and Daniel O'Haire. *Roadside Geology of Alaska.* • *Council Bluffs Nonpareil,* Council Bluffs, IA, July 1873. • Crosley-Griffin, Mary. *Columbia.* Ibid, *Hangtown.* • Cruise, John D. "Early Days on the Union Pacific." In *Collections of the Kansas State Historical Society, 1909-1910.* • *The Daily Gazette,* St. Joseph, MO, April 5, 1882. • *Daily Iowa State Registrar,* Des Moines, IA, July 23, 1873. • Debo, Angie. *Geronimo.* • Dimsdale, Thomas J. *The Vigilantes of Montana.* • Drago, Harry Sinclair. *The Great Range Wars.* • Dykstra, Robert R. *Cattle Towns.* • Earp, Josephine. *I Married Wyatt Earp.* Comp. and ed. by Glenn G. Boyer. • Edwards, J.B. "Early Days in Abilene." Ed. by C.W. Wheeler. Abilene *Chronicle,* 1896. • Erwin, Richard E. *The Truth About Wyatt Earp.* • Farnham, Wallace D. "Grenville Dodge and the Union Pacific: A Study of Historical Legends." In *The Journal of American History,* Mar. 1965. • Foley, Doris. *The Divine Eccentric.* • Gard, Wayne. *The Chisholm Trail.* • Gardner, Mark. *Little Bighorn Battlefield National Monument.* • Gates, Michael. *Gold at Fortymile Creek.* • Gay, Theressa. *James W. Marshall, The Discoverer of California Gold.* • Godfrey, Anthony. *Historic Resource Study: Pony Express National Historic Trail.* • Greever, William S. *Bonanza West.* • Grinnell, George Bird. *The Fighting Cheyennes.* • Guild, Thelma S. and Carter, Harvey L. *Kit Carson.* • Haley, James L. *Apaches.* • Hart, Newell. *The Bear River Massacre.* • Hassrick, Royal B. *The Sioux.* • Hedren, Paul L. *The Massacre of Lieutenant Grattan and his command by Indians.* Drawings by Black Horse. • Hester, Sallie. "The Diary of a Pioneer Girl." In *Covered Wagon Women, Diaries & Letters from the Western Trails 1840-1890.*

Vol. I 1840-1849. Ed. and comp. by Kenneth L. Holmes. • Hittman, Michael. *Wovoka and the Ghost Dance.* • Holliday, J.S. *The World Rushed In.* • Hunter, J. Marvin, comp. and ed. *The Trail Drivers of Texas.* • Hurtado, Albert L. *Indian Survival on the California Frontier.* • Hyde, George E. *Red Cloud's Folk.* • Iverson, Peter. *The Navajo Nation.* • Jackson, Donald Dale. *Gold Dust.* • Jackson, George A. "George A. Jackson's Diary, 1858-1859." Ed. by LeRoy R. Hafen. *The Colorado Magazine,* Nov. 1935. • James, Stella Frances. *In the Shadow of Jesse James.* Ed. by Milton F. Perry. • Jewett, Mendall. *Journal to and from California of Dr. Mendall Jewett.* Ms., Denver Public Library, Western History/Genealogy. • Johnson, Dorothy M. *The Bloody Bozeman.* • *Kansas City Evening Star,* Kansas City, MO, Apr. 4, 1882. • King, Joseph A. *Winter of Entrapment.* • Kloberdanz, Timothy. *The Tragedy at Summit Springs from the Viewpoint of the Indians.* • *The Klondike Nugget,* Dawson, North-West Territories, Canada, 1898. • Kraus, George. *High Road to Promontory.* • Krause, Herbert and Gary D. Olson. *Prelude to Glory.* • Larsen, T.A. *History of Wyoming.* • Lavender, David. *The Great Persuader.* Ibid, *The Overland Migrations.* • Lazarus, Edward. *Black Hills / White Justice.* • Leckie, Shirley A. *Elizabeth Bacon Custer and the Making of a Myth.* • Levy, Jo Ann. *They Saw the Elephant.* • Lewin, Jacqueline A. and Marilyn S. Taylor. *The St. Joe Road.* • *Liberty Tribune.* Liberty, MO, 1850-1882. • Lloyd, Everett. *Law West of the Pecos.* • Lortie, Frank. "The Impact of the Gold Rush on the Native Americans of California." Ms., Marshall Gold Discovery SHP. • Madsen, Brigham D. *The Northern Shoshoni.* Ibid, *The Shoshoni Frontier and the Bear River Massacre.* • Marks, Paula Mitchell. *And Die in the West.* • Mather, R.E. and Boswell, F.E. *Hanging the Sheriff.* • McCann, Lloyd E. "The Grattan Massacre." Reprinted from *Nebraska History,* Mar. 1956. • McCoy, Joseph G. *Historic Sketches of the Cattle Trade of the West and Southwest.* • McCracken, Harold. *The American Cowboy.* • McDermott, John D. "Price of Arrogance: The Short and Controversial Life of William Judd Fetterman." & "Wyoming Scrapbook: Documents relating to the Fetterman Fight." *Annals of Wyoming,* Spring 1991. • McGrane, Martin Edward. *The James Farm.* • Mooney, James. *The Ghost Dance Religion and Wounded Knee.* • Morgan, Dale. *Overland in 1846.* • Muir, John. *Travels in Alaska.* • Nadeau, Remi. *Fort Laramie and the Sioux Indians.* • Neeley, Bill. *The Last Comanche Chief.* • Neufeld, David and Frank Norris. *Chilkoot Trail.* • New York *Daily Tribune.* "1849 Articles from the New York Daily Tribune Describing the Massacre of the Nisenan Indians of the Coloma Vicinity in April 1849." Marshall Gold Discovery SHP. • O'Connor, Richard. *Iron Wheels & Broken Men.* • Pace, Dick. *Golden Gulch.* • Parker, Watson. *Gold in the Black Hills.* • Patterson, E.H.N. "Diary of E.H.N. Patterson." In *Overland Routes to the Gold Fields, 1859 from contemporary diaries.* Ed. by LeRoy R. Hafen. • Paul, Rodman W. *California Gold.* Ibid, *Mining Frontiers of the Far West.* Ibid, *The California Gold Discovery.* • Prucha, Francis Paul, ed. and comp. *Documents of United States Indian Policy.* • Raine, William MacLeod and Will C. Barnes. *Cattle, Cowboys and Rangers.* • Ramsay, Alexander. "Alexander Ramsay's Gold Rush Diary of 1849." Ed. by Merrill J. Mattes. In *Pacific Historical Review,* Nov. 1949. • Rawls, James J. *Indians of California.* • Lamar, Howard R., ed. *The Reader's Encyclopedia of the American West.* • Roberts, David. *Once They Moved Like the Wind.* • Rosa, Joseph G. *They Called Him Wild Bill.* Ibid, *Wild Bill Hickok.* • Russell, Don. *The Lives and Legends of Buffalo Bill.* • Sandoz, Mari. *Crazy Horse.* • Schooley, William Mace. *Alaska Gold Rush Diary and Letters.* Ms., Klondike Gold Rush NHP. • Schultz, Duane. *Month of the Freezing Moon.* • Schuyler, Howard. *Extract from Official Report….* • Seidman, Laurence I. *Once in the Saddle.* • Settle, Raymond W. and Mary Lund Settle. *Saddles & Spurs.* • Settle, William A., Jr. *Jesse James Was His Name.* • Shirley, Glenn. *Belle Starr and Her Times.* • Sonnichsen, C.L. *Roy Bean.* • Spotswood, Ken. *Klondike Gold Rush Centennial Media Kit.* • Steele, Phillip W. with George Warfel. *The Many Faces of Jesse James.* • Stone, Howard M., comp. *Let Us "The Settlers" Tell You About Our Abilene in the 1800s.* • Sturtevant, William, gen. ed. *Handbook of North American Indians.* • *Sutter's Fort State Historic Park.* Pamphlet. • Sweeney, Edwin R. *Cochise.* • Taylor, William O. *With Custer on the Little Bighorn.* • Ten Eyck, Tenodor. "Report…" In *Wyoming Opened,* (Carrington scrapbook). Sheridan County Library, Sheridan, WY. • Thrapp, Dan L. *The Conquest of Apacheria.* Ibid, *Victorio and the Mimbres Apaches.* • *Tribune Extra,* Bismarck, Dakota Terr., July 6, 1876. • Tullidge, Edward W. "The Cities of Cache Valley and their Founders," *Tullidge's Quarterly Magazine,* July 1881. • Turner, Alford E., ed. *The O.K. Corral Inquest.* • U.S. Congress, Senate. "Report on the Secretary of War…respecting the massacre of Lieutenant Grattan and his command by Indians." 34th Congress, 1st Session, 1856. Ibid, "Massacre of Cheyenne Indians." Report of the Joint Committee on the Conduct of the War. 38th Congress, 2nd Session, 1865. • Utley, Robert M. *Billy the Kid.* Ibid, *Cavalier in Buckskin.* Ibid, *Frontier Regulars.* Ibid, *Frontiersmen in Blue.* Ibid, *The Indian Frontier of the American West 1846-1890.* Ibid, *The Lance and the Shield.* • Utley, Robert M., and Wilcomb E. Washburn. *The American Heritage History of the Indian Wars.* • Vestal, Stanley. *Sitting Bull.* • Walker, Paul Robert. *Spiritual Leaders.* • Wallace, Ernest and E. Adamson Hoebel. *The Comanches.* • White, Helen H. *The Biography and Letters of Samuel B. Reed.* • Wilke, Rab and The Skookum Jim Friendship Centre. *Skookum Jim.* • Williams, John Hoyt. *A Great and Shining Road.* • Wilson, Francis L., comp. *A History of Ellsworth County, Kansas.* • Wooster, Robert. *The Military and United States Indian Policy 1865-1903.* • Worcester, Donald E. *The Apaches.* • Young, Fredric R. *Dodge City.*

Published by
The National Geographic Society

Reg Murphy, President and Chief Executive Officer
Gilbert M. Grosvenor, Chairman of the Board
Nina D. Hoffman, Senior Vice President

Prepared by
The Book Division

William R. Gray, Vice President and Director
Charles Kogod, Assistant Director
Barabara Payne, Editorial Director

Staff for this Book
Project Editor, Kevin Mulroy
Art Director, Marianne R. Koszorus
Illustrations Editor, Marilyn Gibbons
Picture Legend Writer/Researcher, Mark Galan
Consulting Editor, Bonnie S. Lawrence
Senior Map Editor, Carl Mehler
Map Research, Joseph F. Ochlak
Map Production, Michelle Picard
Map Relief, Tobor G. Tóth
Production Project Manager, Lewis R. Bassford
Illustrations Assistant, Meredith C. Wilcox
Editorial Assistant, Kevin G. Craig
Staff Assistant, Peggy Candore

Manufacturing and Quality Management
George V. White, Director
John T. Dunn, Associate Director
Vincent P. Ryan, Manager
Polly P. Tompkins, Executive Assistant

Deborah Patton, Indexer

Composition for this book by the National Geographic Society Book Division. Printed and bound by Quebecor Printing, Kingsport, Tenn. Color separations by Digital Color Image, Inc., Pennsauken, N.J. Dust jacket printed by Miken Companies, Inc., Cheetowaga, N.Y.

Visit the Society's Web site at **http://www.nationalgeographic.com**.

Cover—Thomas A. Wiewandt
Inset—Seaver Center for Western History Research, Los Angeles County Museum of Natural History

2, The Denver Public Library, Western History Department. 5, Library of Congress. 6, Marilyn M. Gibbons. 10-11, Chuck Place/The Image Bank. 12, Seaver Center for Western History Research, Los Angeles County Museum of Natural History. 13, Fred Hirschmann/Tony Stone Images. 16, David Hiser. 17, Galen Rowell/Mountain Light. 20, Marc Solomon. 21, Larry Ulrich/DRK Photo. 23, California State Library. 26, Metropolitan Museum of Art, detail. 27, Geoffrey Clifford/The Stock Market. 28, Smithsonian Institution. 29, Corbis-Bettmann. 31, Ed Cooper. 32-33, Tom Bean. 34, Edward S. Curtis/NGS Image Collection. 35, Terry Donnelly/Tony Stone Images. 39, Tom Dietrich/Tony Stone Images. 42, Edward S. Curtis/NGS Image Collection. 43, Patricia Caulfield. 44, Pony Express Stables Museum, St. Joseph, Missouri. 45, Courtesy, Colorado Historical Society. 49, Phil Schermeister/Tony Stone Images. 50-51, Harald Sund/ The Image Bank. 52, Fred Hirschmann. 53, Cosmo Condina/Tony Stone Images. 56, National Archives. 57, Hulton Getty. 59, Michael Melford. 62, Museum of New Mexico. 63, Fred Hirschmann. 65, Michael S. Sample. 68, Ed George. 69, Tom Dietrich/Tony Stone Images. 72, David Hiser. 73, Adrian J. Ebell, Courtesy, Minnesota Historical Society. 74 (low left), Smithsonian Institution; (up left & up right), National Archives; (up center), Corbis-Bettmann; (low right), Library of Congress; 75 (up left), Corbis-Bettmann; (up right), Smithsonian Institution; (low left & low right), National Archives. 76-77, Jack Krawczyk/Panoramic Images. 78, University of Washington, Seattle. 79, Larry Ulrich/Tony Stone Images. 82, Courtesy, The Bancroft Library. 83, Southern Pacific Company. 86, Kansas State Historical Society, Topeka. 87, Kevin Sink/Midwestock. 89 (all), Library of Congress. 92, Corbis-Bettmann. 93, Lowell Georgia. 94-95, William Albert Allard/NGS Image Collection. 96, Edward S. Curtis/NGS Image Collection. 97, John Eastcott & Yva Momatiuk/DRK Photo. 101, Sam Abell, NGS. 104-106 (all), National Archives. 107, Tom Bean/DRK Photo. 110, Smithsonian Institution. 111, Frank Oberle/Tony Stone Images. 113, National Archives. 115, Smithsonian Institution, National Anthropological Archives. 116-117, Jeff Morgan/Midwestock. 118, Library of Congress, Erwin E. Smith Collection. 119, William Albert Allard/NGS Image Collection. 123, Fred Hirschmann. 126-127 (both), Corbis-Bettmann. 128, Western History Research Center, University of Wyoming. 129, William Albert Allard/NGS Image Collection. 132, Corbis-Bettmann. 133, Kansas State Historical Society, Topeka. 137-139 (both), Kevin Sink/Midwestock. 140, Kathy Hamer/Unicorn Stock Photos. 141, Jack Zehrt/FPG Int'l. 144-145 (both), Corbis-Bettmann. 148, Oklahoma Historical Society, Archives & Manuscripts Division. 149, Kevin Sink/Midwestock. 151, National Archives. 153-157 (both), Kevin Sink/Midwestock. 158 (left), Underwood & Underwood/Corbis-Bettmann; (right, both) Corbis-Bettmann. 159 (up left), California State Library; (up right), National Archives; (low right), Corbis-Bettmann. 160-161, John Livzey/ Tony Stone Images. 162, D.F. Barry Photograph From the U.S. Army Military History Institute, Carlisle Barracks, Pennsylvania. 163, Fred Hirschmann. 166, L.A. Huffman, Miles City, Montana. 167, John M. Roberts/The Stock Market. 170, Mathew Brady, Courtesy, National Park Service. 172, Smithsonian Institution, National Anthropological Archives, Bureau of American Ethnology Collection. 173, Fred Hirschmann. 177, Buffalo Bill Memorial Museum. 178, Wyoming State Museum. 179, Michael Melford/The Image Bank. 183, Bruce Stoddard/FPG Int'l. 184 (low right), Corbis-Bettmann; (all others), National Archives. 185 (up left), LDS Church Archives; (up center & low), National Archives; (up right), Courtesy, Colorado Historical Society. 186-187, Fred Hirschmann. 188, Kerry Ross Boren Collection. 189, Fred Hirschmann. 192, Bruce Dale, Courtesy, Burton Devere Collection, Rose Tree Inn, Tombstone, Arizona. 193, Smithsonian Institution. 194, Lippe Studio, Courtesy, Arizona Historical Society Library. 195, Carr Clifton/Minden Pictures. 198, Nick Kelsh. 199, Corbis-Bettmann. 200 (left), Archive Photos; (right), Corbis-Bettmann. 201, Jeff Gnass/The Stock Market. 205-207 (both), Fred Hirschmann. 208, Corbis-Bettmann. 209, George Hunter/Tony Stone Images. 212, Hulton Getty. 213, Alaska State Library. 216, Alaska Historical Library. 217, Paul Robert Walker. 218, Alaska State Library. 219, Fred Hirschmann. 222, Corbis-Bettmann. 223, Fred Hirschmann. 224, Corbis-Bettmann. 227, Fred Hirschmann. 229, Edward S. Curtis/NGS Image Collection.

Copy work provided by Amanda Dunn, Max Reid and the NGS Photo and Digital Imaging Lab